HISTORY
ENCYCLOPEDIA

Om Kidz | Om Books International

Reprinted in 2020

Corporate & Editorial Office
A-12, Sector 64, Noida 201 301,
Uttar Pradesh, India,
Phone: +91 120 477 4100
Email: editorial@ombooks.com,
Website: www.ombooksinternational.com

Sales Office
107, Ansari Road, Darya Ganj,
New Delhi 110 002, India
Phone: +91 11 4000 9000
Email: sales@ombooks.com
Website: www.ombooks.com

ISBN: 978-93-84625-96-2

Printed in India

10 9 8 7 6 5 4 3 2

HISTORY
ENCYCLOPEDIA

Om KIDZ
An imprint of Om Books International

Table of Contents

9. World War I 153

10. World War II 181

11. Independence Struggle of the World's Largest Democracy 225

What is History?

History is the story of people on planet Earth. It begins with human evolution, dating back to 150,000 years and includes everything from politics, faith to cultures. History is a subject that can educate young minds about the past. It can help them decipher the rich past as well as dwell on tragedies.

The importance of history

History is important because it allows us to understand our past, which in turn allows to understand our present. This helps us ascertain why things are the way they are. We need to learn history because it tells us where we came from.

Studying history

History can be read from books; museums can also tell us a lot about our past. Historians study history and write history books. They learn about the past events that have helped shape the present, modern world. They also have fine research skills. They study themes and try to make a complete picture out of it. This enables us to understand our past in a much better manner. Historians aim to provide perspectives, views and analyses to their readers.

Why is history studied?

It is studied because it helps us comprehend the evolution of our world. It enables us to further develop our queries. It also helps shape our opinions. It dives into our roots and gives us information about our ancestors, going all the way back to a simpler time when humans lived in caves. History helps us understand and predict human behaviour.

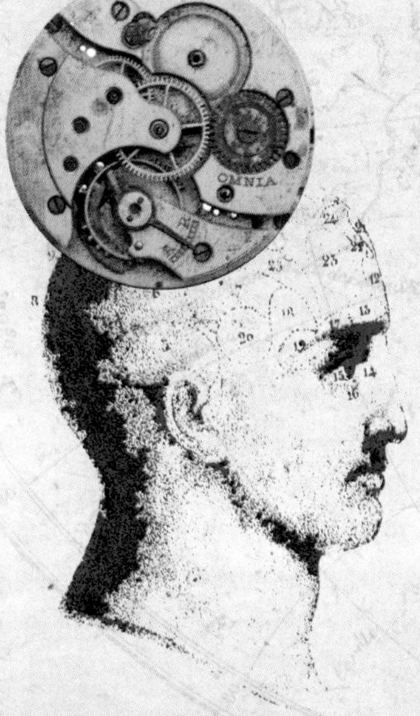

Father of History

In the fifth century BC, a Greek historian, Herodotus, attempted to put down the events of the past to help people recall and remember the past, and hence is known as the "Father of History".

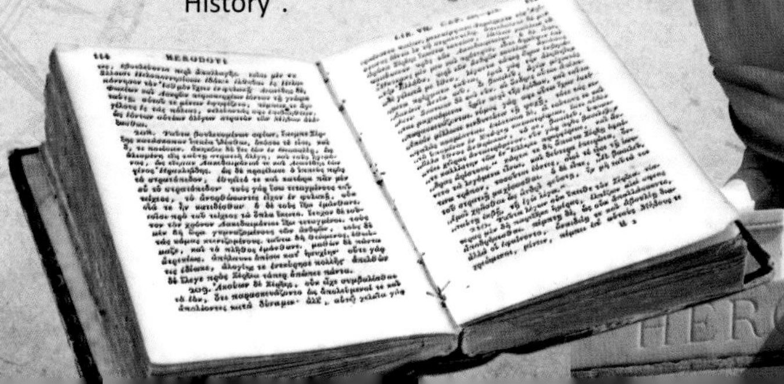

The First Humans

Australopithecus

Although very little is known about early human beings, there has been enough study on the subject to help us generate a few theories and ideas about them. Almost six million years ago, the first humans appeared in East Africa. Back then, they didn't walk on two feet. They walked on all four limbs and often swung from tree to tree. They began to hunt and run away from danger when they finally learnt to walk on two feet. Their bodies changed because they now walked and did not swing from trees. They had relatively smaller brains and were very hairy.

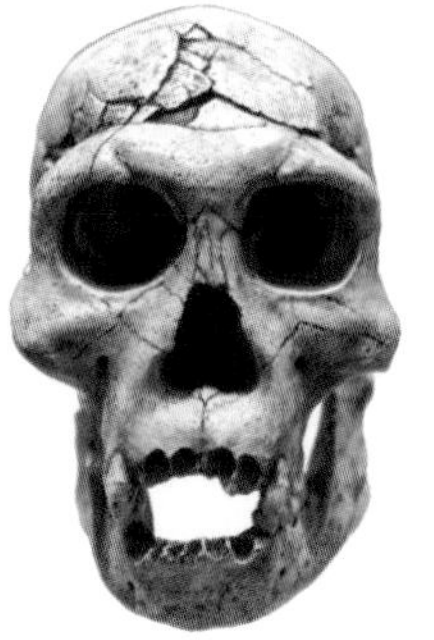
Fossil skull of Homo Erectus.

Life of the first humans

Early humans were only around three to five feet tall. They lived in caves; there is evidence to prove that caves were their first homes. They ate nuts, roots, yams, insects, fish and meat. It took a few million years for them to evolve into modern humans. They developed bigger brains, and used their tongues and voice to talk. They even lost a lot of their body hair. Over time, they understood how to make fire. Soon, they learnt that fire could keep them warm and help them cook food, making it easier to eat. In time, they learnt how to develop and make their own tools. Their tools were very basic, but more often than not, they used sticks and bones to dig and also defend themselves.

Early humans and their survival techniques

Early humans mainly survived by hunting other animals for food. In order to hunt, they built and used different types of tools made of stones. The flint tools, as they were known, were quite useful to cut and scrape flesh from the hides of animals. Later, humans began making hand axes, which were used to chop wood so that they could light a fire in order to stay warm. The first tools were rough and barely useful, but were improved over the years.

Ancient stone tools.

Humans used tools to defend themselves too.

Primitive humans lived outdoors and hunted food.

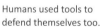

FUN FACT

There is quite a bit of disagreement about when the first humans migrated to other parts of the globe. There is evidence to prove that some of the first humans moved from Africa almost 1.6 million years ago. Interestingly, it is known that early humans reached Asia only around 460,000 years ago and managed to get to Europe only 400,000 years ago.

Prehistoric Period

201 million years ago

Prehistory describes the time that existed before any recorded history, much before writing was discovered. This was prior to the discovery of the pen or quill!

Long before this period, millions of years ago, dinosaurs roamed on Earth. They were a group of animals that came into being around 201 million years ago during the Jurassic Period.

This period is also known as the "age of reptiles". The word dinosaur means "terrible lizard" and was coined by palaeontologist Richard Owen.

Interestingly, the largest dinosaurs were herbivores or plant-eaters, such as the Brachiosaurus! Other dinosaurs like the Allosaurus or Spinosaurus were carnivores or meat-eaters.

People of the Prehistoric Age

All living beings on this planet belong to and have evolved from the Homo sapiens. These are the people that walked upright and straight. They were called hominids. "Homo sapiens" is the Latin term for "wise human", owing to human beings' developed brains, bipedal gait (where one moves using the two rear limbs or legs) and opposable thumbs. Evidence of this species was found in Africa, Middle East and in Europe.

A Homo sapien man.

Homo sapiens

The Neanderthals, a subspecies of the Homo sapiens, lived between 300,000 to 1,000,000 years ago. They knew how to hunt and build shelters. They were food gatherers and hunters. They also wore animal skins. They used rock and bone to scrape off flesh and fat from skins to use them as clothing. There were certain physical differences such as a larger brain, receding chin and a projecting nose. Most importantly, they stood fully upright.

Climate change

The world climate was witnessing remarkable changes around 1.5 million years ago. The climate became very cold. The drop in temperature led to the four periods of cold temperatures called the Ice Age. Each age is known to have lasted anywhere between 40,000 years and 60,000 years. This impacted man's activities.

People of the prehistoric age

Towards the end of the second "Ice Age", with the climate getting warmer, many tribes of hunters and gatherers travelled to different parts of the continent. These people had no definitive literature, but they believed in some rituals that emphasised the manner in which the dead were buried. Hence, burial chambers with artefacts in them have been found in numerous places including Great Britain.

A stonehenge in Great Britian.

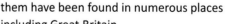

FUN FACT

The first detailed genetic analysis of the Neanderthal genome reveals that some modern humans may have mated with Neanderthals because of which an imprint of the Neanderthal genome was found among modern humans. In fact, biologists say that about 1–4 per cent of the present day human genome was derived from the Neanderthals!

Art of the Prehistoric Age

FUN FACT

Did you know that abalone shells, ochre, bone, charcoal, grindstones and hammer stones were used for different works of art in the prehistoric period? In fact, ochre, which is made from soft rock (either red or yellow pigments) was first powdered then mixed and heated with the crushed stones and/or bones!

The prehistoric art is the oldest form of art, appearing much before literature or sculpting.

Around 20,000 BCE, human beings had settled in all the different parts of the globe and various art forms were discovered from all the different continents from Africa to Europe. From cave paintings in Lascaux and Chauvet in France to the engravings of humans in Asia to the rock art in Australia, the art during this age gives us a glimpse of the life of that period.

20,000 BCE: Human settlement

15,000 BCE: Cave paintings, Lascaux

Cave painting

The Lascaux cave paintings were made with brushes that were made from the fur of animals. Artists from the Palaeolithic age used five different colours including black, violet, yellow, red and brown. Most art that can be recognised dates back to 15,000 BCE and it generally depicted animals, humans and certain symbols. With people engaging in farming activities, art of domestic animals, maps and other landscapes made their presence felt. Pots with different decorations were also made. However, despite this, ceramics were only utilised for domestic purposes since the sixth millennium.

Terracotta vases and goblet bowls are examples of this art.

Children also painted

There has been some evidence of children also using the medium of art to express themselves some 13,000 years ago. In France, the Rouffignac caves have markings called "finger flutings" made by a child, where the art consists of simple lines. The lines have some symbolic meaning. These flutings or meandering lines depict the everyday lives of the people of this time. Some are shaped like animals or have a hut-like appearance called "tectiforms".

Art in all its forms

Art from South Asia is comparatively documented little less than their western counterparts. The cave sites of the Pachmarhi Hills in India amply showcase the life of the people during the Mesolithic period. Central and East Asia have numerous examples of art with carved figurines found in Malta. The archaeological site of Jiahu in China hosted bone flutes that represented the culture and their appreciation for music.

Ice Age and Stone Age

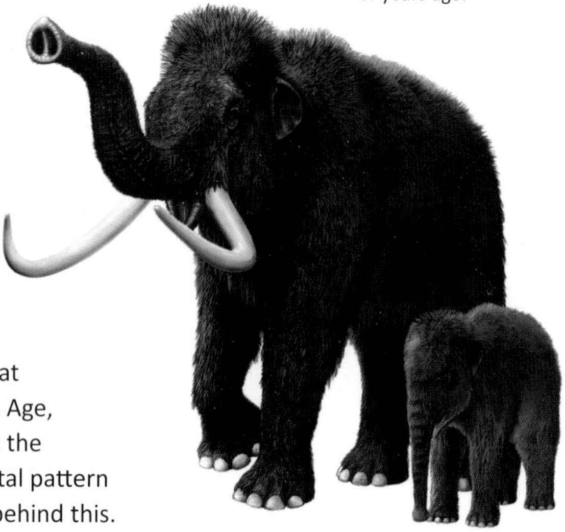

Mammoths walked on Earth thousands of years ago.

The Ice Age occurred during the Pleistocene Epoch (2.6 million to 11,700 years ago) when huge glaciers formed and spread from the North Pole towards the south.

What are glaciers?

A glacier is a large mass of perennial (permanent) ice that is formed by the re-crystallisation of snow. During the Ice Age, such glaciers existed all over Canada, the USA and even the north-western part of Europe. Glaciers continue to exist even today, but are slowly melting as the temperature on earth has been increasing.

Sometimes, the ice was a thousand feet deep. But even in these sub-zero conditions, both plant and animal life existed. Some flowering plants and trees could be seen when the weather turned a little warm. Animals like reindeer and giant mammoths roamed the earth. Mammoths are similar in appearance to today's elephants.

What made Earth cold?

Scientists have not been able to state what exactly caused the Ice Age, but some believe that the change in Earth's orbital pattern could be one reason behind this. A few others believe that the reason could be attributed to the huge amounts of dust and fewer gases that could have made Earth cold.

A melting glacier.

Rise and fall of sea levels

The most recent Ice Age entered its coldest period about 22,000 years ago, when ice sheets covered a great part of North America and Northern Eurasia. As the seas froze, the sea level fell by over 100 m in certain places, exposing bridges of land between land masses. For example, the Bering Strait between Siberia and Alaska became a dry land, allowing animals such as mammoths and deer to move between Asia and North America. They were followed by human hunters, the first humans to colonise North America. When the climate became a little warm, the ice melted, sea levels rose and this as well as other land bridges disappeared. Conditions were extremely harsh for the people who lived near the ice sheets.

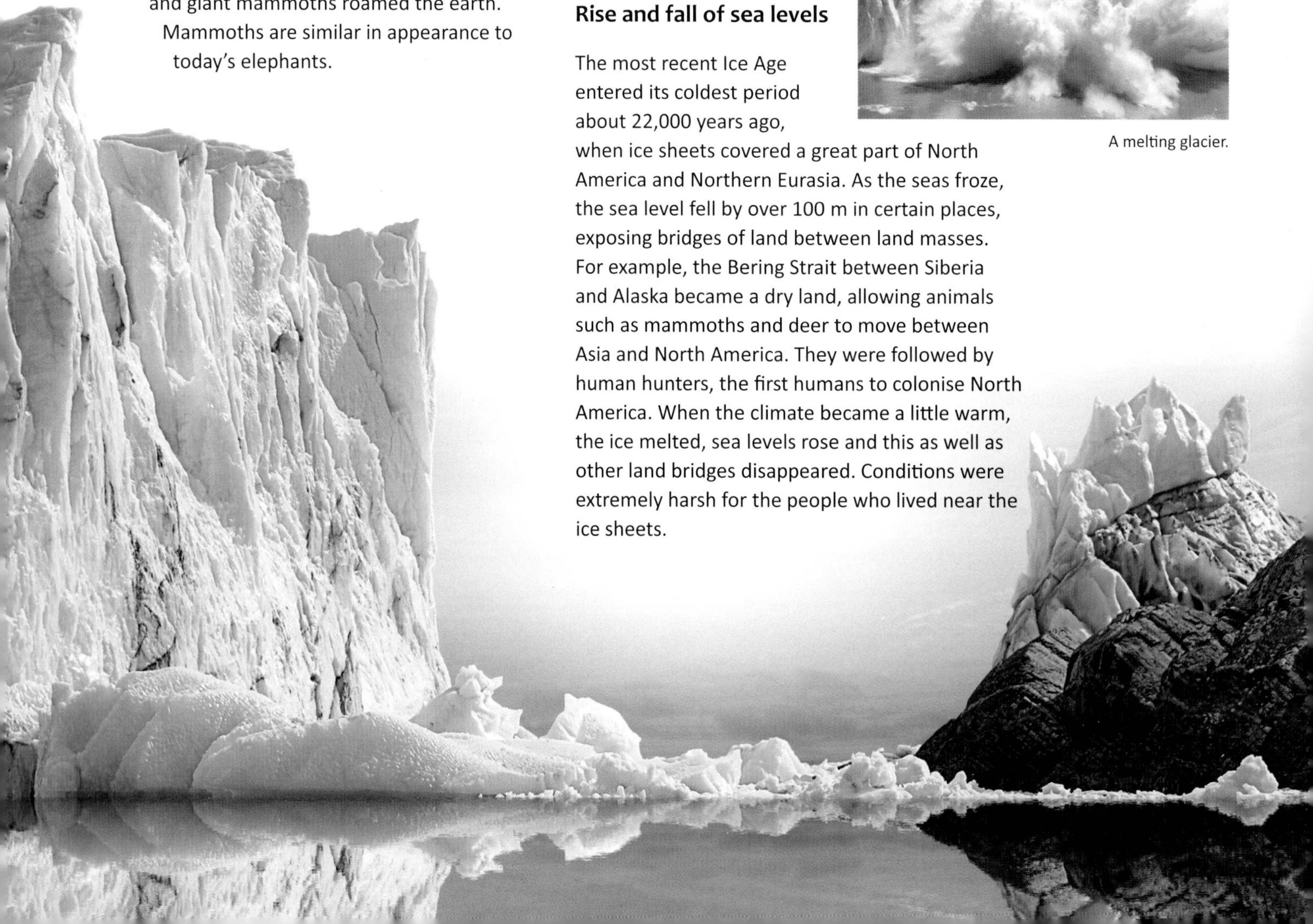

The Stone Age is divided into three separate periods: the Palaeolithic Period, the Mesolithic Period and the Neolithic Period. These divisions are based on the styles of different tools.

The three age system

The term "Stone Age" was coined by the Danish scholar Christian J. Thomsen, who also came up with the "Three Age System". This system is based on the idea of three successive periods, namely the Stone Age, the Bronze Age and the Iron Age. Thomsen arrived at this system after observing the artefacts that were found in archaeological sites.

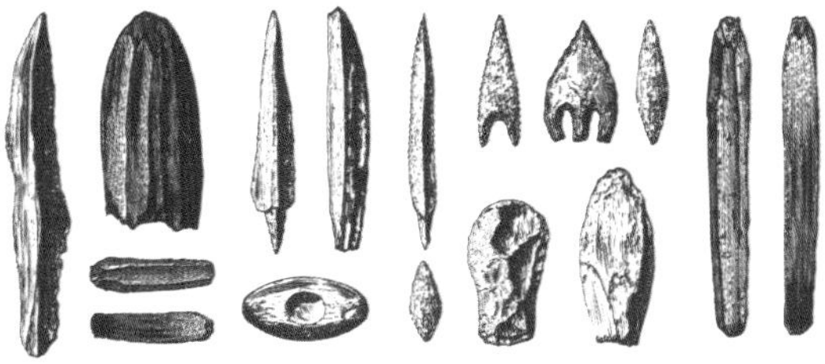

Stone Age tools.

The Stone Age began around 2.5 million years ago and continued till around 3300 BCE, when the Bronze Age began. The Stone Age is the earliest period of human development and the longest phase of humankind's history. It approximately coincides with the Pleistocene geologic period, beginning about two million years ago and ending in various places between 40,000 and 10,000 years ago, when it was succeeded by the Mesolithic period.

FUN FACT

Did you know that when ice melted, different ridges, piles and other formations consisting of gravel, sand and soil were formed? The melting caused huge lakes to be formed and the sea level also rose, while some land sunk!

A Palaeolithic man using a spearhead against a wild animal for his defence.

Stone Age tools

The first known tools were made by the Homo habilis around two million years ago. These were very simple tools made from pebbles. Over time, the tools became more advanced. People soon discovered that flint was one of the best tool-making materials available. It was extremely hard and it could be chipped into several pieces of various shapes and sizes. Stone Age people used flint blades to remove animal skin. The hides were used to make clothes, tents and bags. They would sew the pieces of skin together using needles made of antler or bone.

The tools during this period were made of stone, though other organic materials such as antler, bone, fibre, leather and even wood were used. These tools were used for the purpose of hunting as well as cutting roots, tubers and so on, to be used as food.

Stone Age man making a stone tool. As humans became smarter, they started to make even more complex tools.

1.8 million years ago: Ice Age

2.5 million years ago: Stone Age

Palaeolithic Age

A man from the Palaeolithic Age.

The Palaeolithic Age is also known as the "Old Stone Age", when the use of stone tools was very basic. This age saw the advent of the stone axe. During this period, the main task for humans was to protect themselves from wild animals and to gather food. Stones were also used to make fire.

Palaeoliths

The Lower Palaeolithic period occurred between 2,500,000 to 200,000 years ago. During this period, the hand axe was discovered. Stone flake tools also made an appearance. Around this time, humans preferred to live near water sources, enabling the formations of many river valleys and terraces. Palaeolithic people often lived together in small groups or societies called bands and survived on hunting and gathering plants. The artefacts found from this period are called "Palaeoliths".

2.5 million years ago: Palaeoliths

35,000 million years ago: Neanderthals

Stone tools of the Palaeolithic Age

A sophisticated Lower Palaeolithic tradition, known as the chopper/chopping-tool industry, is widely distributed in the Eastern Hemisphere. This tradition is believed to have been the work of the hominine species named "Homo erectus". Although no fossil tools have yet been found, it is believed that Homo erectus perhaps made tools of wood and bone as well as stone. Some of the earliest known hand axes were found at Olduvai Gorge in Tanzania with the remains of Homo erectus. Besides the hand-axe tradition, a distinct and different stone-tool industry developed, which was based on flakes of stone. Special tools were made from worked flakes of flint that were carefully shaped.

An example of Palaeolithic stone tools.

FUN FACT

Did you know that the stone axe that was unearthed at the Lower Awash Valley in Ethiopia, Africa, was 3.4 million years old?

Life in different Palaeolithic periods

The people in the lower Palaeolithic period ate wild plants, fruits and meat. They were called "Neanderthals". During this age, people developed their creative skills, which was evident from the discovery of pendants, necklaces and other forms of jewellery made from shell, bone and ivory. During this period, humans showed an inclination towards arts. They engaged in religious and spiritual activities.

Hunting and gathering

Typically, women would gather wild plants and wood for fire, while men would hunt. Group hunting was also practiced for big animals like mammoths. Researchers believe that the people around this time knew about herbs and plants. Hunting was often geared to the seasonal killing of one or two species: mammoth or reindeer in Eurasia and wildebeest or zebra in Africa. Additionally, the Upper Palaeolithic bands of Europe and Northern Asia attained a degree of hunting efficiency unsurpassed even by advanced specialists such as the Eskimo or some of the North American Indians.

Technological advancement

This was a time of great advancement. The hunting populations became regionally specialised and improved their social and economic behaviour by using a greater variety of raw materials. They used the raw materials rigorously and introduced efficient means of obtaining food.

A group of Palaeolithic people living in a cave.

Growth of cultures

There was a growth of diverse human cultures: Aurignacians, Gravettian, Perigordian, Solutrean and Magdalenian. Aurignacians migrated from Asia to Europe. Solutreans came to Europe from the east. The Magdalean culture was perhaps the most impressive. Their remnants show that the Magdalenian people painted in caves and used tools made from microliths.

FUN FACT

A group of humans called "Homo heidelbergensis" settled in Europe from Africa. They eventually evolved into Neanderthals.

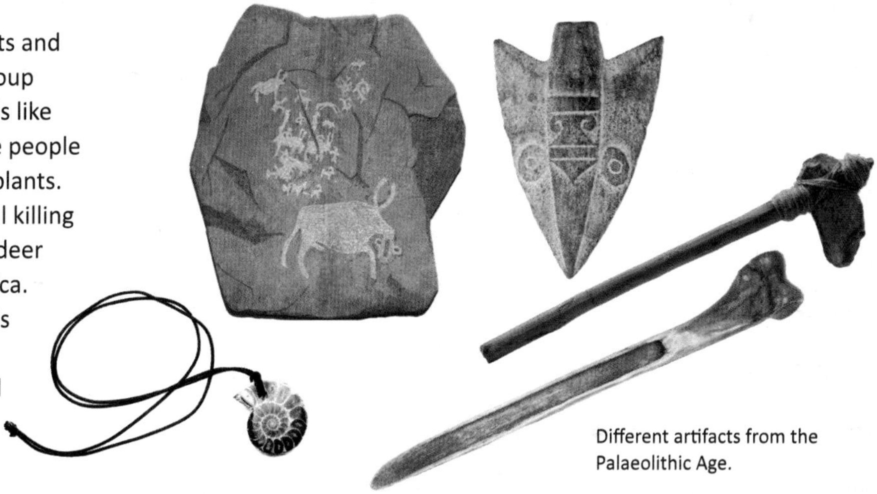

Different artifacts from the Palaeolithic Age.

Palaeolithic art

Two forms of Palaeolithic art are known to modern scholars: small sculptures and monumental paintings, incised designs and reliefs on the walls of caves. Evidence suggests that small sculptured pieces dominated the Upper Palaeolithic artistic traditions of Eastern Europe. The purpose of art in Palaeolithic life continues to be a debate.

A Venus figurine from the Palaeolithic Age.

Mesolithic Age

The Mesolithic Age is also known as the Middle Stone Age. It existed between the Palaeolithic period, where chipped stone tools were developed and the Neolithic Period, where polished stone tools were made.

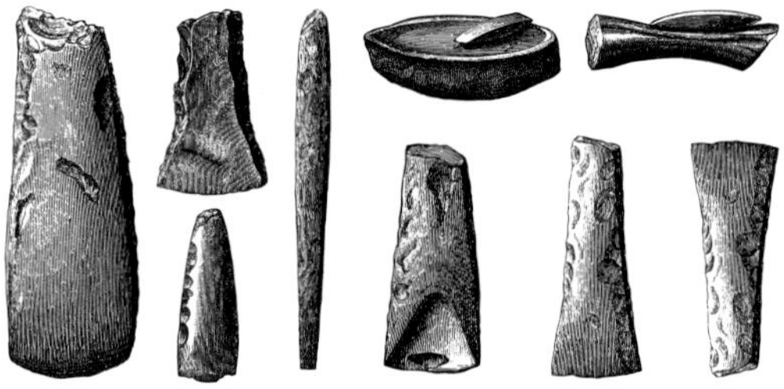

Collection of different types of stone tools.

Tools of the Mesolithic Age

During this period, chipped stone tools called "microliths" were used. These microliths were very tiny stone tools, often of geometric shape, made from a bladelet and mounted singly or in series. The different tools included small flint microliths almost the same size as the human thumb. These microliths were used to make lightweight spears and arrows. The tools were made from bones and were to be used as fish hooks. Deer antlers were used for digging.

People of the Mesolithic Age

People during this period hunted, fished and lived along rivers and lakes. Pottery and the bow were developed during this period. Evidence of people living during this period was found in the Pyrenees region and later spread to Switzerland, Belgium and Scotland.

Tent houses

The nomadic Mesolithic people lived in temporary "tent houses" made from animal skins on poles. They were also known as hunter-gatherers because of the constant gathering and hunting for food. They hunted wild animals and gathered wild berries and nuts.

Evolving living conditions

Their nomadic style of living transformed due to favourable climate, good rainfall and warm atmosphere, which led to better food security conditions.

Climate during the Mesolithic Age

The retreat of the Pleistocene glaciers, the rising sea levels and the extinction of megafauna (large-bodied animals) was accompanied by a growth in forests and a major redistribution of animals and plants. After the climate stabilised, people moved northward into previously glaciated areas and adopted new subsistence methods. The climate during this period was warmer as compared to today and the landscape was made up of trees such as oak, elm and alders.

FUN FACT

The word "Epipaleolithic" is also used besides Mesolithic, which describes the various groups that lived during this period.

Mesolithic people are said to have forced most of the megafauna into extinction.

Pottery

The people of this time made distinctive pots with a point or knob base and flared rims. Evidence shows that the earliest forms of pottery from the Mesolithic era could be found in the areas around Lake Baikal in Siberia. There are diverse Mesolithic sites that include Star Carr, Newbury, Aveline's Hole and Howick House in England, Franchthi Cave in Greece, Cramond in Scotland, Mount Sandel in Ireland, Pulli Settlement in Estonia, Swifterbant culture in the Netherlands, Lepenski Vir in Serbia and Shigir Idol in Russia. The remnants of evidence found in these sites date back to 7500 BCE.

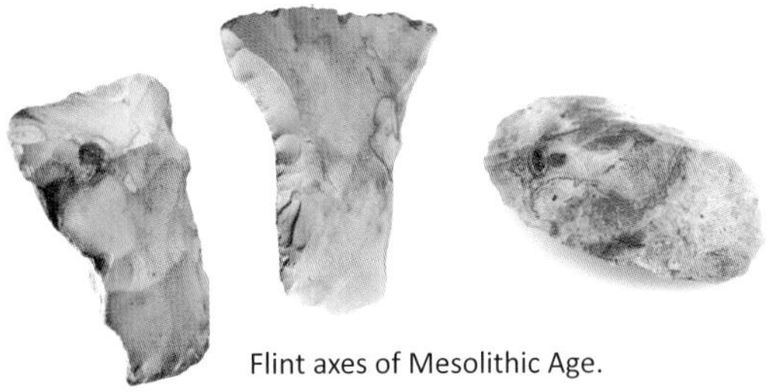

Flint axes of Mesolithic Age.

Cultures during the Mesolithic period

The Azilian culture is believed to be one of the early forms that emerged during the Late Paleolithic and Early Mesolithic Europe. It originated around the Pyrenees region and then spread to Europe. The culture that followed was the Tardenoisian culture, which also spread across Europe. The Maglemosian culture, named after a site in Denmark, is found in the Baltic region and North England. It was prevalent during the mid-Mesolithic period. It is here that hafted axes (an enhancement over the Palaeolithic hand axe) and bone tools were found. The Ertebolle culture during this period was centred on Denmark. The other cultures that closely followed the aforementioned cultures were the Campignian and Asturian cultures, which spread across the Middle East, while the Capsian culture spread across North Africa. The last one was the Natufian culture that brought about the beginning of the Neolithic era.

Emergence of farming

During this period, humans learnt the use of seeds of certain grasses, such as barley and wheat, as food. It is believed that humans may have thrown seeds into the soil and realised that these grow into plants. This is how humans began to grow their own crops. Humans also needed water for the crops to grow, so they began settling near plains with an extremely good supply of water.

FUN FACT

It was during this period that "polished" stone was first discovered.

End of the Mesolithic period

This period ended as farming spread across Europe. Cereal crops such as wheat and barley were introduced. Cattle and sheep were domesticated. Burial and ritualistic monuments began to be made and used for the first time. People also began making and using pottery full-fledged. It is unclear if this period ended with the influx of people who replaced the indigenous hunters and gatherers or with the initiation of new ideas and technologies, which was slowly adapted by the local population. Interestingly, this period was one of the most long-lived periods that lasted for over 6,000 years.

These pottery-making Mesolithic cultures can be found peripheral to the sedentary Neolithic cultures.

Neolithic Age

The word "Neo" comes from the Greek word "*Neos*", meaning "new". Therefore, the term Neolithic means "New Stone". The New Stone Age people used more sophisticated tools that were made from different types of stones such as jadeite or schist. Quite similar to the Old Stone Age, the New Stone Age humans also used stone tools.

Importance of wood

It was during this period that wood played a key role in the life of human beings. It was made a universally accepted building and hunting material. Canoes, paddles and other such materials were made during this period. Huts began to be made out of branches and stones. Slowly, the people settled in communities. Huts that seemed huddled together allowed for better defence. A contributing factor for this change was the emergence of agriculture.

Transition from food collecting to food cultivation

People slowly understood how to farm and domesticate animals. This created a huge shift in the way they lived because now they had a stable source of food and did not need to travel in search of food. This also gave them more time to explore other arts and crafts. The Neolithic people showed an interest in pottery, which mainly started in their quest to make vessels to store food. Soon, they also started living in bigger settlements and with larger communities.

A seamless pattern with petroglyphs.

Food cultivation

This period witnessed the cultivation of different crops like barley and wheat. The transition was long and gradual. It spread over Europe and the Indus Valley around 3000 BCE.

Grains of rye.

Around this time people were less dependent on plants for food, but with the growth of grain cultivation, cereals slowly began to be included in their diet. However, grains were mostly used for rituals.

Domestication of animals

Around this time, humans observed that some animals would come close to human habitation in search of food and would eat food that humans disposed. They learnt to tame these animals and use them for their own advantage. Animals like cow and sheep were domesticated during this period, to ensure a ready supply of meat, milk, wool and leather. The dog was the first animal that was domesticated during this period. Dogs would help humans and warn them of any danger as well.

3000 BCE: Food cultivation

3000 BCE: Stonehenge causeway enclosure

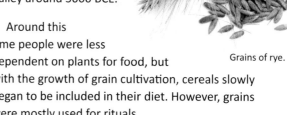

Neolithic people began to cook food.

Change in lifestyle

Farming and herding improved the living conditions of people to a great extent. Growing crops assured a continuous supply of food to man. Hunting provided him with a continuous supply of meat, milk and animal skin for clothing. Now that man did not have to be on the constant look out for food, he had time to improve and develop new skills. To take care of his crops, he needed to remain at one place for a long time. Therefore, permanent human settlements began to be established and community life began to emerge. Mud houses with thatched roofs began to be built during this time.

Neolithic houses had no windows, but had one doorway.

Emergence of communities

Communities began to emerge over time. The beginning of community life led to the concept of families being introduced. Families living in a Neolithic village were closely related and shared similar customs, beliefs and ways of worship. These people carried out farming, herding, hunting, gathering honey and fishing in groups. They jointly owned land, forests and water sources among other natural resources. As a result, there was equality of resource use and ownership.

Inventions and discoveries

People made significant progress during this time. Humans discovered basalt, a type of rock that they used to make tools which could be sharpened and polished. Humans also created many spindles and bone needles.

The problem of surplus food came about as humans started farming on a large scale. This is how they developed the idea of making pots. As time passed, Neolithic people learnt how to bake clay vessels on fire in which they could store liquids as well as cook.

FUN FACT

Most clothing was made from skins of animals during this period. In fact, a well preserved corpse from 3300 BCE found in the Tyrolean Alps, revealed that Otzi the Iceman wore clothing made entirely from animal skins.

Neolithic art

During this period, art was geometric and not representational, except among the hunter-fishers of the Taiga. Pots, which were always handmade, were painted in Southeastern Europe, Southern Italy and Sicily. In other places, they were adorned with carved, impressed or stamped patterns. Many designs are "skeuomorphic". This means that they enhance the pots' similarity to vessels of basketry or other material.

Stonehenge, England is believed to be a remnant of the Neolithic age.

Iron Age

Iron Age was a time when humans used tools and weapons made of iron. This age started somewhere in 1200 BCE in the middle and southeastern part of Europe. Around this time, iron was mixed with other materials to fortify it.

Iron anvil and tools.

Iron shaping

Iron was first extracted from rocks. This extracted material was worked into a shape by heating it repeatedly and then hammering it against an anvil. This process of shaping the raw material was called "smiting".

An anvil is a block of heavy iron that is flat on the top and has hollow inward facing sides on which different metals, particularly iron, can be hammered and made into different shapes.

Uses of iron

During the Iron Age, iron was not just used to form tools. It was used to make ploughs. These iron-tipped ploughs helped the farmers tackle heavy clay-like soil with ease, which led to significant progress in farming and the introduction of various new crops.

Iron was also used to make weapons and create armours like shields and helmets. These were created to protect the soldiers fighting in battles. The use of iron to create weapons also enabled people to create arms against each other for the first time, thus beginning the history of battles and warfare.

Iron was also used to make coins. In fact, coins were first minted in Britain around 100 BCE.

Discoveries and innovations

It was during the Iron Age that forts and bridges were being constructed for the first time. During this period, humans discovered the concept of mining to find salt and other precious minerals. The use of horse chariots was also first introduced during this period.

A new type of wheat was grown during this age. This wheat was called "bread wheat" and it was ground using rotary querns. Querns are stone tools that are used to grind (sometimes by hand) different kinds of materials like grains and cereals.

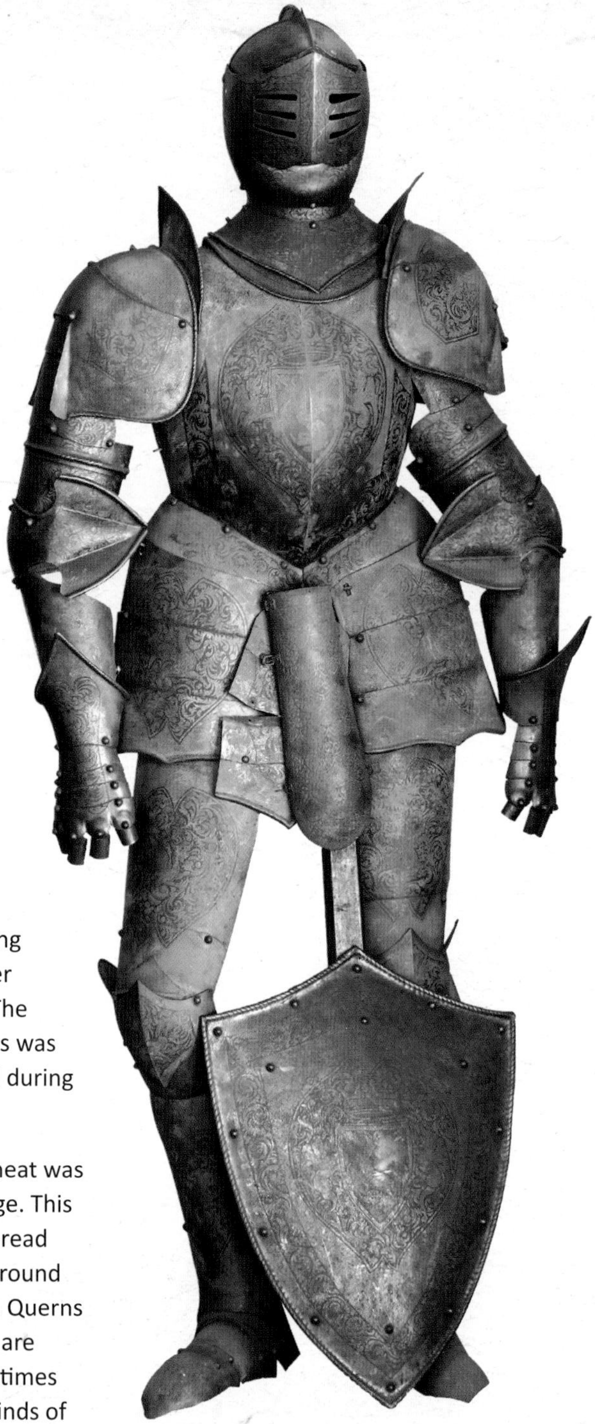

Shields were often decorated with a painted pattern or had an animal representation.

A quern stone with grain.

Life expectancy

During this period, the life expectancy of humans was just around 30 years, a hurdle that we have been able to overcome thanks to the advanced medical technology that we possess today. Back then, only around a quarter of the children born actually survived to experience adulthood.

During this period, people had small farms and increased farm yields. The Iron Age also marked the start of trading, when people began to sell and buy grains.

Weapons became a requirement for all households between 1900 and 1400 BCE, just when the tempering technique was invented. The Hittite rulers tried to keep the iron workings a secret, but after their downfall, migration movement ensured that the secret of iron forging soon spread to South Europe and the Middle East.

Emergence of farming

Before the Iron Age, human farming was dependent on temperate forests. Due to this, the cultivation of crops was limited. The Iron Age led to the creation of various tools that enhanced farming. Ploughs drawn by oxen also became common, thereby changing the agricultural patterns. These ploughs could dig through tough soil with ease, enabling the growth of new types of crops.

Villages were made more secure during the Iron Age. A farm during this period would have a hedge and ditch to deter any intruder, human or animal. Timber also became an equally important crop after wheat, barley and beans. It was used for fuel, building houses, carts, etc. As farming itself offered so many opportunities, everyone worked in the farms and very few chose to be artisans or take up another occupation.

During this period, animals herded were kept close to human dwellings.

However, it must be noted that the women during this period made skilled earthenware which were used for cooking as well as trading purposes. Women also did farmwork.

Their actual life expectancy, too, was short. In a family consisting of five girls and five boys, only two or three would actually survive and most people did not live longer than 45 years.

Iron tools used for farming.

An old iron pot and pewter spoon.

FUN FACT

Did you know that the Early Iron Age in Central Europe from 800 BCE to 500 BCE was called the "Hallstatt" period, while the later Iron Age was called La Tène?

Ancient Greek Civilisation

This civilisation existed from the end of the Mycenaean civilisation (1200 BCE) until Alexander the Great's death. The Greek empire spread from Greece to Europe. The Greeks were mainly involved in agriculture. Owing to a shortage of land, they were forced to look at sea-borne trade routes for more land. This led to clashes between the rich and poor, which paved the way for the beginning of democracy.

Olympic Games were held in elaborate stadiums.

Olympic Games

The first Olympic Games (as per records) were held in 776 BCE. As per a popular Greek legend, however, Heracles or the Roman Hercules, the son of Zeus, started the ancient Olympic Games. These Games were played every four years for around 1,200 years, but the Roman Emperor Theodosius I believed that the Games were unchristian and hence abolished them. Pierre de Coubertin proposed the Modern Olympic Games 1,500 years later.

Ancient Greeks started the Olympic Games. The first Olympic Games were held in 776 BCE at the Greek City of Olympia. It is said that Pheidippides ran from Athens to Sparta to request for help against the Persians before the Battle of Marathon.

Largest city-state

Athens, the largest city-state in Greece became a commercial centre and banker for the Greek world. During the fifth century BCE, the coin of Athens became the international currency of the Mediterranean.

People and their lives

Most Greeks lived in multi-storey apartment blocks equipped with bathrooms and toilets. Greek men wore a large piece of cloth that was draped over a woollen tunic, while women wore tunics that would reach their ankles. Both genders wore leather sandals on their feet.

The clothes worn by the men and women of Ancient Greece.

Ancient Greece and the three periods

The three chronicled periods of Ancient Greece are the Archaic Period, from the 700 BCE to 480 BCE, when democracy emerged; the Classical Period, when philosophers like Socrates and Plato existed. This period ended with the death of Alexander the Great in 323 BCE and soon after this period came the Hellenistic Period from 323 to 146 BCE, when Greece was conquered by Rome.

The Parthenon was built for Athena, the patron Goddess of Athens.

FUN FACT

Did you know that the English word "politics" has its origin in the Greek word "polis", which stands for the term city state?

Democracy and its Origin in Greece

FUN FACT

Did you know that Ancient Greeks developed the word "alphabet"? The words "alpha" and "beta" make "alphabet"!

Theseus fighting the Centaur.

Athens was the one of the most known and biggest democracies. Citizens met, chose members of the government and formed a small council. The council discussed public matters by laying it before the assembly. In fact, this council also selected public officials whose positions were constantly rotated.

Greek mythology

Greek mythology would often feature very interesting characters, both human and beasts or creatures, to showcase different qualities from bravery to intelligence and greed to ego. Many of these creatures featured in stories of brave battles including the one with the "Minotaur" where the brave King Theseus kills the monster who devoured children and killed people with its deadly horns.

People during the ancient Greek civilisation

Women had very little independence during this period. They had slaves working for them who cooked, cleaned and looked after the crops. Slaves were a part and parcel of the ancient Greek life. Male slaves looked after the women, while the men were away. Ancient Greeks dressed in a long cotton cloth called "chiton". However, slaves were allowed to wear just a loincloth or a small cloth strip that was tied around the waist. The Greeks were polytheistic, that is, they believed in many Gods and Goddesses. The Greeks built statues of these Gods temples. One of these is the Parthenon temple, which was built for Goddess Athena, the protector of the city of Athens. Of these Zeus was the most important God.

Story of Medusa

Another battle story featured the horrible monster Medusa who had snakes for hair. She had tusks and a face that could turn anybody who saw it into stone! The brave warrior Perseus killed Medusa by wearing a helmet of invisibility. He looked at her reflection from his shiny shield. Greek mythology had many stories with interesting mythological characters such as the three-headed dog "Cerberus" who was the watchdog for the underworld. Another story was that of Pandora who was very curious about a box that Zeus had left behind. The box had a note that said "Do not open". But Pandora's curiosity made her open the box which is said to have released disease, pain and death in the world.

Perseus with the head of Medusa.

Aegean Civilisation

The Aegean Sea, a branch of the Mediterranean Sea, had the Greek mainland to its west and the island of Crete to its south. Present day Turkey was to its east. This region had entered the Bronze Age even as the rest of the region was in the Stone Age. Knossos in Crete Island was the home of King Minos the son of Zeus and Europa. Therefore, this civilisation is called the Minoan civilisation. There is evidence to prove that by 1600 BCE the Minoans had become predominant residents of the Aegean region.

Archaeological site of Phaistos, Crete, Greece.

Etymology

The origin of the name "Aegean" is said to come from the Greek town of Aegae or Aegea—named after the Queen of the Amazons who died at sea. Others believe that the name comes from "Aigaion"—which is the name of a sea goat. Some others believe that it is named after Aegeus, who is the father of Theseus who drowned in the sea believing his son had died during the Crete expedition on his way to defeat Minotaur.

Emergence of bronze

A lot of artefacts, especially pottery, from the Bronze Age has been found in Crete. Radiocarbon dating proves that these items were imported to Egypt as well. In fact, noted poet Homer's works contain certain customs of this civilisation, such as the warriors using bronze weapons and helmets.

Decoding the Aegean civilisation

The Aegean people lived near the sea. Much about them came to be known from the excavations carried out in sites near Crete. Unfortunately, many of the early writings found there could not be deciphered. It is known that an earthquake that devastated the Thera Island affected Cretan cities.

FUN FACT

Radiocarbon dating is a method of age determination of organic matter that is dependent on the decay of radiocarbon or carbon 14. Carbon 12 is formed continuously in nature by carbon's interaction with nitrogen 14 and neutrons. Tree rings are often used for radiocarbon measurements.

Urns from archaeological sites dating back to the Minoan civilisation.

Bronze helmets with tusks from the wild boar.

Homer is the author of the poems, *The Iliad* and *The Odyssey* known as "Homeric Epics".

Greek literature

The Greeks have a rich history of literature. Greek literature includes the form of epic poems like Homer's "*The Iliad*" and *The Odyssey*. A theory suggests that Homer did not make the stories in these poems, rather just wrote them down. The content is said to be from legends that other poets and bards had been narrating for hundreds of years. Other works such as Hesiod's "*Theogony*" or poems by Archilochus and Sappho were also from this culture. Next, come the plays that were essentially either tragedies or comedies. Among these were the ones written by Aeschylus or Sophocles and Euripides. Menander and Aristophanes wrote comedies. Philosophy also originated in Greece from the philosophical writings of Plato. Aristotle, a student of Plato, also wrote philosophical prose.

Ancient Greek sarcophagus decorated with scenes from *The Iliad*.

Commodity production

The Aegean archipelago produced various commodities including grapes, figs, raisins, honey, wheat, vegetables, wine and certain herbs. Marble became an intrinsic aspect of their commerce. With the export of marble, the ancient Greeks became quite wealthy.

Prominent civilisations

Two different civilisations were prominent during this period, the Minoan and Mycenaean. A devastating earthquake resulted in the complete destruction of cities in Crete. By 1400 BCE, the Minoan civilisation completely disappeared. The Mycenaean's invaded the Greek mainland. They built huge fortresses, which provided refuge during battles and wars. The Dorians defeated them. The Dorians had a distinct dialect and were subdivided into tribes called "Dymanes", "Pamphyloi" and "Hylleis". They brought about the infamous "dark age", which spread poverty. This lasted for nearly 300 years. In 750 BCE, the Ionians were responsible for introducing cultural elements including writing, art and reading. A new period now known as the Hellenic period emerged, which made the Greek civilisations, one of the most powerful.

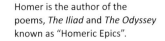

Round tower of Spinalonga fortress, Crete, Greece.

1600 BCE: Aegean Civilisation

1400 BCE: Minoan Civilisation ends

Hellenistic Age

Back in 336 BCE, Alexander the Great began his rule over the Greek kingdom of Macedonia. He died 13 years later. He had built an impressive empire that stretched from Greece all the way to India. This great expansion spread Greek ideas and culture to different parts of the world. This period was called the Hellenistic Age. The word Hellenistic originates from "Hellazein", which means "to speak Greek" or "to identify with the Greeks". The period lasted until the Roman troops began to conquer all the territories that the Macedonian king had ruled over.

Alexander the Great.

Warfare during this age

Towards the end of the Classical period in 360 BCE, the city-states were very fragile and jumbled owing to 200 years of fighting when the Athenians fought against the Persians. Then, the Spartans fought against the Athenians and finally the Thebans and Persians fought against the Athenians. This constant warfare made it easy for Macedonia to rise to power under the leadership of King Philip II.

It was during King Philip's reign that the expansion of the Macedonian empire started. Advanced tools of warfare aided them in this pursuit. These include the long-range catapults that had pikes called "sarissas" and were almost 16 feet long that were used as spears by the soldiers. King Philip was assassinated and his son Alexander took over the imperial expansion project. After Alexander's death, the conquered lands were divided into three powerful dynasties including the Ptolemies of Egypt, Antigonids of Greece and Macedonia and the Seleucids of Syria and Persia.

A silhouette of Macedonian soldiers.

Ancient Greek warrior in combat.

Spread of culture

Alexander was responsible for the spread of the Greek culture throughout the Persian Empire. However, Alexander gave importance to the local culture and ensured that the local customs continued. He was one of those kings who embraced local customs and encouraged his soldiers to marry Persian women. Alexander is said to be responsible for the Hellenistic age.

FUN FACT

Did you know that in the Hellenistic age items like ivory, gold, ebony, spices, cotton and sugars were imported from India?

A sculpture from the Hellenistic period.

The Hellenistic People

During this age there was a constant need to show and display the wealth for everyone to see—as a result, elaborate palaces were built. Museums, zoos, universities and libraries were sponsored. The university at Alexandria was home to noted mathematicians such as Archimedes, Euclid and Apollonius. People spoke a language called "Koine"—a colloquial form of Greek. Some people joined religions like the cults of Fortune and Isis that promised its followers wealth and immortality. This period ended in 31 BCE when in the Battle of Actium, Romans defeated Marc Antony's fleet.

Growth of cultures

This was a time of great learning in different fields from math and arts to architecture. It was a time when Archimedes, Hero and Euclid made discoveries. This period was also a time of relative peace, which is one of the reasons why travel and trade grew. Antipater from the city of Sidon is credited with a poem that sites down the Seven Wonders of the World. He picked these buildings and statues for the beautiful architecture and art that they exhibited. The different places of prominence in the Hellenistic period include Alexandria in Egypt, Antioch in Syria and Pergamum in Asia Minor. An interesting fact is that though none of these cities were in Greece, they were all influenced by Greek architecture.

Greek architecture was also visible in the universities of Taxila and Nalanda in India.

End of the Hellenistic period

The Hellenistic Period ended in 31 BCE. With the death of Alexander the Great, there was no strong leader left to protect his kingdoms. This was brought about by the conquest of the remaining Hellenistic kingdoms by the Roman Empire. The wars between its rulers also weakened the Hellenistic kingdoms, leaving them open for the attacks by the Romans.

336 BCE: Alexander's rule over Macedonia

31 BCE: The Hellenistic Period ends

FUN FACT

The Hellenistic Period is usually defined as a transition period between Alexander the Great's death and the expansion of the Roman Empire.

The fortress in Alexandria, Egypt.

Ancient Italic Period

Ancient Italic people inhabited Italy prior to the Roman Italy, as we know it today. It was a region that was greatly influenced by Greek culture. In fact, Etruscans were a powerful nation and it was them who taught the Romans the alphabet and numbers.

Etruscan gravestones, "Pietra fetida" funerary sphinx, middle sixth century BCE.

Carvings of ancient Etruscans.

The Etruscans

The Greeks knew the Etruscans as Tyrsenoi, while the Latins called them Etrusci. The Etruscan region consisted of the areas that bordered the Tyrrhenian Sea in the west, the Tiber River in the south and east, while in the north was the Arno River. This region was rich in metal ores such as copper, iron and tin.

They dominated the western coasts of Italy and prospered. The Greek connect started around 775 BCE when the Greek Islanders of Euboea moved near the Bay of Naples and settled there. The Etruscans traded with the Greeks. They traded lumber and fur to the east and purchased spices and perfume. The Etruscans had a government system, where the control was held by the central government.

The origin of the Etruscan civilisation is unknown. However, the people from this period are said to have come from the Villanovan culture or from invasions that took place in the East of this area. Etruscan expansion was focussed both to the north beyond the Apennines and into Campania.

The Toga

The Etruscans created the Toga, which became the official costume of the Romans. It was made from a semi circular white wool cloth piece. Only emperors or senators used purple coloured clothing. They were known for their gold and semi-precious stoned jewellery. These ancient Italic people played board games including checkers and chess. They influenced Roman architecture, particularly the grid plan city system. The Etruscans followed a Polytheistic religion. The Etruscan language does not figure in any literary work. There is a playwright named Volnius who wrote the "Tuscan Tragedies".

FUN FACT

Did you know that the Ancient Romans used oil instead of soap while bathing? A metal tool called "strigil" was used to scrape off the oil that was scrubbed into the skin.

Ancient roman man and woman wearing the Toga.

Etruscan inscriptions

These inscriptions were found in the Zagreb mummy wrapping during the nineteenth century in Egypt. The wrapping was a book of linen cloth and was cut into strips and wrapped around the mummy. It had some 1300 words written in black ink and is known as the longest existing Etruscan text. More than 10,000 Etruscan inscriptions were found on vases, statues and jewellery as well as on tombstones. But there is still no clarity on the pronunciation of the Etruscan letters. There was also some evidence that they had some music notation system as well. The Etruscan language was in use by the people up until the first century CE, but later became the language in which priests and scholars conversed and studied.

A commemorative plaque.

FUN FACT

Did you know that the Tuscan region is named after the Etruscans? Tuscany comes from the Latin word "Tuscanus", which is derived from the word "Tuscas", meaning an Etruscan.

Ancient Italic people and their customs

Religion became a uniting factor for the diverse Etruscan cities. These people had a strong belief in life after death. The beliefs can be amply gauged from the frescoed paintings in Tarquinia in northern Rome. The Etruscans were deeply influenced by mysticism, which we could even call "superstition".

Unlike Greek and Roman societies, women sat with their husbands to eat at banquets and had their own possessions. They were also very active in politics. The Etruscans were both economically and geographically rich. They controlled the Tyrrhenian Sea, and thereby controlled the Mediterranean and the continent of Europe.

Downfall of the Etruscan cities

After 400 years of Etruscan rule, they could not hold against the force of the reorganised Romans, who had managed to unite themselves and gained over their opponents quite easily.
By 265 BCE the Romans had already claimed the Etruscan cities.

Ancient Etruscan art.

Etruscan warrior riding a chariot.

Etruscan Roman archeology museum.

Barbarian Invasions

There are numerous reasons that led to the barbaric invasion. One of them was the decline of the Roman military and also lead poisoning through water and food. Few historians claimed this could have caused lower births, anaemia and gout among the Roman citizens. Another cause was the split of the empire and the failing economy. Even as the Roman Empire got divided, not a single emperor could withstand the invasion from the different tribes of Northeastern Europe.

Anglo Saxon stone monument

Germanic tribe invasion

In 410, Rome was attacked by Germanic tribes who moved across the Roman Empire in a destructive and barbaric manner which earned them the name. These tribes settled down over the vast empire in different regions. For instance, the Angles and Saxons settled in England, while the Franks in France and Lombards made Italy their hometown. The Huns were a nomadic group who plundered the Roman Empire, but eventually lived in Eastern Europe, Central Asia and the Caucasus.

The Franks, Angles and Saxons

The Franks ruled in the northern part of France from 481 to 511. Clovis ruled over the tribe and also followed Christianity. In time, the Franks married the native Gallo-Roman people and soon the cultures merged. While in Spain, the Alans, Sueves and Vandals occupied Spain after crossing the Pyrenees, but when the Visigoth King crushed Sueves tribes, Spain came under the Visigoth rule. In England, the Saxons conquered Sussex in 492 and by the sixth century Angles and Saxons conquered an entire part in Eastern England. Not all Saxons and Angles were interested in war as some even traded with the Romans. Pope Gregory managed to convert the Angles and Saxons to Christianity.

An artist's imagination of the Franks, Angles and Saxons.

FUN FACT

These people were originally from a place called "Gaul", which was the name given to their military area. They were believed to have come from a common background and had similar religious faith.

Attila the Hun

Being a warrior race, the Huns were very good horse riders. They were feared because they plundered kingdoms and were very violent. Led by King Attila, they were dreaded by the European Empire. The Huns devastated the Gaul region and the other barbarians joined the Goths and Franks. The Burgundians joined hands to defeat the Huns at the "Battle of the nations"—as the battle was called.

Defeat of the Huns

They were defeated, but Attila did not give up, he marched through Italy, leaving in his wake a devastated Rome. Pope Leo I, assisted by St Peter and St Paul were left with the job of making Attila see sense, and thereby ensured that he halted and did not go further with his plundering of Rome. It also did not help that the Huns soon found themselves troubled by famine and plague and the numbers in their armies began to drop. Attila's retreat was soon followed by his death—he died after he choked to death from a nosebleed. After the death of Attila, his sons split the empire amongst them, but the Huns never returned to their former glory. Soon, this clan mixed with others including Germans and Slavs.

Decline of Rome

In 537 CE, the aqueducts (water supply stations) of Rome were destroyed and the Romans died without water. The population fell by almost 90 per cent, putting the city to an end. Gibbon, the historian wrote in his *History of the Decline and Fall of the Roman Empire*, "the decline of Rome was the natural and inevitable effect of immoderate greatness. The story of its ruin is simple and obvious, instead of inquiring why the Roman Empire was destroyed we should rather be surprised that it existed for so long."

Painting of the Huns attack in Turkey.

Romulus and Remus

According to an old legend, Rome was founded by twin brothers named Romulus and Remus in 735 BCE. At birth, they were left to die at the bank of the Tiber river in Italy. They were saved by a she-wolf who also fed them. They were later discovered by a shepherd who raised them. Years later, as adults, they decided to build a city in honour of the she-wolf that rescued them. The city was to be built on the Palatine Hill where they were found by the she-wolf.

410 CE: Germanic Tribe invasion on Rome

537 CE: Decline of the Roman Empire

A mosaic depicting the Sword of God, the legendary weapon of Attila the Hun.

Old map of Barbarian kingdoms before Clovis I.

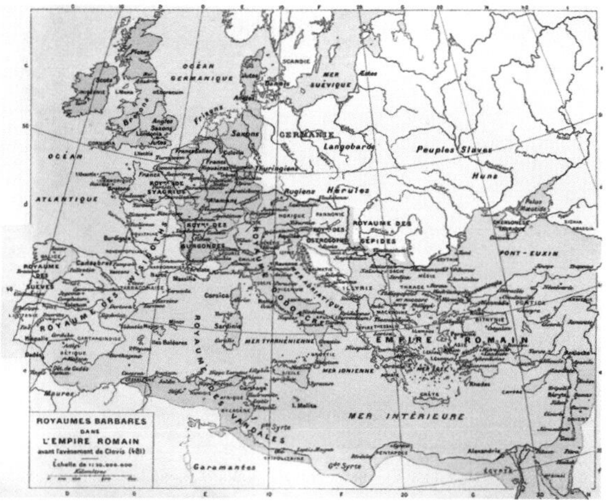

FUN FACT

Rome was named after Romulus, the first king of Rome. He won this title after a quarrel with his brother Remus, where the latter was killed.

Configuration of the Roman Empire

The Roman Empire was a feudalistic monarchy and it consisted of parts of France, Italy, Slovenia, Austria, Belgium, Germany, Holland, Luxembourg and the Czech and Slovak Republics. In 753 BCE, Rome's first king Romulus was credited with being the founder of Rome. Over the next hundred years, the Roman Empire grew into a successful and powerful city. Till up to 117 CE, the Roman Empire had spread to include Italy, the Mediterranean, Europe, England, Wales and even parts of Scotland.

She-wolf suckling Romulus and Remus - the traditional founders of the city and empire of Rome.

Origins of Rome

Another legend on the origin of Rome says that the brothers could not agree with where the new city should be built. They had each picked a place. They decided to consult with some birds to find out who had picked the better place. Romulus won, and thus became the king of Rome. Rome began developing during the sixth century BCE near the River Tiber. Close to the river were the seven hills of Rome: Capitol, Palatine, Caelian, Esquiline, Viminal, Quirinal and Aventine. Soon, the hills were cleared of trees to make room for houses and temples on its hilly slopes. Communities started living in these areas and trade also began.

Roman Empire and the Romans

The Romans were decent architects and engineers. They built many elements like roads and walls. They also built aqueducts that could transport water for public baths and toilets. The farming methods were very advanced and had used water mills, manure and mechanical reapers. They built fantastic roads; in fact the saying that "All roads lead to Rome" comes from the road that was built in London to Wroxeter in Shropshire.

FUN FACT

Did you know that even as the Romans built their huge empire, they owed its speed to its army that had the ability to march up to 40 km a day?

A picture from an archaeological site of Ancient Rome.

Remains of the public baths in Pompeii.

Antique illustration of Roman Forum, Italy.

753 BCE: First Roman king, Romulus

1453 BCE: End of the Roman Empire

Public baths

They had big public baths and toilets where 60 people could be easily accommodated. The Romans invented concrete and they were the ones who used it to make the Pantheon that still exists even today. They liked to live a luxurious life, which explains the villas that had bath suites, mosaic floors and under floor heating.

Religion followed by the people

They believed in the power that God held over nature; hence, they would perform different sacrifices. It was only during the rule of Emperor Constantine that Christianity became the religion of the empire. Before the spread of Christianity, Romans believed in many gods and goddesses like the Greeks. All of these gods were said to have come from one family and represented different things.

End of the Roman Empire

Everything from anarchy to barbaric invasions to plague, the decline of the empire slowly began during the third century, but eventually it ended after a few centuries. While the Eastern Roman Empire was called Constantinople and lasted till 1453, the Western Empire was devastated by the barbaric invasions.

The once strong Roman military slowly became inefficient and failed to safeguard the borders of the vast city. The internal rebellions failed the government which was unable to collect taxes and safeguard the economy. Foreign powers such as the Visigoths also weakened the Roman Empire.

FUN FACT

The Senate in the USA is in charge of making laws there. It is actually named after the Roman Senate.

The gladiator

The Romans enjoyed gladiator contests complete with swordsmen. The gladiators would generally be prisoners or slaves. Each gladiator had his individual way of fighting and each style would be different. Armed with swords and armours, the gladiators would fight till either one of the men died. Those who were about to lose would beg for pardon from death, but it was up to the emperor and the crowd to decide if the gladiator would live or die. This made the contests very thrilling and exciting for the crowd.

The contests were held in big amphitheatres and people would come to watch the fights between them. Sometimes the men would also fight with animals. Men in armour would fight against animals like bears, bulls, alligators, lions and tigers.

A Roman gladiator.

Civilisations of Africa

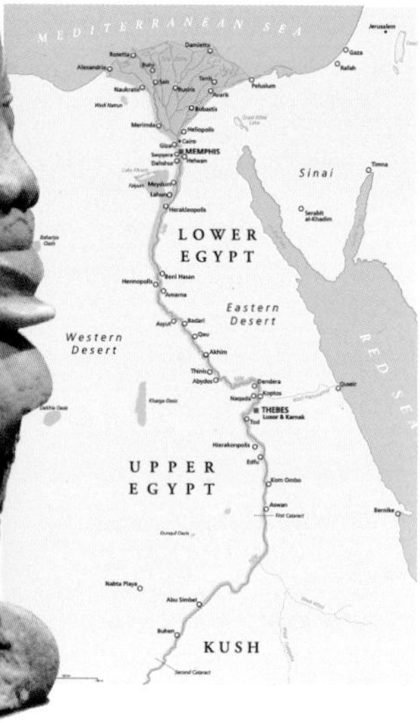

Besides the Egyptian civilisation there was another great civilisation that grew during pre-historic times. It emerged in Nubia, currently Northern Sudan, which existed around 2000 BCE. It was called the "Kingdom of Kush". It was conquered by Egypt in 1500 BCE.

Diverse Africa

Africa can be divided culturally between sub-Saharan Africa and the northern countries from Egypt to Morocco. The northern countries mostly follow the Arabic culture. The southern parts of the Sahara belong to the Bantu group. Within Africa there are divisions between French Africa and the rest of Africa, there are groups who still follow the traditional living style of Africans till date.

A new capital

During the third century BCE, the capital of Kush moved to Meroe, which was on the banks of the river Nile. This city became an important centre for iron working. The people of this region were known as the "Nok". Their culture developed until 200 CE. These people engaged in occupations such as iron mining and smelting of clay. They used the iron to make tools such as hoes and axes. They used the tools to clear land for cultivation. They also made iron arrowheads, spears and knives.

The Nok people from the Meroe region.

Kush nobility

The nobles lived along the River Nile. They believed that they were similar to Egyptians, although the Egyptians would not accept this. They lived in houses similar to the Egyptians and worshipped the same Gods, with few Gods of their own such as the three-headed lion God. They had queens as rulers rather than kings or pharaohs. They mummified their dead. They built tombs with flat roofs.

FUN FACT

The "Nok" is a name given to the people from Meroe. It came from the art of this region, which later influenced West African art.

The commoners

The common people also mummified their dead copying the nobility. They also worshipped the same Gods. However, they did not consider themselves as Egyptians. The common people lived in villages. They were farmers and were proud of their village. Each village had a leader, but the leader was not a king, queen or chief. The leader did not rule; rather, the leader suggested and led discussions. The villagers took decisions together along with their leader.

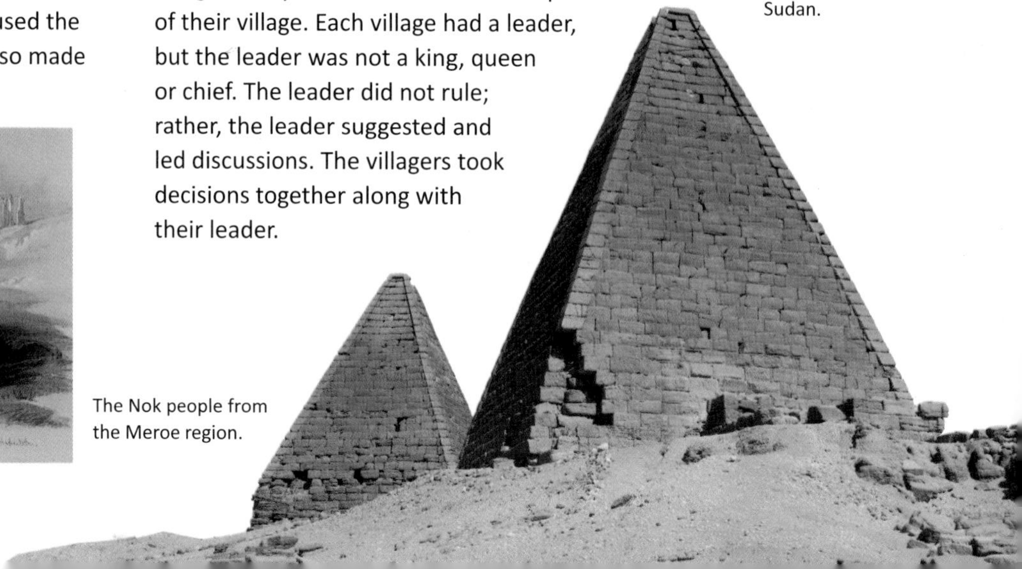

Karima Pyramids, Sudan.

Prominent Civilisations, Dynasties and Religions

3000 BCE–1707 CE

The Indus Valley Civilisation was one of the oldest civilisations to flourish in Asia. Existing around 2500 BCE, this civilisation flourished along the flood plains of the Indus river in present day Pakistan and northwest India. People belonging to the Indus valley civilisation, also known as Dravidians, had a prosperous commerce and trade industry. By around 1700 BCE, the civilisation began to decline.

Many other civilisations, such as the Chinese, Persian and Egyptian give us a glimpse into the lives of people in bygone eras, their politics, religion and way of life. Many of these are well recorded and we have visible evidence of those periods. This period also saw the birth of prominent religions like Buddhism and Jainism.

Ancient Japanese Civilisation

Right from 50,000 BCE, indigenous tribes occupied Japan. It was only around 12,000 BCE that the Ice Age brought about the end of the Paleolithic Age in Japan. Different periods marked the history of ancient Japan, each leaving behind a legacy that impacted the culture of the Japan that we know today.

Jomon Period

The period of time from 13,000 BCE to approximately 300 BCE is known as the Jomon Period to historians. This essentially encompasses Japan's Neolithic period. It was known for its pottery and ceramics, which had a unique "cord marked" pattern. The word "Jomon", in fact, represents these cord-like patterns. It is believed that the Jomon people were semi-sedentary and obtained their food through hunting, fishing and gathering.

Remains from the Jomon period

Yayoi Period

The Jomon Period was followed by the Yayoi Period, which flourished from 300 BCE to 250 CE. During this period, Japan began using metals like bronze and iron. People also discovered newer techniques of agriculture (wet rice cultivation) and weaving. They began to live in permanent communities and clusters of thatched houses.

Kofun Period

The documented history of Japan starts with the Kofun Period from about 250 CE to around 538 CE. It got its name from the Kofun burial grounds that were discovered in Tanegashima Island located to the south of Kyushu. The Shinto culture prevailed during this period and still exists in Japan.

Sumo wrestling is an ancient Japanese art which originated in the Shinto religion.

A famous Shinto shrine.

Asuka Period

The Asuka period existed from about 552 CE to 645 CE. This period was characterised by its strong administration, clear boundaries and trade ties with South Korea. It also marked the beginning of Buddhism. The rulers, Empress Suiko and Prince Shotoku, spread the teachings of Buddha. Other ideas that appeared during this time were the documenting of history, using coins as currency, standardising weights and measures, and a central bureaucratic Government.

Nara Period

Also known as the Golden Era of Japanese history, the Nara period extended from 710 CE to 782 CE. It was named after the city of Nara, which became the base of culture and political power. This period saw its people settled in villages and focussed primarily on agriculture. But the establishment was overtaken by greed and imposed heavy taxes, leading to protest and unrest during the closing decades of this period.

Heian Period

The capital moved from Nara to Heian-kyo (known as Kyoto today) in 794 CE. This was followed by almost 400 years of peace, overseen by the aristocratic Fujiwara family, who dominated both politics and culture. An awareness of their own heritage led the Japanese to express themselves in both literature and art. The kana script, which became the Japanese writing system; the waka style of poetry; the monogatari, or narrative tales; and nikki, or diaries, evolved during this period.

The painted Japanese fan is indicative of the delicate artistry prevalent in Japan.

Kamakura Period

The feudal era came into play during the Kamakura Period (1192–1333 CE). It was during this period that the Samurai class came to power. The royalty became figureheads with the real power being vested in the samurai, shogun and military aristocracy. Mongol invasions in 1274 and 1281 drained the economy, which heralded the disintegration of this period.

The samurai warriors of ancient Japan.

Muromachi Period

The period that followed, that is, the Muromachi Period (1392–1573) saw economic and artistic revival, and economic progress. Transportation and urban development were the key themes of this period. Zen Buddhism made an appearance and impacted all aspects of life – art, commerce, education and politics. Kyoto became the hub of power once again. The shoguns built elegant villas and performed the elaborate tea ceremony. Garden designs, architecture, flower arrangements, calligraphy and preparing and serving food gained much importance. The Noh dance drama, a slow and elaborate performance, also gained popularity.

The tea ceremony is an elaborate ritual that takes years to master.

The Noh dance drama.

Azuchi-Momoyama Period

The internal conflicts of Japan came to an end with the Azuchi-Momoyama period. By the beginning of the sixteenth century, Christian Missionaries made an advent, but they were not too successful with conversions. This was followed by the Edo period (1603–1868) where Japan began to isolate itself from the rest of the world in terms of trade and missionaries, largely due to the fear of European invasion.

The Kabuki – an ancient dance form

The Kabuki dance form first was seen during the early seventeenth century. It is believed that a female dancer called Okuni would perform with wandering troupes of female performers. Women were banned from performing this dance during 1629. For a while, young boys, dressed as women, performed. Finally, in the eighteenth century, it was accepted again. It depicted historical events and grand love stories. The Kabuki is famous for its elaborate costumes and subtle movements.

Kabuki originated in the seventeenth century in Kyoto. It is still widely performed in Japan.

Martial arts

The martial arts are deeply connected with Japan's history. Ancient Japan saw much conflict. With the Samurai playing a significant role, ancient Japanese were great students of weaponry and combat techniques. Over a period of time, they developed martial arts into a science, backing it up with deep study. From the twelfth century, combat techniques began to be formalised. Even today, many Japanese martial art forms are practiced. Kyūdō, or the art of archery; Sōjutsu and Naginatajutsu, or combat with the spear; and Kenjutsu or sword fighting were among some of the martial arts that held sway. Judo is yet another form that is practiced even today, though it finds its origins in Jujutsu. The most popular form, Karate, is believed to have originated from Okinawa, where natives would simply call this form "te".

Karate, an ancient martial art, is widely practiced even today.

The kimono is a traditional Japanese dress worn by women, that is popular even today.

Historical attire

The Kimono first came into existence during the Jomon period, when there was no great difference between what men and women wore. The word kimono literally means "thing to wear". As trading with the outside world began, newer ways of wearing clothes made an appearance. Until the fifteenth century, people wore kimonos that were made of hemp or linen. Traditionally, the art of wearing a kimono was passed on from mother to daughter. Today, this art is also taught in schools. Western clothing was first adopted by soldiers of the shogun's army and navy, who found the style more flexible and convenient.

FUN FACT

Sushi, a popular Japanese dish, needs to be made delicately. It is said that the blade of a professional sushi chef needs to be sharpened every day – just like the sword of a samurai.

The Mesopotamian Civilisation

Relief of an ancient assyrian king.

The name Mesopotamia is derived from the Greek language and means "between rivers". This basically refers to the land that lies between the rivers of Tigris and Euphrates. However, in reality, Mesopotamia includes areas that are more commonly known as eastern Syria, southeastern Turkey and a large part of Iraq today. The Mesopotamian civilisation is the longest one in history and is known for giving birth to many of the European states that we see today.

Establishing boundaries

The first evidence of people occupying this land goes back to 6000 BCE, when early settlers built villages in Northern Assyria. As the population grew, the area began to get politically divided into smaller independent "city-states". This was followed by a forced unification under the rule of King Lugal-zage-si of Uruk (a city in ancient Sumer). In 2000 BCE, the country was divided into smaller units once again, after repeated wars. Finally, Babylon established a state in the south and Assyria, in the north. Assyria went on to build an empire that, for a period, consisted the entire ancient Middle East. This remained steady under various Neo-Babylonian and Persian kings, up to Alexander the Great's conquests in 331 BCE.

Religion through the years

Mesopotamia, as a region, was influenced by many different cultures and invasions. Despite these, it maintained a tradition of its own. Nature was worshipped along with deities that appeared to meet different kinds of needs, such as power, fertility, wealth, etc. Slowly, concepts like sin and forgiveness also made an appearance.

Literature of Mesopotamia

Mesopotamian literature is possibly the oldest known literature in the world. The literary evidence provides a storehouse of information in the form of clay tablets inscribed with texts written in cuneiform script.

The ancient city of Babylon.

Key themes included religious texts, hymns, prayers, incantations, descriptions of rituals, etc. Many songs and stories talk about life in that period. There is evidence of legal or medical texts. As writing became more precise through the third millennium BCE, a considerable body of literature found its way into written form. Much of this found its way into Sumerian scribal schools, indicating an organised education system. Mesopotamian literature abounded in myths, laments, prayers and stories of war and bravery.

Writing of the ancient Sumerian or Assyrian civilisation.

Major achievements

Mathematics and astronomy flowered during this period. Some concepts used even today include the sexagesimal system to calculate time and angles; the 12 "double-hours" Greek day; the zodiac, sunsigns, etc. The Pythogoras law, though credited to Greek mathematician Pythogoras, made an appearance in early Babylonian tablets during 1900–1600 BCE, indicating a knowledge of this logic. Legal theory during this period also flourished and much of it was documented in various collections termed as "codes" by historians. The most famous of these is the "Code of Hammurabi". These codes focussed on concern for the weak, widows, orphans, etc.

Changing life over centuries

Buildings were made of mud-brick and were thus vulnerable to weather vagaries; over centuries, layers of settlement created mounds that characterised the ruins of Mesopotamia. Over the centuries, life in ancient Mesopotamia underwent changes. Humans moved from a nomadic to sedentary life. This was followed by the emergence of an agricultural economy with deliberate farming methods. The erection of permanent houses, temples and burial grounds indicated the organisation of society. Specialised craft, division of labour, use of new materials like metals were indicative of the transition from the late Neolithic to a Chalcolithic period.

Bee-hive houses in Mesopotamia (present-day Turkey).

FUN FACT

In the Mesopotamian religion, people believed that after death, everybody would become a ghost.

Tablet with cuneiform script

5000-3500 BCE

Sumerians set up the first city states in southern Mesopotamia.

Map of Babylonia, Mesopotamia.

3500 BCE

The evolution of writing begins. At first, it appears in the form of pictograms, but takes about a thousand years to evolve into a full cuneiform script.

The Code of Ur-Nammu, the first complete law code.

2300 BCE

King Sargon of Akkad starts conquering the first empire in world history. The empire reaches its height in 2220 BCE.

Statue of King Sargon.

2100 BCE

The city of Ur becomes the centre of a powerful Mesopotamian state. It soon falls into decline. This marks the decline of the Sumerians as the Amorites, a nomadic people, start moving into Mesopotamia.

King Cyrus at a Babylonian temple.

1530 BCE

Babylonia is conquered by the Kassites, who rule the area for 400+ years.

Portrait of an old Chaldean man.

1100 BCE

Nomadic peoples such as the Aramaeans and the Chaldeans over run much of Mesopotamia. The kingdoms of Babylon and Assyria go into temporary decline.

1792-49 BCE

King Hammurabi of Babylon conquers a large empire. Hammurabi is famous for the law code which he issues. His empire begins to decline immediately after his death.

Law code of Hammurabi.

1500 BCE

The Mitanni (Indo-European people) conquer northern Mesopotamia and areas of Syria and Asia Minor. After 200 years, the kingdom of Assyria conquers northern Mesopotamia from the Mitanni.

Map of Syria.

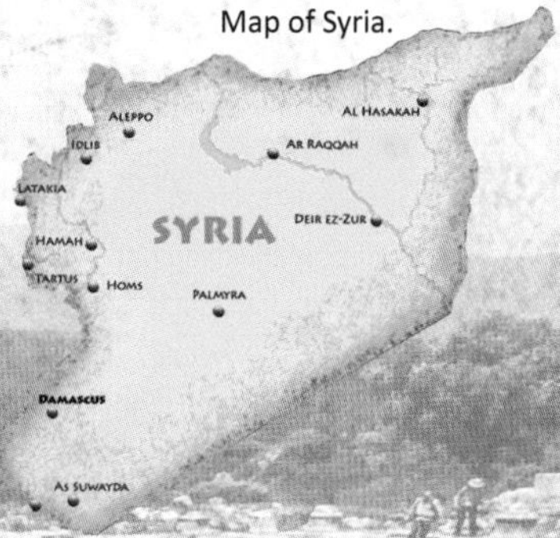

Ancient Egyptian Civilisation

The ancient Egyptian civilisation is one of the longest civilisations in human history. It lasted for more than 3000 years from 3150 BCE to 30 BCE. Today, Egypt is a small country in the north-eastern corner of Africa. Yet, its history is great and powerful. The monuments and tombs of the Pharaohs of Egypt, called pyramids, which are over 4000 years old, continue to stand even today. Till date, over 130 pyramids have been discovered in Egypt.

The Great Nile

The River Nile, the longest river in the world, flows through Egypt. A land of deserts, barely receiving any rainfall, Egypt would have been a barren land, had it not been for the Nile. The river allowed the ancient Egyptian civilisation to thrive and flourish. Every year, the rain in southern Africa would cause the Nile to flood. However, the floods brought in the rich soil of the mountainsides, causing the land to be extremely fertile. Naturally the vegetation in Egypt thrived, giving life to its civilisation.

Earlier, Egypt was made of two kingdoms, on either side of the Nile. In the 3rd millennium BCE BCE, Pharaoh Menes conquered the other kingdom and Egypt was united.

Practices of the afterlife

The afterlife was very important to the Egyptians. They preserved their dead bodies by mummifying them. The bodies of the dead would be oiled and their internal organs would be removed. The bodies would then be wrapped in long strips of cloth. The dead were buried with their personal belongings, which the Egyptians believed would be needed in the afterlife.

The Pharaohs were given a more elaborate burial. Pyramids were built for them, where they would be buried with all their riches. Over the centuries, many objects have been retrieved from the pyramids. The wall paintings on the tombs have also depicted the daily lives of ancient Egyptians.

An Egyptian mummy.

FUN FACT

The Pharaoh always covered his head as his hair was not to be seen by regular people.

Pyramids of Egypt.

Royal temples

The rulers of Egypt considered themselves to be gods and built temples in their honour, celebrating important events during their reign. For example, in Queen Hatshepsut's temple, a wall relief depicts her expedition by sea.

Ruins of the Hatshepsut temple, Egypt.

Gods and Goddesses

Apart from royalty, the Egyptians worshipped several gods and goddesses and built temples in their honour. The most important God was Ra, the Sun God. He had the head of a hawk and a headdress with a sun disk. Other important gods were Isis, Osiris, Horus and Thoth.

Egyptian writings

The alphabet of the ancient Egyptians was in the form of pictures, called hieroglyphics. The Egyptian alphabet contained more than 700 hieroglyphs. Some of the symbols represented sounds, while some depicted entire words.

Hieroglyphic carvings on the walls of an ancient Egyptian temple.

Games and entertainment

The Egyptians enjoyed various activities for entertainment. Festivals and games were an important part of their daily lives. They enjoyed hunting, board games, storytelling, swimming, archery, wrestling, chariot racing, dancing, as well as playing with toys.

FUN FACT

Cats were considered sacred in Ancient Egypt. The house cat was a symbol of grace and poise.

Mayan Civilisation

The Mayan civilisation primarily existed in and around the lowlands of the area that is present-day Guatemala. It was at the pinnacle of its existence during the sixth century CE. The Maya are believed to have been an advanced people and were known for their hieroglyphic writing, mathematics, pottery, agricultural techniques and calendar-making. They left behind a stunning body of work that has helped us learn about their skills, way of life, religion and politics.

A visual depiction of the Mayan calendar.

Evolution

The earliest known Mayan settlements have been said to exist around 1500 CE. Over the next several centuries, till about 300 CE, the Maya extended their influence across both highlands and lowlands.

The Golden Age of the Mayan civilisation began approximately around 250 CE. During this period, the Maya built over 40 cities, each with a population ranging from 5000 to 50,000 people. At its height, the Mayan population is believed to have crossed 2,000,000 people.

Architecture

The Mayan cities had names like Tikal, Uaxactún, Copán, Bonampak, Dos Pilas, Calakmul, Palenque and Río Bec. These cities were surrounded and supported by agricultural communities and villages. The Maya followed modern techniques of agriculture like terracing and irrigation, which can be seen from the remains of their cities. The evidence of the architectural brilliance and advanced imagination of the Maya is visible in the palaces, pyramids, temples and plazas that have been discovered during archaeological excavations.

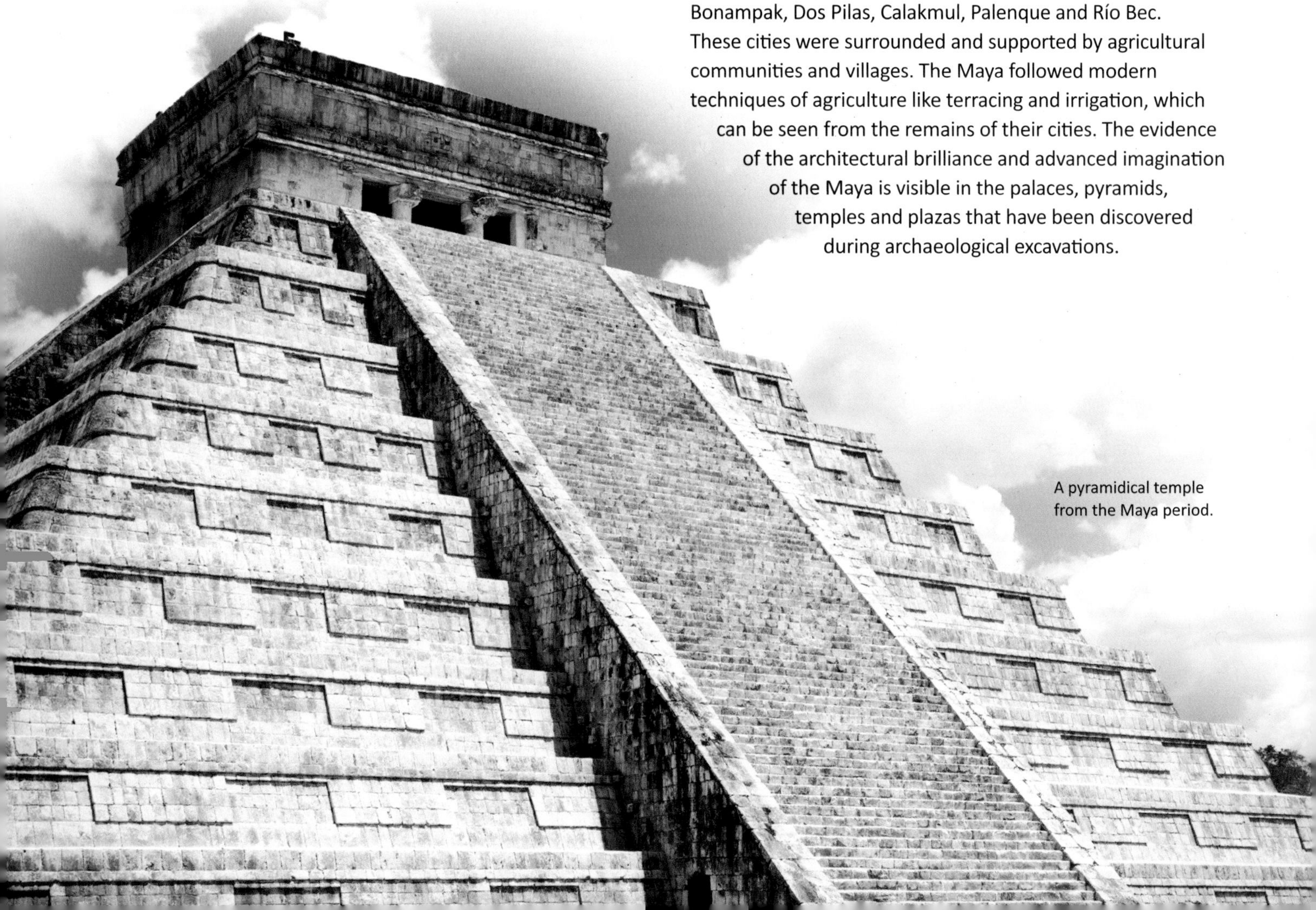

A pyramidical temple from the Maya period.

Religion

The Maya had deep religious beliefs. They prayed to many Gods and their Gods were especially related to nature. These included sun, moon, rain and corn Gods. The importance of art in Mayan life and religion is evident from the detailed work on their many temples and palaces. Many temples were pyramidical and decorated with inscriptions and relief work.

While evidence has already proven that they were great thinkers, the Maya also made strides in mathematics and astronomy – including the use of zero. They also developed a detailed calendar, with 365 days. Another significant discovery was the discovery of the system of hieroglyphic writing. The Maya used paper made from tree bark. They converted this paper to books known as codices. Four codices have survived over time, which have helped us discover more information about the Mayan way of life.

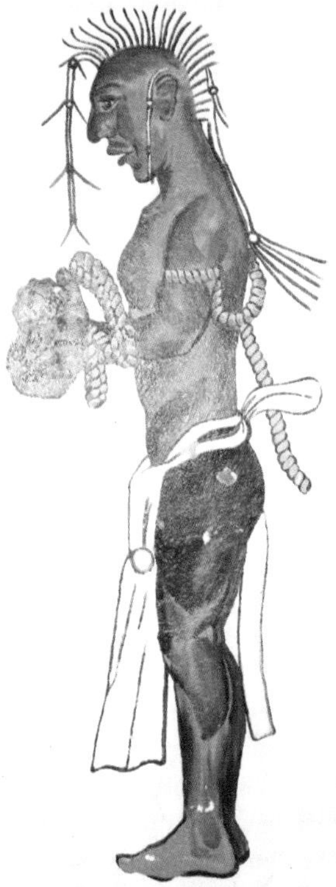
The typical clothes of a Mayan man.

Attire

The Maya were well-known for their use of colourful clothes as well as the unusual body modifications they created. Based on the material available to them, the Maya had a wide variety of clothes for different occasions—elaborate costumes for ceremonies, vibrant dance outfits, elaborate armour for protection and simple flexible clothes for everyday wear. During public events that were attended by large crowds, the ruling class would wear elaborate headdresses, jewellery made of jade and clothes made from the skin of animals that were considered to be "dangerous". This elaborate attire was a mark of their own status and power.

For everyday wear, most of the Mayan people wore a simple outfit that usually comprised a loin cloth or a short skirt for men; and a long skirt for women. These were elaborately embellished with jewellery like bracelets, anklets and neck pieces. Their hair was almost never left loose; it was often tied together with bands and decorated with feathers.

FUN FACT

The Maya had advanced medical practices. They are known to have performed surgery and made artificial limbs with jade and turquoise; they even used human hair for suturing.

Decline

The Mayan civilisation flourished extremely well, which is why historians feel that its disintegration appears to be a mystery. Between the eighth and ninth century, many Mayan cities were abandoned and the reason behind this event remains unknown even today. By 900 CE, the Mayan civilisation had virtually collapsed.

Use of natural resources

A factor that has both mystified and amazed historians is the ability of the Mayan people to create such a large, thriving civilisation in the inhospitable rainforest regions, which is where this civilisation flourished.

When one sees the history of ancient civilisations, it can be observed that most of them existed in drier climates, mainly because they did not have the technology to battle elements. This perhaps worked in favour of the Mayan people, for many foreign invaders left the Maya to their own devices, finding the climate unfavourable with no marked riches, silver and gold to attract them. However, the Maya made the most of the natural resources available to them. They used limestone for construction, volcanic rock deposits for making tools, and jade, quetzal feathers, etc., for decorating royal costumes and shells as trumpets during formal ceremonies, as well as war.

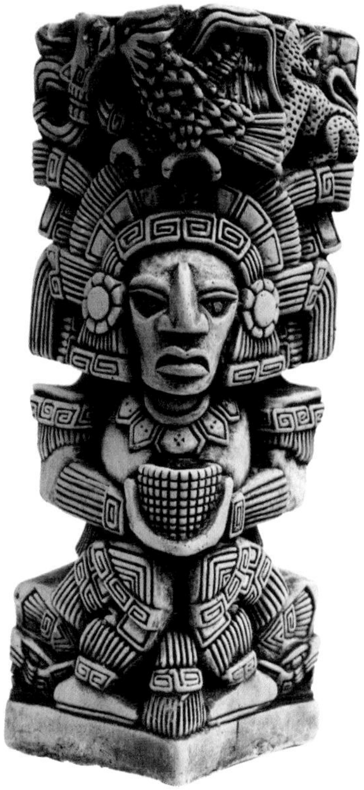
Statue of a Mayan god.

Indicators of Early Civilisations

Cave paintings in the Cueva de las Manos, Patagonia, Argentina.

Cave paintings are paintings that are found on the walls and ceilings of caves. These prehistoric paintings were made over 40,000 years ago. They are an important source of information about the early civilisations. Many such cave paintings have been found in Europe and Asia. While very little is known about why the paintings were made, historians believe that the cave paintings were a way of expression for the prehistoric people, either to communicate with each other or as part of a religious custom.

FUN FACT

The oldest known cave paintings were discovered on the island of Sulawesi in Indonesia. The paintings are around 35,000 years old.

Universal similarity

The paintings are remarkably similar around the world, with animals being common subjects of the cave paintings. The paintings often include images of human hands, mostly hand stencils. Scientists believe that to make the stencils, the early humans held a hand to the wall and blew pigment on it.

Paintings at Bhimbetka

The Bhimbetka rock shelters in India are an archaeological site dating back to the Stone Age. Located at the foothills of the Vindhya Mountains in the south of the central Indian plateau, the Bhimbetka rock shelters are five clusters of natural rock shelters. Historians estimate that human beings occupied the shelters more than 100,000 years ago.

The paintings on the wall of the shelters date to the Mesolithic period. They consist of geometric patterns and figures made in red and white, with some use of yellow and green. They depict the daily lives of the people with scenes of childbirth, dancing, drinking and rituals of burial among others.

Prehistoric rock petroglyphs in Usgalimol, India.

Lion plate with lion man and other bushman prehistoric rock engravings.

Indus and Sarasvati Civilisations

Mohenjo Daro is a city in the Indus valley civilisation that was built around 2600 BCE and flourished till 1900 BCE. It was discovered in the 1920s.

The Indus valley civilisation was one of the largest civilisations of the ancient world, bigger than Sumer and even Egypt. The Indus valley civilisation was discovered during the 1920s. Its two great cities were Harappa and Mohenjo Daro. Each of these cities had a population of more than 40,000. It had a well organised system of trade. Merchants traded grains along with other agricultural produce that grew along the fertile river banks.

River Sarasvati

The Indus valley civilisation was one of the world's major ancient civilisations that included Egypt, Mesopotamia, South Asia and China. All these civilisations emerged on the banks of rivers. For example, Mesopotamia flourished on the banks of the river Tigris and Euphrates.

The Indus valley civilisation developed on the banks of the river Indus—Sarasvati. There is evidence to prove that similar to the Mesopotamians, the people from the Indus valley civilisation were also culturally rich and seemed to have had some form of writing in existence.

Course of Sarasvati

The Sarasvati River is the Ghaggar stream that ends in the Thar Desert. It used to flow into the Arabian Sea till 1900 BCE when it dried up because the Yamuna changed course and started flowing into the river Ganga.

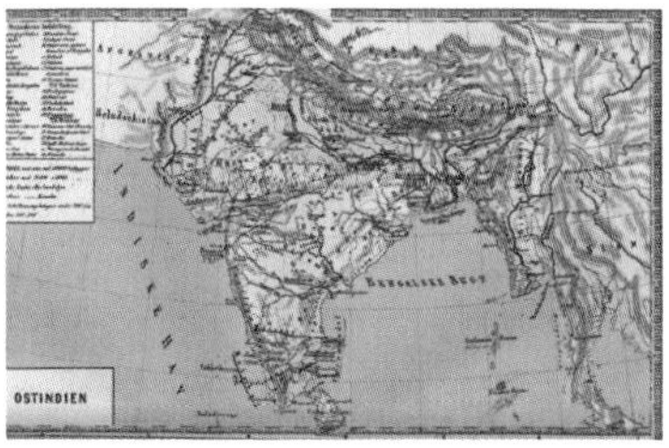

Old map of the Indian sub-continent, 1867 showing rivers.

Decline of the civilisation

Unfortunately, from 2000 BCE, the Indus valley civilisation began to decline. This is attributed to the devastating floods that destroyed the crops or because the river Indus changed its course making the once fertile land barren. Interestingly, it is believed that overgrazing may have also contributed to the decline as the land became too dry, rendering it impossible to grow any crops.

Confluence of Zanskar and Indus rivers – Leh, Ladakh.

Harappa and Mohenjo Daro Communities

Mould of a seal, Indus Valley Civilisation (2500–1700 BCE).

The Indus Valley Civilisation spanned across different parts of India, such as present-day Punjab, Haryana, Sindh, Baluchistan, Gujarat and Uttar Pradesh. Artefacts from this civilisation show that its inhabitants followed a number system. This civilisation was perhaps the first of the settlements in the Indian subcontinent. Cities such as Mohenjo Daro and Harappa also had citadels (fortress above a city), proper drainage and sewage system.

Life of the people

The people of the Indus Valley Civilisation subsisted on farming. They reared cattle, pigs, sheep and goats. They also practised hunting and fishing. They grew wheat, cotton, chickpeas, mustard and sesame among other crops. They also traded gold, copper and silver.

Archaeologists have found several toys during the excavations, such as toy carts, rattles, whistles, pull-along animals, etc. The toys were made of clay and terracotta. They also played dice games and board games. Evidence suggests that they enjoyed the sport of cock-fighting. The seals found in the Indus valley show us how the men and women dressed. The men wore loincloths and women wore dresses. Both men and women wore jewellery, such as beads.

They traded goods, such as pots, gems like turquoise, seashells, gold and silver. They also knew the craft of building boats. Indus valley seals have been found in Mesopotamia. This suggests that they had trade relations with Mesopotamia.

Evidence of writing

Artefacts, such as seals found at these sites, prove that the people from this civilisation were literate. Unfortunately, the Indus Valley writing has still not been deciphered. The writing has around 400 picture symbols.

Ruins of Mohenjo Daro, Pakistan.

Aryan Migration

The word Aryan is derived from the Sanskrit word Arya, meaning noble. It was also used to refer to the Indo-Iranian tribes that lived during the prehistoric times in ancient Iran and the Indian subcontinent. Today, the word "Aryan" is used as part of the term "Indo-Aryan languages in South Asia."

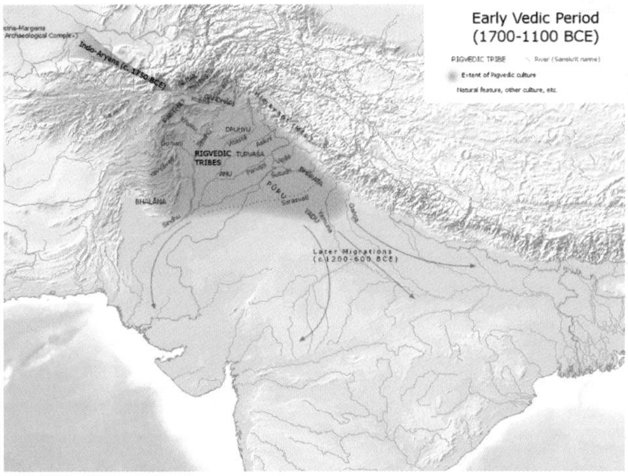

Map showing early vedic India and the extent of the Aryan migration.

Indo-Aryan migration theory

In the nineteenth century, German linguist and Sanskrit scholar, Max Muller, proposed the Indo-Aryan migration theory when a similarity between European and Indian languages was discovered.

The theory suggests that the Indo-Aryan group of languages were introduced in the Indian subcontinent when people from central Asia, that is, the Indo-Iranians migrated here around 1800 BCE and brought the Indo-Aryan languages with them.

The Indo-Aryan languages are a part of the Indo-European group of languages. The theory aims to explain how the Indo-European languages developed and spread over different parts of the world. Thus, the theory is a meeting point of archaeological, anthropological and linguistic research.

Migration to India

The Aryan migration is believed to have occurred during the Indus valley civilisation. Coming from Central Asia, these large groups of nomadic cattle herders crossed the Hindu Kush mountains. In fact, some researchers believe that this settling down near the Indus valley civilisation could be one of the reasons for its collapse.

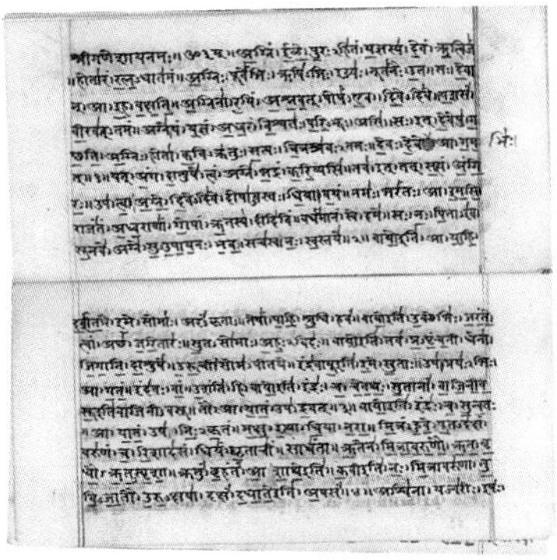

Rig veda was written during the Vedic period somewhere between 1500 and 1000 BCE.

Illustration of Aryans entering India during the Indus Valley Civilisation.

FUN FACT

It is theorised that the language of the Aryans soon gained popularity over the local languages and they too turned to agriculture to survive. There is, however, mention of the Aryans in the Vedas, the Indian religious books that contain stories of struggles and conflicts.

Hinduism and Vedic Period

Hinduism does not have a particular founder or a particular date of origin. Hinduism refers to many different beliefs, philosophies and perspectives that originated in India. It is also called the Sanatana dharma. It is a polytheistic religion, that is, it involves worship of several gods.

Hazarar Rama temple, Hampi, Karnataka, India.

Temple in Karnataka state, India.

Vedic period

The word Hindu is derived from the Sanskrit word "Sindhu", which was the name given to the river Indus by the Persians. The Indus valley civilisation was followed by the Vedic period (1500–500 BCE) during which an emphasis on religious sacrifice or yajnas and other religious rituals began to gain prominence.

The Vedic period saw the worship of various Gods, such as Indra, Vayu, Marut, Varun, Rudra, Agni, etc. During this period, the Vedas were written in Vedic Sanskrit. They are ancient texts that contain Hindu teachings. The word Veda means knowledge in Sanskrit. The Vedas were compiled by Vyasa Krishna Dwaipayana around 1500 BCE.

The four Vedas

There are four Vedas: the Rigveda, the Yajurveda, the Samaveda and the Atharvaveda. Collectively the four Vedas are known as Chathur Veda.

The Vedas are called Shruti, that is, which need to be heard. While other religious texts are called Smriti, that is, which need to be memorised.

Each Veda has four parts. The primary section is the mantra or hymn section, also known as Samhitas, next are the Brahmanas containing commentaries on rituals, followed by the Aranyakas explaining rituals and sacrifices. The Upanishads discuss philosophy and meditation.

The Rigveda means Veda of praise. It is supposed to be the main Veda. It contains 1028 hymns or suktas and 10,600 verses and is divided into 10 mandalas or books. The Samaveda means the Veda of sacred songs. It is a collection of melodies. The Yajurveda means the Veda of sacrifice. It explains various mantras to be sung and religious rituals to be followed by priests. The Atharvaveda means the Veda of the Fire Priest. It is a collection of spells and charms to treat diseases.

FUN FACT

As per the Rigveda, the universe emerged from Prajapati, who is the earliest God and the creator of this world.

Palm leaf manuscript (top). Dried palm leaves were used as writing material in ancient India to record events, right from horoscopes to mythological stories (left).

Rise of Jainism

Statue of Jain god Gomeshvara in Shravanabelagola, India.

During the sixth century BCE, many great thinkers like Buddha, Mahavira, Heraclitus, Zoroaster, Confucius and Lao Tse propagated their ideas. The thinkers and their followers rose as one voice against orthodox religion, which followed rigid rituals and rites. Jainism also emerged due to the orthodox practices and rigid dogma of religion.

Time of social flux

It was a time of great social, political and intellectual flux when the old tribal structure of the society began to change. Some groups, known as republics, came into existence. The old social order began to slowly disintegrate and soon a conflict within religions arose. Further, many complicated rituals and sacrifices during the late Vedic period remained inaccessible to the common people and were also expensive. The beliefs confused many people and some of the teachings in the Upanishads were very philosophical, which could not be easily understood. All these factors led to disillusionment amongst the common people. They wanted a simple way towards salvation in a language that was known to them. Mahavira managed to do just that.

Caste system leading to rise of Jainism

Carvings in a Jain temple in Ranakpur, India.

Apart from the inaccessible religion, other equally important social and economic factors also gave rise to Jainism. One such factor was the caste system. The four castes were Brahmins, Kshatriyas, Vaishyas and the Shudras. The upper castes lived a life of privilege while the lower castes were discriminated against and denied many resources. This led to resentment against the upper castes. Mahavira belonged to the Kshatriya tribe. The Kshatriyas and Vaishyas wanted to improve their condition, but the rigid caste system denied them the chance. This led to the merchant class embracing Jainism.

Chaumukha Mandir–Jain Temple, Ranakpur, India.

Jain Tirthankaras

Jainism originated between the seventh and fifth centuries BCE. Followers of Jainism are known as Jains. Jainism does not have one founder, but 24 tirthankaras. The word tirthankara means a teacher who has surmounted the cycle of birth and death, and who shows others the path to attain moksh (salvation). The first tirthankara was Rishabhanatha. The 23rd Jain tirthankara was Parshvanatha. During the seventh century BCE, he developed a community based on the renouncement of worldly concerns.

Rockcut statue of Jain tirthankara in rock niches near Gwalior fort, India.

The one who leads

Parshvanatha was the 23rd tirthankara or the one who leads the way towards salvation. The twenty-fourth and final tirthankara was Vardhamana, also known as Mahavira (great hero). Mahavira was a contemporary of Gautam Buddha. Just like Buddha, Mahavira was a Kshatriya chieftain's son who renounced his princely status at the age of 30 to live the life of an ascetic. Mahavira spent around 12.5 years as a devout ascetic and attained enlightenment (kevalnyan).

He had 11 disciples or ganadharas. Of these disciples, Indrabhuti Gautama and Sudharman were the founders of the historical Jain monastic community. Mahavira is believed to have died at Pavapuri, near Patna.

A group of Digambar Jain nuns, sadhvis, attend a religious ceremony at a Jain temple.

Principles of Jainism

As per Jainism, right knowledge, right faith and right conduct can help a person attain moksha. For this, the five great vows—non-violence (ahimsa), truth (satya), non-stealing (asteya), celibacy (brahmacharya) and non-attachment (aparigraha)—should be followed.

Hutheesing Jain Temple, consecrated in 1848 AD, is one of the best known in Gujarat, India.

Rise of Buddhism

During the sixth century BCE, the Vedic religion had become orthodox and inflexible. An emphasis on expensive religious rituals made the common man feel disenchanted and alienated. The rigid caste system made the life of the people belonging to the lower castes miserable. Further, the religious texts were in Sanskrit, which the common people could not understand as they spoke Pali and Prakrit. This made the common man feel even more alienated. These factors helped in the rise of Buddhism.

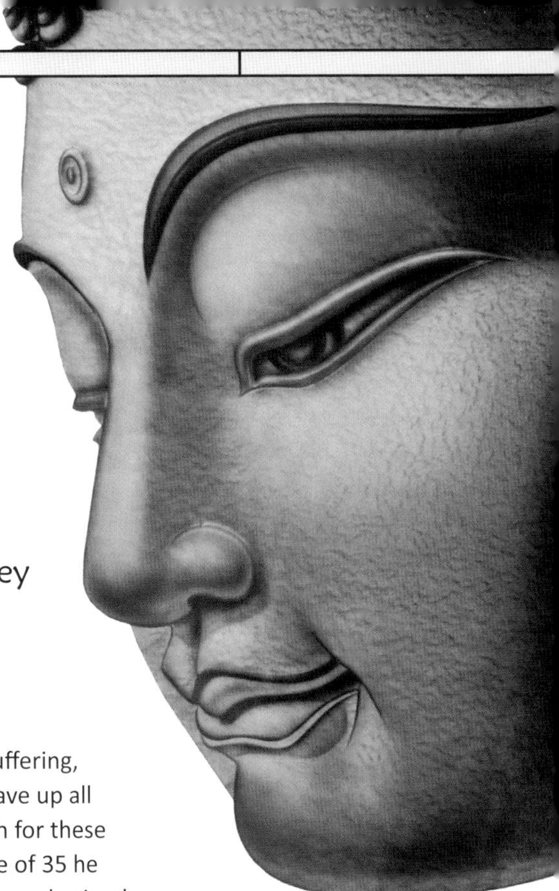

Face of Buddha.

Buddhist monks praying.

A protected life

Buddhism is derived from the Hindi word "buddhi", meaning wisdom. Gautam Buddha was the founder of Buddhism. His real name was Siddhartha and he was a prince. Born into a royal family in Lumbini, as a child Siddhartha was protected from all negative things in the world. However, one day after leaving the royal household, Siddhartha saw—an old man, a sick man, a corpse and a monk, for the first time. He realised that old age, sickness and death were a part of human life.

Becoming the Buddha

He renounced his kingdom to seek answers as to why there is so much sorrow and pain, why people age and how one can get rid of his or her sorrows and pain.

Thai Buddhist monk.

Seeking a way to end human suffering, Gautam became a monk and gave up all worldly possessions. The search for these answers ended when at the age of 35 he meditated under the Bodhi tree and gained enlightenment. Afterwards he came to be known as the Buddha (awakened one).

First sermon at Sarnath

Five weeks after attaining enlightenment, Gautam Buddha travelled to Sarnath where he delivered his first sermon to five monks, teaching them what he had learnt. This was the beginning of the Buddhist sangha or community of monks. Over the next 40 years, Gautam Buddha travelled around north India to spread his teachings.

FUN FACT

Gautam Buddha's wife Yashodhara and son Rahula also joined the Buddhist sangha or monastic community.

Young Buddhist novices pray at Shwezigon Pagoda near Bagan.

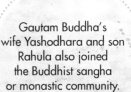

Principles of Buddhism

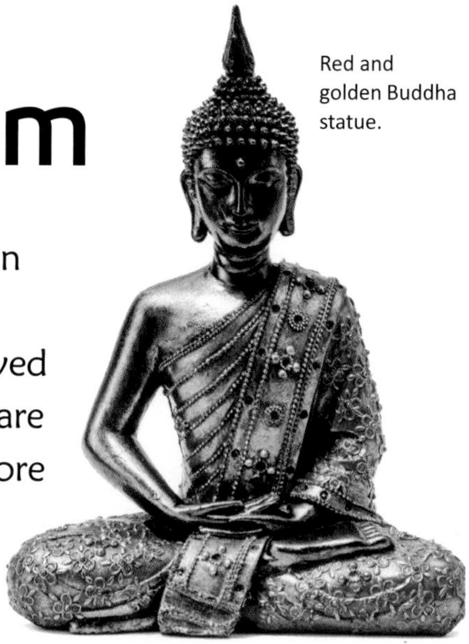
Red and golden Buddha statue.

Buddhism aims to achieve nirvana by following the path laid down by Gautam Buddha. Buddhists don't believe in a personal god. Karma, or action, is an important element of Buddhism. It is believed that if we do good in this life, we will have a better life when we are reborn. Although Buddhism originated in India, it presently has more followers in countries like Thailand, Japan and China.

Tibetan prayer wheels in a Buddhist temple.

Four noble truths of Buddhism

Buddhism revolves around the four noble truths: (1) suffering, (2) origin or cause of suffering, (3) cessation of suffering and (4) the path to the cessation of suffering. The Buddha prescribed the eightfold path that to end suffering. It includes right views, right intention, right speech, right action, right livelihood, right effort, right concentration and right mindfulness.

Reason behind the noble truths

In the first two noble truths, Buddha diagnosed the problem (suffering) and identified its cause (desire). The third noble truth is the realisation that there is a cure to human suffering. The fourth noble truth is a prescription or detailed method through which humans can achieve a release from suffering.

The Middle Path

In his first sermon at Sarnath, Buddha called the Eightfold Path as the Middle Path because it prescribes a life of moderation, a middle way between the two extremes of austere ascetism and indulgence of desires.

Tibetan buddhist Mani wheel or hand prayer wheel.

FUN FACT

The pink lotus is the supreme lotus, which is generally reserved for the enlightened one or Buddha. The white lotus symbolises the Bodhi or the awakened state.

The different colours of the lotus represent the different stages of the spiritual journey.

Spread of Buddha's Word

Old Buddhist Temple Wat Yai Chai Mongkhon in Ayutthaya Province, Thailand.

King Ashoka was a follower of Buddhism and played an important role in the spread of this religion. He used oral announcements to spread Buddha's teachings and also had them inscribed on rocks and pillars at various sites, such as Sarnath.

Ashokan pillar with four Asiatic lions on top.

262–261 BCE: Kalinga war

250 BCE: Placing of the Lion capital in Sarnath

Impact of the Kalinga War

After fighting a brutal war to conquer Kalinga in the third century BCE, Ashoka felt deep remorse when he saw the bloodshed and destruction caused by the war. Consequently, he denounced any form of violence. Ashoka became a devout follower of Buddha and vowed to follow the path of non-violence or ahimsa.

Ashoka and Buddhism

Ashoka himself practised Buddhism, but he respected his people's wishes and gave them the freedom to follow the religion of their choice.

He undertook tours to preach Buddhist philosophy and also asked his officers to participate. He built hospitals for people and animals, planted trees along the roads and gave orders to reduce taxes and prevent cruelty to animals.

The Buddhist council

Ashoka organised the Third Buddhist council and supported Buddhist missions that travelled as far as Greece, Egypt and Syria.

There is a mention in the Buddhist Theravada tradition of a group of Buddhist missionaries who were sent by Emperor Ashoka to a Buddhist school in Sri Lanka in 240 BCE.

Due to his efforts, the religion gained prominence, particularly after he made Buddhism his state religion. Thus, Ashoka helped to spread Buddhism far and wide.

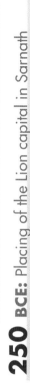

Great Stupa (ancient Buddhist monument) in Sanchi, Madhya Pradesh, India.

The Mauryan Dynasty

Alexander's campaign in northwest India lasted from 327 to 325 BCE. A few years later, in 321 BCE, Chandragupta Maurya founded the Mauryan dynasty.

Temple 18 and the Great Stupa (Stupa 1) at Sanchi.

Mauryan empire

After Alexander's death, Chandragupta Maurya, the founder of the Mauryan dynasty, created an empire that would go on to cover most of India. However, this did not include present-day Tamil Nadu. The empire had a well-organised army and civil service. Chandragupta was assisted by his advisor Chanakya, who was a teacher at Takshashila. Chanakya authored the treatise Arthashashtra that explains the duties of a king, methods to manage the economy and administration of the Mauryan empire and steps to maintain law and order.

Statue of Chandragupta Maurya.

Ashoka the Great

The Buddhist Mauryan emperor Ashoka ruled from 265 to 238 BCE. He was the third ruler of the Mauryan empire, which was the largest empire in the Indian subcontinent. After the Kalinga war, Ashoka maintained friendly relations with his neighbouring kingdoms.

He worked towards extending Buddhism and spreading Buddhist teachings across the world. He commissioned some of the finest works of ancient Indian art. He built several Buddhist monuments, such as stupas, sangharama, viharas and chaityas. Ashoka set up clinics for people and animals, and had wells dug out for the benefit of his people. Further, he abolished hunting and fishing. After Ashoka's death, the Mauryan empire began to decline. Brihadratha was the last Mauryan ruler, who was assassinated 50 years after Ashoka's death.

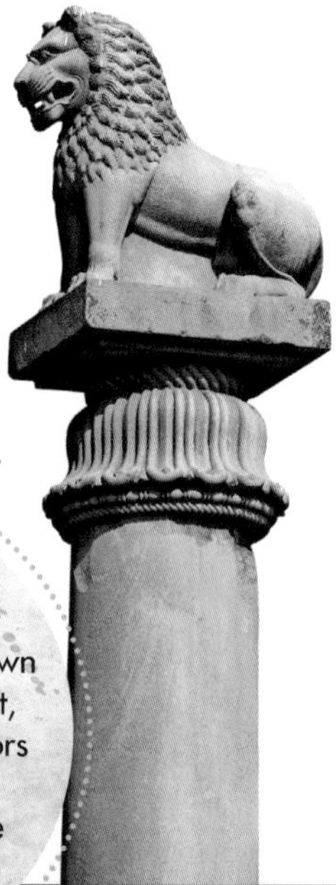

Ashokan lion pillar at Vaishali in India.

FUN FACT

Ashoka in Sanskrit means "the one without sorrow". He was also known as Chakravartin Samraat, or the emperor of emperors and sometimes as Priyadarshin, or the one who looks at everyone with love.

Chandragupta Maurya and his bride from Babylon.

Persian Empire

The Persian Empire rose in Western Asia after the fall of the Babylonian Empire. Lasting less than 250 years, it was the largest empire in the ancient world.

Stone bas-relief of Persian soldiers in Persepolis, Iran.

FUN FACT

The name "Persian" comes from the tribal name "Parsua". This was the name given to the land surrounded by the Tigris River where the Persians originally settled.

Cyrus the Great

The Achaemenid Empire was founded by Cyrus the Great. His name was derived from Kuros, meaning "like the sun". He founded Persia by uniting the Medes and the Persians - two original Iranian tribes. He then went on to conquer the Lydians and the Babylonians. Under his rule, the people were allowed to practise a religion of their choice. They could keep their customs as long as they paid taxes and obeyed the rulers.

The Great Cylinder

Cyrus the Great was known for creating the first Charter of Human Rights known to humankind. It was written on a clay cylinder, which was excavated in 1879 by an Assyro-British archaeologist called Hormuzd Rassam. It is said that the script on the cylinder was written by Cyrus himself. It was written in the Akkadian language with a cuneiform script. Passages in the text express the emperor's humanity, religious tolerance and freedom. Today, Cyrus the Great is remembered as a wise, peaceful leader and a liberator of his people.

Fighting the Greeks

After the death of Cyrus the Great, the next strong emperor to come into power was Darius I. Under his rule, the Persians tried to expand their empire by conquering Greece. King Darius first attacked Greece in 490 BCE. However, he only managed to conquer a few city-states, before he was defeated at Athens. His dream of conquering Greece was fulfilled by his son Xerxes I in 480 BCE when he won the Battle of Thermopylae against a strong army of Spartans.

Ruins of the city of Persepolis, the capital of the Persian Empire.

The Cyrus Cylinder, now preserved at the British museum, London.

The Vikings: A Warrior Civilisation

It is a popular misconception that Vikings wore helmets with two horns when in fact their helmets were likely made of iron or leather.

Large numbers of Scandinavian seafaring warriors raided and colonized several settlements between the eighth and eleventh centuries. These warriors were known as Vikings or Norsemen. For three centuries, they made their mark on large parts of England, Europe, Russia, Iceland, Greenland and Newfoundland.

Landowners and farmers take to the sea

The Vikings basically comprised heads of clans or landowners who were in search of adventure and loot. On their own lands, they were farmers, but once they set out, they turned into violent raiders and pillagers. Thus, power-hungry chieftains would organise bands of armies, set forth on longships and raid coastal cities and towns, plundering, burning, and killing at will.

Making inroads into England and Europe

By the middle of the ninth century, the Vikings had made significant inroads into Ireland, Scotland and England. They brought much of Scotland under their control; they established Ireland's early trading towns of Dublin, Waterford, Wexford, Wicklow and Limerick. Only the kingdom of Wessex withstood the Vikings.

Turning their attention to Europe, the Vikings took advantage of Europe's internal conflicts, realising that many European rulers were willing to pay richly to keep the Vikings away from attacking their subjects. They attacked and occupied large parts of France (the name Normandy comes from The Land of the Northmen), Italy, Denmark, Greenland and Iceland.

Longships were seagoing vessels used by the Vikings for their seafaring adventures.

The Viking legacy

Even though the Viking age ended over nine centuries ago, some legacies of the Norse civilisation remain. The Viking society believed in law and democracy. The "Althing" was believed to be Europe's first national assembly, with powers akin to parliament. Though women could not vote, they did enjoy tremendous equality, running farms and businesses while their husbands were at sea. They could inherit property and even initiate divorce.

The Viking age was also known for its art forms and craft. The Vikings wrote with a set of alphabets called "runes". The Vikings also appeared to have high hygienic standards, as is evident from excavations of tweezers, razors, ear cleaners and combs that were made from bones. The importance of boats in the Viking way of life is evident from the fact that sometimes they buried their dead on boats or wagons.

FUN FACT

The Vikings considered swords as their most precious possession and even gave them names like "Fierce" or "Leg biter".

Famous Vikings

Rollo—First ruler of Normandy
He was either of Danish or Norwegian origin and raided France in the tenth century.

Erik the Red
He was possibly called so due to his red hair and fiery temper. He set his sights and conquered Greenland.

Olaf Tryggvason
Great-grandson of Viking leader Harald I Fairhair, Olaf led a Viking attack on England. He forced his subjects to convert to Christianity. In 1000, he was defeated and is believed to have jumped over the side of his ship.

Leif Eriksson
Son of Erik the Red, he is believed to have landed in North America much before Columbus. However, he was unable to establish himself successfully.

Cnut the Great
He was the son of Denmark's King Sweyn Forkbeard. He helped his father conquer England in 1013.

Harald (Hardrada) Sigurdsson
He led 300 ships to challenge William the Conqueror and gain control of Northern England. He was killed at the battle of York. "Hardrada" means hard ruler.

Chinese Civilisation

Portrait of Emperor Qianlong of the Qing dynasty, the last dynasty to rule China.

Ancient China is one of the oldest civilisations of the world. Its history can be traced back to over 7000 years. Like the Indus Valley Civilisation, the Chinese civilisation was cut out from the rest of the world—as it was bounded by oceans, mountains and deserts—making it inaccessible to outsiders. Being cut off from others gave rise to a feeling of nationalism among the Chinese. They believed themselves to be the strongest empire, ruled by powerful families called dynasties. The first recorded Chinese dynasty was the Shang Dynasty, which is said to have ruled China from 1766 to 1122 BCE.

Mongols and the Great Wall

The Mongols were the greatest enemy of the Chinese, frequently attacking them from the north. To keep the Mongols from invading, the Chinese built a huge wall, stretching for miles on its northern border. Started by the Qin dynasty, the wall continued to be built by the dynasties that followed. Most of the wall, as we see it today, was built by the Ming dynasty. It is the longest man-made structure in the world, stretching up to 8900 km. The wall also had towers, where soldiers would stand to keep guard.

Chinese technology and inventions

The Chinese are known for their inventions. They invented silk and paper. Printing was first practised in ancient China on wooden blocks. Their other inventions include gunpowder, crossbows, hand fans, fireworks, ploughs, kites, harnesses, umbrellas, wheelbarrows, paper money, the compass, the abacus and the Grand Canal.

The wheelbarrow was invented by the Chinese.

The Great Wall of China.

Traditional Chinese medicine

Medicine in China was developed almost 5000 years ago. They devised various healing methods, many of which are still in use. Some of these are acupuncture or the science of healing through needles pierced at critical points; acupressure or the science of healing by applying pressure at key points; and herbs made from thousands of medicinal plants or even dried animals parts.

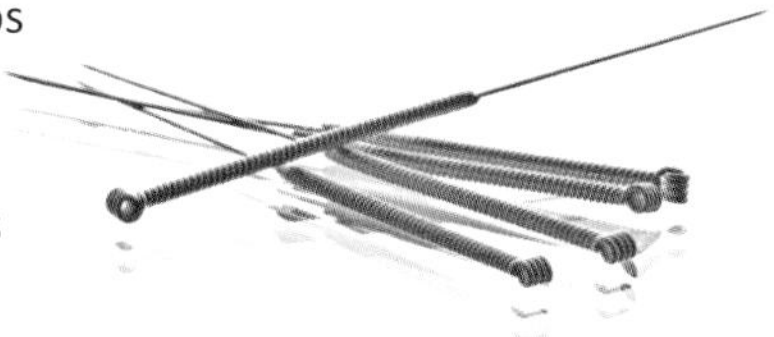
Needles are used for acupuncture.

Languages in China

There are many languages and dialects in China, which are known as Sinitic languages. The main language group, Chinese Han, comes from the Sino-Tibetan area. Other languages are Mandarin, Wu, Gan, Hakka, Xiang and Cantonese. The languages differ in grammar, vocabulary and pronunciation. Today, Modern Standard Chinese has been accepted as one of the six official languages by the United Nations as an outcome of a programme for the unification of the national language, based on Mandarin.

Calligraphy is a known art in China with elaborate and delicate strokes creating virtual pieces of art.

The history of Chinese cuisine

Chinese food is among the most popular cuisines in the world. The importance of food in Chinese ancient culture dates back to the days of the emperor. Chefs were in high demand. Yi Yin, Prime Minister in the seventeenth century, began his life as a cook. Typically, food was cut into small pieces before being cooked, so that it cooked fast. This was primarily because of low fuel supply. Each area of China had a distinct style of cooking and ingredients differed based on local availability. In northern China, wheat was used for noodles and dumplings; whereas in the south, there was a greater prevalence of rice.

The Chinese eat sticky rice with chopsticks even today.

The Chinese Terracotta warriors

Ying Zheng became an Emperor at the age of 13 in 246 BCE. Over the next several years, he unified a number of warring kingdoms and became the first Emperor of Qin dynasty. A lot of achievements like the standardisation of coins, weights, measures, building of canals and roads, etc., are attributed to him. He commissioned the creation of an army of terracotta warriors to accompany him into the afterlife. Over 700,000 workers were involved in the creation of the famous Terracotta Warrior

The army of terracotta warriors was intended to serve the emperor in the afterlife.

Army. Archeologists excavated four pits that were filled with terracotta soldiers, weapons and horsedrawn chariots. The fourth pit remains empty, suggesting that the task was never completed. There are estimated to be over 6000 soldiers. These give us an idea of the life, army, clothes and social structure of that time.

A terracotta horsedrawn carriage as a part of the terracotta army.

The Dynasties of China

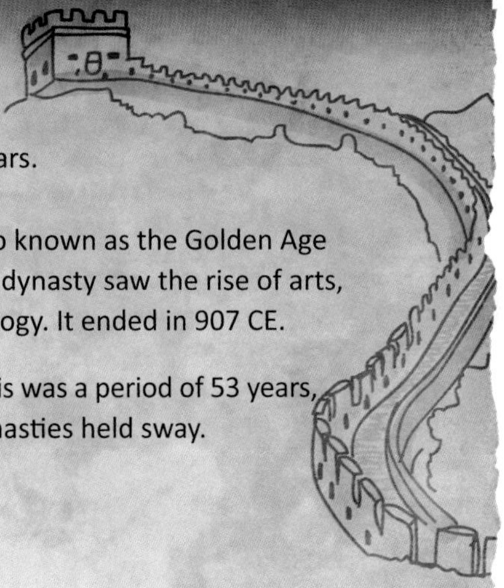

Ancient China was ruled by 13 main dynasties for over 3000 years.

1. **Xia dynasty** – Considered to be the first dynasty in ancient China, it lasted for nearly 500 years under the rule of 17 emperors.

2. **Shang dynasty** – This dynasty lasted for 600 years and was ruled by 30 emperors. It was also known as the Yin dynasty.

3. **Chou (Zhou) dynasty** – This dynasty was founded by Wuwang. It was the longest dynasty and saw 37 emperors over 800 years.

4. **Qin dynasty** – It came into power in 221 BCE, ruling for only 15 years.

5. **Han dynasty** – It ruled from about 206 BCE to 220 CE and was a period of peace and prosperity.

6. **The Six Dynasties rule** – During this rule, six smaller dynasties held power for the next three and a half centuries. These were:
- Wu (222 CE–280 CE)
- Dong (Eastern) Jin (317 CE–420 CE)
- Liu-Song (420 CE–479 CE)
- Nan (Southern) Qi (479 CE–502 CE)
- Nan Liang (502 CE–557 CE)
- Nan Chen (557 CE–589 CE)

7. **Sui dynasty** – Lasted for only 38 years during which the Great Wall of China was built.

8. **Tang dynasty** – Also known as the Golden Age of Ancient China, this dynasty saw the rise of arts, literature and technology. It ended in 907 CE.

9. **Five Dynasties** – This was a period of 53 years, when five specific dynasties held sway. These were:
- Later Liang Dynasty
- Later Tang Dynasty
- Later Jin Dynasty
- Later Han Dynasty
- Later Zhou Dynasty

10. **Song dynasty** – It was founded by General Zhao Kuangyin in the 960s by unifying many warring kingdoms.

11. **Yuan dynasty** – Also known as the Mongol dynasty, this dynasty was founded by Mongol nomads.

12. **Ming dynasty** – It was the last of the great Chinese dynasties and it came into power after it overthrew the Mongols.

13. **Qing dynasty** – It was set up by the Manchus, who invaded China in 1644 CE and overthrew the last Ming emperor.

A porcelain vase from the Ming dynasty.

FUN FACT

The name China was most probably derived from the name Qin (pronounced as Chin) dynasty.

The Inca Civilisation

Considered to be one of the largest in pre-Columbian America, the Inca civilisation came into being during the twelfth century. The Incas took over large parts of Western South America; sometimes through peaceful methods but often through violent conquests. The land was combined into a state almost as large as some of Eurasia's historical empires. Having made Cuzco (now Peru) their capital in the twelfth century, within a hundred years, the Incas brought almost twelve million people in the region under their control.

Inca icon

Expanding boundaries

It is believed that Manco Capac, the earliest known leader of the Inca tribe, settled his tribe in Cuzco. It was under the fourth emperor, Mayta Capac, that the Inca began to truly expand their influence. They plundered neighbouring villages and brought them under their control. Over the succeeding generations, the Incas established themselves in a position of superiority.

It was during the reign of Topa Inca Yupanqui (1471–93) that the Inca empire was the most widespread. When he died, there was a struggle for succession and Huayna Capac (1493–1525) came to power. Huayna Capac further extended the northern boundary of the empire, but his death brought about another succession struggle. This remained unresolved when the Spanish arrived in Peru in 1532. By 1535, the Inca civilisation came to an end.

Advanced architecture

At the helm of the Inca society was the emperor, who ruled ruthlessly and harshly with the help of an aristocratic bureaucracy. Technology and architecture during this period were fairly advanced. Excavations have unearthed evidence of fortifications, places of worship, palaces and irrigation systems from this period.

Inca's water canal in the archeological site of Ollantaytambo, Sacred Valley, a major travel destination in the Cuzco region of Peru. Inca terraces can be seen in the background.

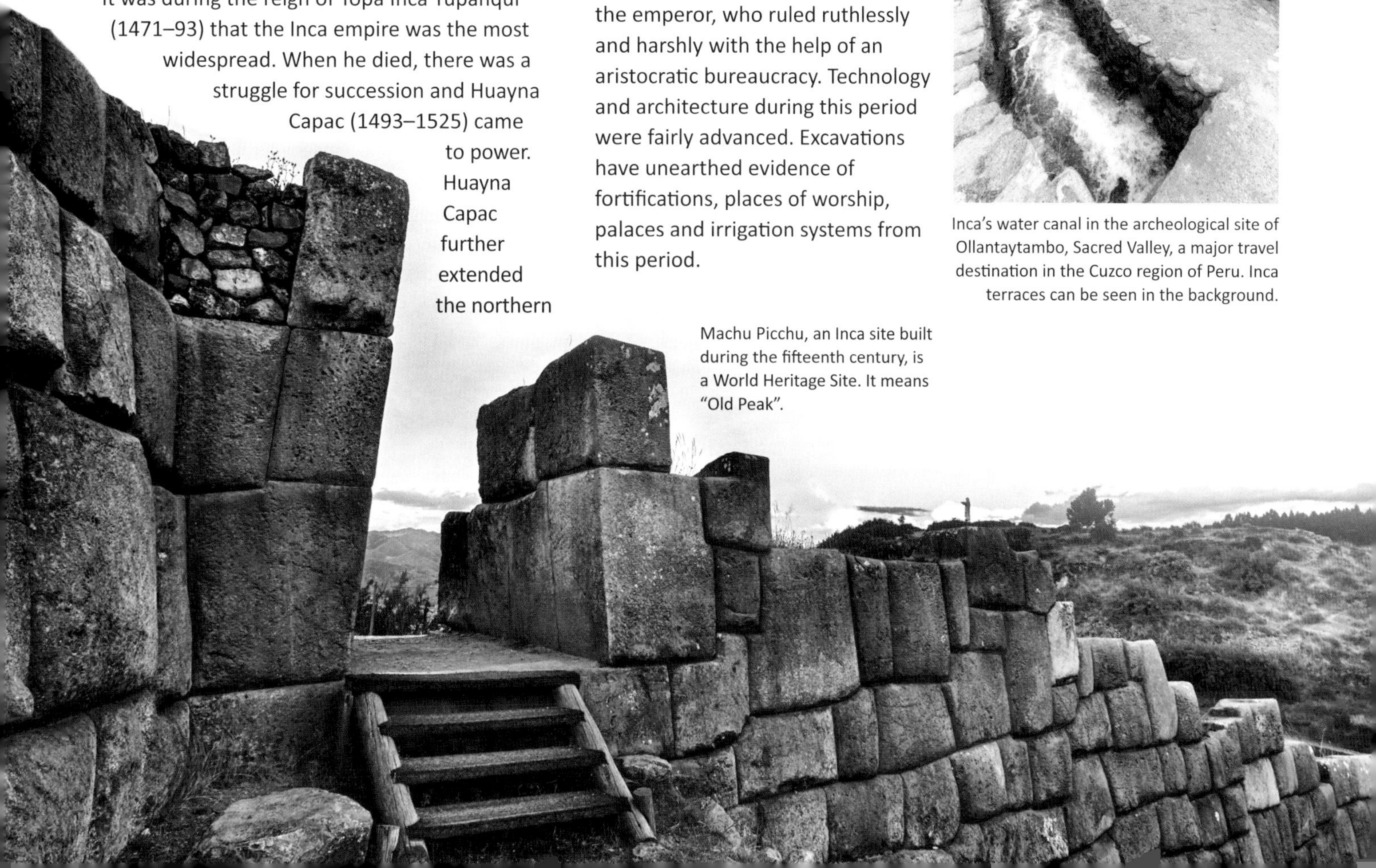

Machu Picchu, an Inca site built during the fifteenth century, is a World Heritage Site. It means "Old Peak".

The Inca economy was primarily agricultural, with a predominance of crops like maize, potatoes, peanuts, cocoa, cassava, cotton, etc. Domestic animals were raised and utilised in farms. Clothing was largely made of llama wool, as well as cotton.

Ancient Inca circular terraces suggest organised farming.

The Inca religion

The Incas worshipped animals and nature gods. Inti, the Sun God; Apu Illapu, the rain God; and Viracocha, the God of creation were among the chief Gods they worshipped. They conducted elaborate rituals that included both animal and human sacrifice. Many of these rituals were discontinued after the Spanish conquest.

The Incas believed that the Earth, the moon, the stars and the Sun were all created by the God Viracocha. The legend claimed that he plucked them from an island in the middle of Lake Titicaca. The official ruler of the Incas was said to be Sapa Inca, which meant "Son of the Sun". The high priests chose women to serve the religion. Girls were sometimes chosen when they were very young. These girls or women were called "acllas".

A sacrificial ceremonial axe made of either wood, bronze or copper.

Evidence of the advanced architectural abilities of the Incas lies in the vast road network they built. Not much is left of the original Inca culture today. However, their lineage seems to have been carried forward by the peasants living on the Andes, who are believed to be descendants of the Inca. The peasants speak a language called Quechua and account for almost 45 per cent of Peru's population. Primarily farmers, they follow a version of Roman Catholicism with a pagan hierarchy.

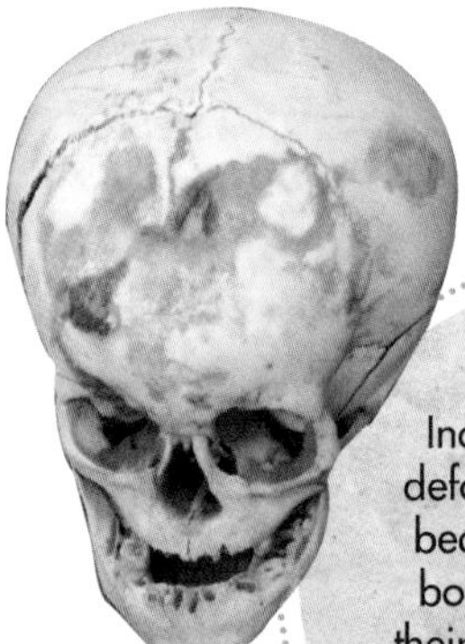

FUN FACT

Incas believed that deformed skulls were beautiful. They even bound the heads of their children tightly to change the shape of their skull.

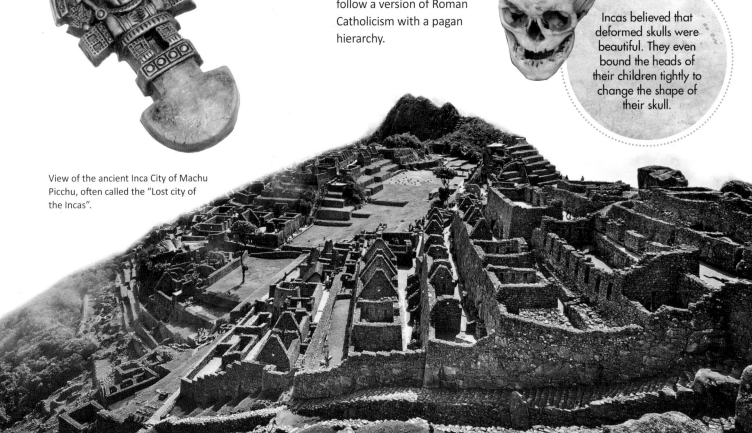

View of the ancient Inca City of Machu Picchu, often called the "Lost city of the Incas".

The Mughal Empire

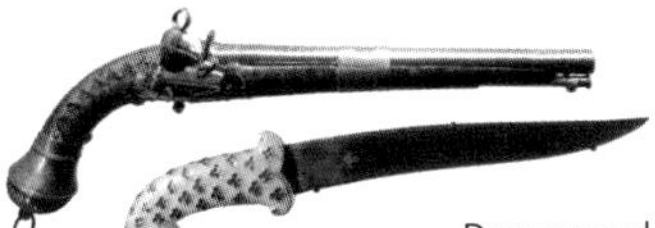

Dagger and flintlock pistol from the Mughal dynasty.

Illustrations from the manuscript of Baburnama (Memoirs of Babur)—late sixteenth century.

The word Mughal is derived from the Arabic word for Mongol. Seven generations of the Mughal dynasty ruled for 200 years, from the sixteenth to the eighteenth centuries, over northern India. Babur, the founder of the empire, was a Mongol warlord descendent. Under the Mughals, roads were built, trade prospered and the arts flourished.

The Mughal dynasty

Babur was the first Mughal Emperor; he was the descendent of Genghis Khan and Tamburlaine. He became a ruler at the age of 12. In 1524, he turned his sights towards India when he disposed the ruler under whose invitation he had come to India and soon became the ruler himself. In 1526, he captured Delhi after ousting the forces of Ibrahim Lodhi in the first Battle of Panipat and defeated Rana Sanga of Mewar. Soon, Babur controlled the entire northern India from the Indus river to present-day Bihar, from Bengal in the east and Himalayas in the north to Gwalior in the south.

Emperor Babur

Religious tolerance

The Mughals had to fight against the Afghans and many regional Hindu rulers. The early Muslim emperors allowed the practise of all religions, but Aurangzeb offended the Hindus and caused the Sikhs to rebel. He also fiercely clashed with the western kingdom of the Marathas and its ruler, Shivaji. However, it was the growing political power of the British traders in India that brought about the final decline and collapse of the Mughal Empire in the eighteenth century.

Emperor Aurangzeb

FUN FACT

Babur was a broad-minded emperor who stopped the killing of cows because it was against the beliefs of the Hindus. His autobiography is called the Baburnama.

Diorama of Battle of Panipat (1526) displayed at Indian War Memorial Museum, Naubat khana, India.

Prominent Mughal Rulers

Maharaja Hemu

The Mughal dynasty began their rule in India in 1526 CE. These early Mughal rulers; the young prince Babur, Humayun and later Akbar were known for their efficient administrative organisation. This glorious dynasty that ruled India for over 300 years, came to an end during the reign of emperor Bahadur Shah. The decline of the empire had already begun after the death of Aurangzeb. The advent of the British reduced the later rulers to mere puppets.

A painting from the period of Akbar's rule, showing a minaret being built using the beheaded skulls of the relatives and supporters of King Hemu.

Tolerance policy

Akbar was succeeded by his son, Emperor Jahangir. He followed his father's policy of religious tolerance, which pleased those of the Hindu faith. His son, Shah Jahan, was a great admirer of architecture. The Taj Mahal and the Great Mosque of Delhi were built under his patronage. Emperor Shah Jahan was succeeded by Aurangzeb, who annexed the Deccan states of Bijapur and Golconda, which were under the rule of Muslim leaders. Though Aurangzeb followed religious tolerance, he excluded those of the Hindu faith from this policy. During his reign, he plundered and destroyed several temples and schools attended by Hindu children. Those who followed Sikhism also suffered under his reign. Aurangzeb persecuted them, which caused several rebellions to break out against him. These were mostly led by the princes of annexed or enemy territories. The Rajputs, Sikhs and Marathas were at the forefront of these rebellions. Aurangzeb also levied heavy taxes on farmers who were already suffering. All these factors added to the slow decline of the Mughal Empire. Aurangzeb died in 1707, after his attempt to defeat the Marathas was crushed.

Muhammad Shah, who succeeded the throne, did not make much impact though he ruled from 1719 to 1748. By the end of his rule, the Mughal empire was confined to only some parts of Delhi. Bahadur Shah II, who succeeded him, was exiled to Yangon, Burma, by the British for his participation in the Indian Mutiny of 1857.

Diwan-e-Khas, the hall of private audience in Fatehpur Sikri.

A photo from Musamman Burj, where Shah Jahan spent the final years of his life placed under house arrest by his own son Aurangzeb.

1540 CE: Akbar defeats King Hemu

1707 CE: Aurangzeb dies after the Maratha defeat

The Middle Ages

1500 years ago

The Middle Ages refers to the time after the decline of the Roman Empire (476 CE) and until the beginning of the Renaissance in the fourteenth century. Researchers call it the medieval period, since the term "Middle Ages" gives the wrong notion that the period is not significant enough and it simply lies between two otherwise important periods. The Middle Ages are a period of great transition in the world.

All over the world during this period there existed a feudal system of society, where people were grouped based on the money they made and the land they owned. Here, there were two main players—the lord, who owned the land, and the vassal who wanted the land. He worked for the lord because he either owed him money or needed to make money. This age is infamously also remembered for the deadly Bubonic plague or "Black Death", which killed around 20 million Europeans from 1347 to 1350.

The main form of art during that time was Byzantine art produced by artists from the Eastern Roman Empire, also called Byzantium. It was during this period that the Catholic Church became the most supreme, especially after the fall of Rome, in fact Pope Leo the 3rd had named Charlemagne, the Frankish King and the Emperor of the Romans. It was often referred to as the Holy Roman Empire. The Church was exempt from taxes and since the common folk were expected to devote 10 per cent of their earnings to the Church, it became powerful and rich.

Rise of Islam

Prophet Mohammed stamp on a metal ring.

After Prophet Mohammed's death in 632 CE, the Muslim armies had captured large parts of the Middle Eastern cities like Baghdad, Damascus and Cairo. All of these were ruled by the Caliph. It was also a period where great works of Greek, Indian and Iranian origin were translated into Arabic. Also, a period of several inventions including the soap, windmills, the numerical system and even an early version of a flying machine. The Islamic world was created during the seventh and eighth century Arab conquests, and Islam spread far and wide from Turkey and Middle East to India.

The new Caliph

After the death of Prophet Mohammed, the united tribes of Arabia and the followers of Islam were faced with a dilemma—who would be their next leader? They had two people to choose from. One of whom, was a man named Ali, Prophet Mohammed's cousin and son-in-law. The other was Prophet Mohammed's father-in-law and longtime friend, Abu Bakr. The latter of the two received support from many of the elders and he was chosen to become the first caliph of Islam. Although Abu Bakr died two years later, he managed to convert the entire Arabian Peninsula to Islam with his words and charm.

Concerns of the Church

Cathedral of Burgo de Osma, Soria, Spain. It is a Gothic temple built on an area previously occupied by a Romanesque Church.

The rise of Islam brought forth concerns among the people of the Catholic Church who began to authorise military crusades against the Muslims. These began in 1095 when Pope Urban urged the Christian Army to fight its way to Jerusalem. While no one won the crusade, it did bring about a feeling of purpose to the Catholic communities. The Church during this period built grand cathedrals across Europe in the Romanesque style—wherein round arches and barrel vaults supported the roofs. The walls were made of thick stones. In 1200, churches began to change and then the Gothic styled structures were seen in churches.

FUN FACT

The occupation of Spain by the Moors actually led to the advances made during the Middle Ages; in fact, words like "algebra", "magazine" and "orange" have their roots in the Arabic language. The Moors also introduced chess to the Europeans!

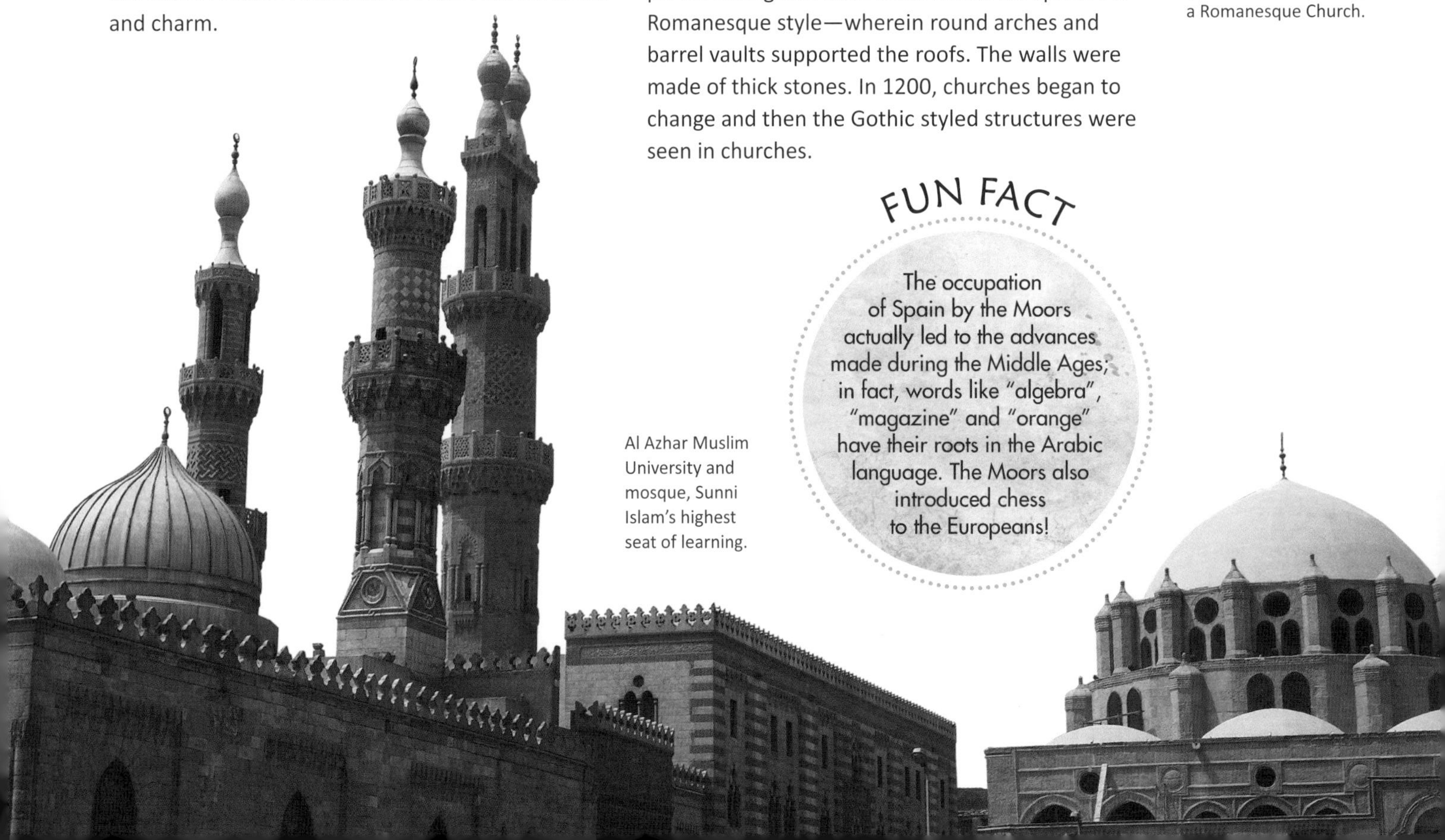

Al Azhar Muslim University and mosque, Sunni Islam's highest seat of learning.

Norman Legacy

The legacy of the Norman Conquest has shaped British History. In 1066, William the Conqueror and his army defeated King Harold in the Battle of Hastings. That was when power shifted to the Normans from the Anglo-Saxons. As per the Domesday Book, William changed the hierarchical structure and gave his trusted people large plots of land. The nobles were expected to collect taxes. He also built more than 80 castles in his lifetime.

Scene of the Battle of Hastings of 1066.

The Normans

Vikings were raiding France in 1000 CE and soon were allowed by the French king to settle down and live in France. In return, they were to assist the king against other raiding Vikings. These Vikings were also supposed to convert to Catholicism. The Normans were Vikings who had settled along the coast of France where they were known as the Norseman from Norway. Eventually, they came to be known as Normans after they settled down in Normandy.

Art during the Norman legacy

The Norman architectural style found its way in cathedrals across Ely and Durham in England. It was in the Norman legacy that Latin as a language was introduced. Though it was only in the fourteenth century when Old English would regain its hold in England. There was a political change with the focus moving away from Scandinavia and towards France—a country with whom England would enter into battles with. Soon, after the Norman invasion of England, after winning the Battle of Hastings, the Normans marked the event by making the Bayeux Tapestry. It was a large embroidery made up of small stitches that was used to outline diverse images on cloth and showcased the events that unfolded during the Battle of Hastings.

Detail of the famous Bayeux Tapestry depicting the Norman invasion of England in the eleventh century.

The Normans were similar to the Romans and Greeks. They were great organisers, like the Romans, and excellent city planners. Like the Greeks and Romans, they were patrons of art and music. They took forward the culture and beauty left behind by the Anglo-Saxons, also called the founders of England as they contributed greatly to its culture.

The Battle Abbey medieval gate building.

FUN FACT

Did you know that William the conqueror could not speak English when he became the King? It was during the Norman Conquest that French names like William, Robert and Henry entered into the English culture. In fact, the name quickly became popular and even today it ranks among the most popular names in the world!

The Domesday Book

The Domesday Book is a grand survey with details of land ownership and census. It was commissioned by William the Conqueror to mark the Norman conquest. It continues to remain one of the few older historical records of this period. Historians opine that the root of feudalism started in the Dark Ages when the Duke of Normandy confiscated all the land from the Saxons and then distributed the same to the Norman Barons.

Elements of the Domesday Book

Ordered by William the Conqueror (William I) in 1085 to assess England's wealth to help the tax system, the Domesday Book was legally binding and had no system of appeal. Written in Latin it was made up of two separate works, which included Little Domesday that covered East Anglia and Great Domesday that covered the rest of England and parts of Wales. Close to 13,000 places were covered in the book. This book was also called the Book of Winchester when it was kept at the Winchester Royal Treasury. It tells us that the government of King William I was interested in retaining information about its people. It also showed how advanced their methods and technologies must have been to collect this "Grand Survey".

Preparing the Domesday Book.

King William I of England

King William introduced the tradition of building castles to show his control over the land. He invaded Scotland and Wales to fortify England. He died at the age of 60 and he will be remembered for the different social and economic traditions that he brought into the country. He ensured the supremacy of the Church in England and his Norman legacy remained etched into the English aristocracy and royalty. He was credited with having altered land tenures.

Young William was made king at the tender age of eight. His father had taken a pilgrimage to Jerusalem. During this time, the nobles of the kingdom swore to put William at the throne. As his father did not return, King William I took to the throne right when his kingdom entered into a civil war. From a very young age, William saw a lot of blood and war.

1085 CE: The Domesday Book was written

13,000 years ago: Places covered in the book

A page from the Domesday Book.

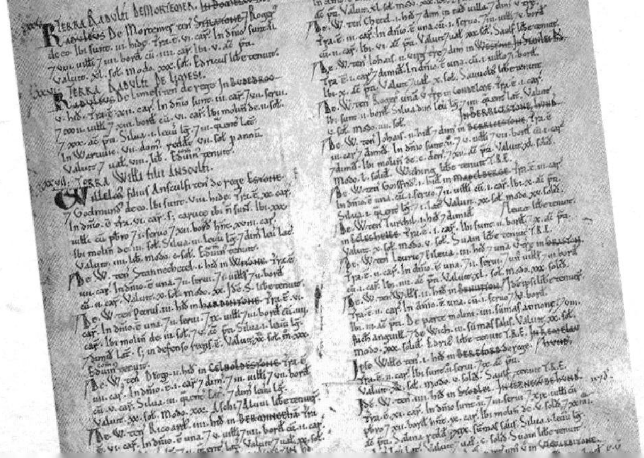

FUN FACT

William the Conqueror was illiterate and could not speak English. In fact, after his invasion, French was the preferred language in the courts.

In 1169, England started its colonising and began its conquests with Ireland. It all began with Henry II marrying Eleanor, who brought the Lordship of Aquitaine with her. But things were not that easy for him, when he took over as the King, he found that the authority of the King was fraught with the effects of civil war and power tussle between the other feudal lords.

King Henry II, Queen and courtiers.

English Quest for Dominance

After Henry II

King John was the youngest son of Henry II, but his reign was disastrous. First, he was faced with the loss of Normandy to the French King Philip, who eventually also invaded Aquitaine. King John finally came to terms with the Pope and tried to get him to be on his side and support him against any possible invasion. It was perhaps as a response to the poor rule of John that the Barons disapproved of him and his exploitation led to the formation of the Magna Carta that protected the Church's rights. It also ensured that the powers of the king were limited.

What is "Magna Carta"?

The Magna Carta was not a small document and had 63 clauses that outlined the laws, which the barons wanted the king to put into practice. The rights included the church rights, ability to avail justice quickly, no imposition of new taxes without agreement from the Barons, feudal payment limits and so on.

Magna Carta Memorial at Runnymede, Surrey, England, UK.

"Magna Carta" is Latin for "the Great Charter". It was signed by King John on 19th June, 1215. The Magna Carta was put forth with the intention of curbing the powers of the king, so if he were a corrupt king, these laws could limit his word or could overthrow him. The Barons were keen on this charter as before it, the daughters and widows of Barons could be sold for profit. The Magna Carta was written in Medieval Latin on parchment paper. The writing was made by scraping a sharp knife against dry parchment. As this process and paper was expensive, scribes would abbreviate words and write in small letters.

FUN FACT

There was confusion as to what the people who came to Ireland during its invasion should be called. Quite a few came from England and others from France. Some historians called them Anglo Norman or Anglo French or simply Norman. Today, they are known as the English.

Tomb of Henry II and Catherine de Medici, from Saint Denis gothic cathedral, Paris.

Famine and Plague or the 100 Years' War

The term "100 years' war", refers to the conflict between the kingdoms of France and England. The kings of England were eager to acquire Aquitaine. They wanted to rule the kingdom of France. Although the French kings seemed to have more advantage over the much smaller English Kingdom, but in reality the disciplined and much experienced army of England did manage many a victory both at sea and on land as is noticed in the battles at Sluys, Crecy and Poitiers. To maintain his supremacy and save his crown, in 1360 King John signed the Treaty of Calais, which made the Duchy of Guyenne independent.

The Battle of Crecy, Edward III of England defeats Philip VI of France, 26th August, 1346.

The renewed war

The Treaty of Calais gave Edward III the power over the lands. After the death of John II, his son Charles renewed the war and again the two kingdoms fought over their territories even as they suffered from their own internal power struggles. The English King Henry V got the crown; he wanted to take advantage of the French internal strife and again renewed the campaign to claim the French throne. Henry V was made prince at the time of his father Henry IV's coronation in 1339.

King of England, Henry V.

Joan of Arc

After the death of King Henry V, the English army faced the might of a force led by the Joan of Arc. The people of Southern France opposed the English rule. In 1428, as the English began to invade Southern France, a peasant girl called Joan of Arc decided to battle it out with the forces based on a vision she had from God. She won the battle at Orleans in 1429 and remained unbeaten in many such victories until she was captured by the Burgundians who sold her to the English and executed her. Paris again came under the king of France.

FUN FACT

During the Middle Ages, animals were tried for smaller crimes and sometimes locusts and mice were charged with the crime of spoiling crops or eating the agricultural produce.

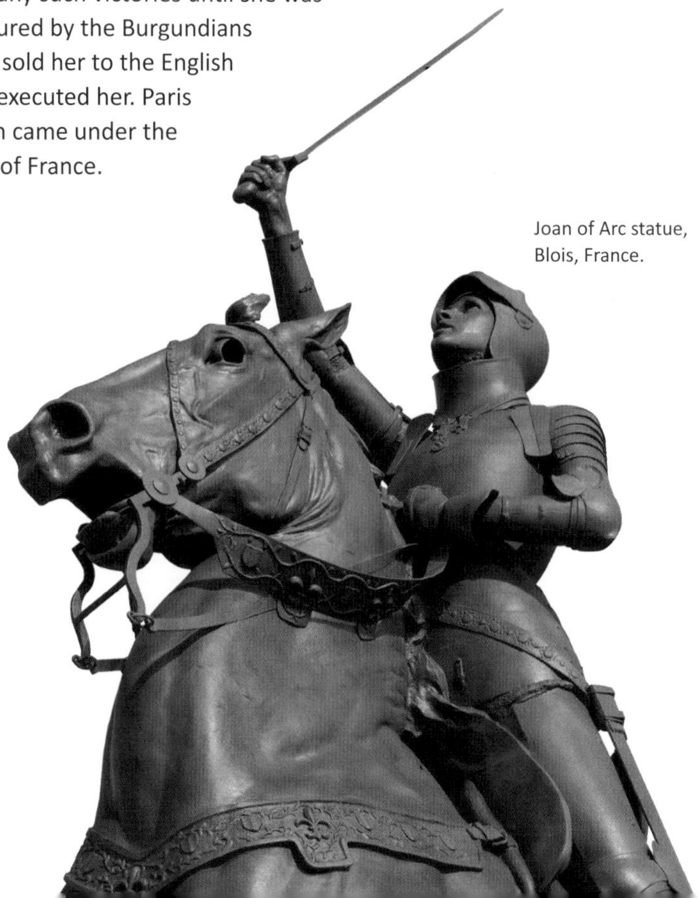

Joan of Arc statue, Blois, France.

A painting showing the people of Europe suffering from the "black death".

The famine

In the backdrop of the terrible wars between the kingdoms of France and England, the people were suffering from the after effects of the famine. The climate had taken its toll on farming and the scarcity of grain led to acute starvation. Around 15 per cent of the population suffered and finally succumbed to diseases like bronchitis, tuberculosis and pneumonia. Plague ravaged the populations and earned its name as "black death". By 1348, it had decimated populations in Europe.

The Black Death

The Black Death was the name given to the pandemic that spread across Europe from 1347 to 1350. At the time, the plague was a disease that had no cure and unfortunately was very contagious. It is said that the plague may have travelled from Asia and moved via the silk route. The carriers of the disease were essentially fleas that travelled with or lived on the bodies of rats.

The hundred years' war did not have any set winners or losers; in fact, the wars ensured that Louis XI could remove the sceptre of feudalism from France and unite the kingdom under the royal power. For England too, it re-oriented its focus and finally England decided to cease its continental hold and seek to reinforce its naval authority. The hundred year's war re-evolved the two kingdoms into looking more internally and into setting things in order before seeking expansion.

Even though historians refer to this constant power war between France and England as the 100 years' war, it must be noted that the war actually lasted for 116 years. It began in 1337 and ended in 1453. As the plague began to hit a large number of the population, it spread panic among the people who mostly experienced nose bleeds and began to grow paler, experiencing swellings in the groin and armpit.

FUN FACT

Plague is an infectious fever caused by bacteria that is passed from rodents to humans via the bite of infected fleas. Did you know that there was a plague epidemic in India as recent as 1994, in Surat, Gujarat. The Surat Plague epidemic claimed 52 lives.

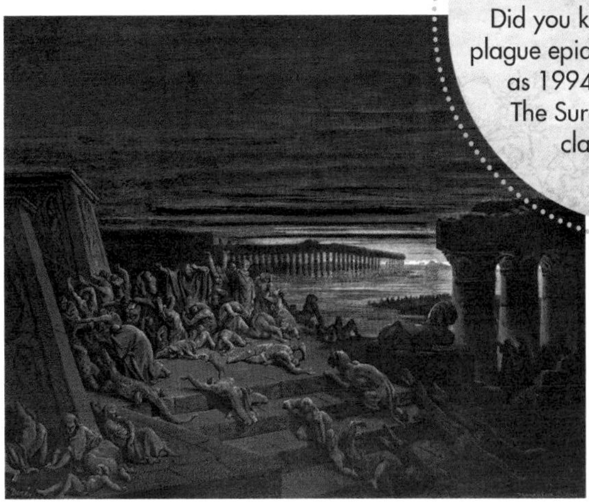

Artist's imagination of the black death.

The Magna Carta

The Magna Carta was signed in 1215 between King John and the Barons of England. This royal-sealed document became one of the most important documents of medieval England. It contained a series of promises to the subjects of England, on the King governing the land and people as per the feudal law. The charter was seen as a document that would bring a stop to the abuse of the power of the king.

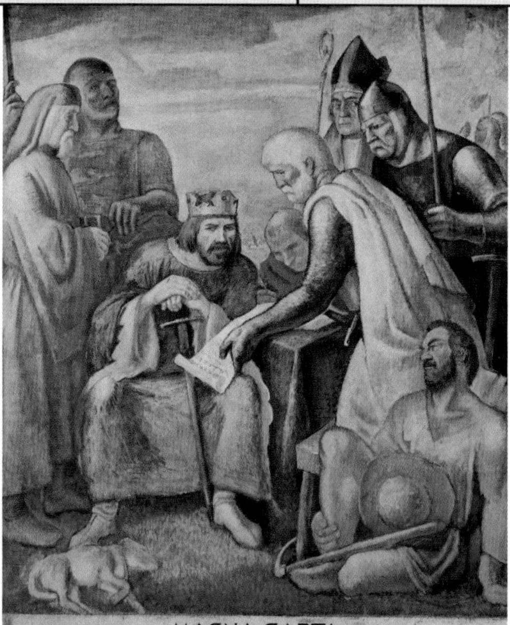
MAGNA CARTA

What was the Magna Carta?

The Magna Carta was a document which stated that a king needed to follow the law of the land and also to assure the people of their rights. The document stated that people should not be imprisoned or arrested for any other reason except as per the law of the land. It was what made way for the trial by jury, wherein people could be tried and then as per the judgement of the jury they could be assured of their rights. Moreover, the Magna Carta put in place that the Barons could effectively limit the king's power if he was involved in harming the country.

King John and the Roman Catholic Church

King John angered the Roman Catholic Church, and troubled by his behaviour of unfairly adding taxes and asking for money from the Barons, they stopped all church services. Afraid of being excommunicated by the Pope, King John finally accepted the power of the Church and gave in to their demands for different privileges and powers.

The start of the crusades

Eastern Europe was under attack from the Islamic forces. In particular, the area of Jerusalem became a point of contention owing to its significance to both Jews and Christians. It remained under protection from the Byzantium's, the term used for the eastern Roman Empire, who appealed for the Pope in Rome to intercede and that was the start of the crusades.

Doors of the Milan Cathedral depicting conquest of Jerusalem by crusaders.

1215 CE: The Magna Carta is signed

1095 CE: The start of the crusades

Magna Carta Libertatum, is an English legal charter that required King John of England to proclaim certain rights, respect certain legal procedures and accept that his will could be bound by the law.

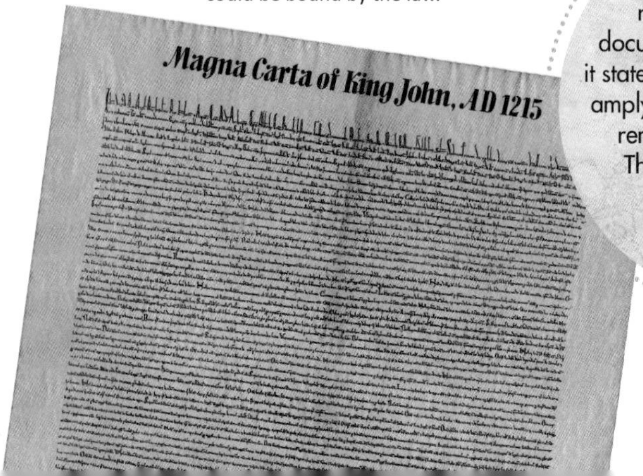

FUN FACT

Magna Carta remains a significant document owing to the limits it states on royalty and makes it amply clear that even the king remained below the law. The charter was written entirely in medieval Latin.

Jerusalem exists even today as a city in Central Israel to the west of the Dead Sea. It is a site of great importance to Jews, Muslims and Christians. The Dome of the Rock, for Islam and the Temple Mount for Judaism is still operational in the Old City of Jerusalem. Jews, Christians and Muslims still visit Jerusalem for pilgrimage and to pay honour to their religion.

Renaissance

Renaissance is a word that you might see mentioned often in your history books. What is so special about this French word that means "rebirth"? The Renaissance period extended from the fourteenth century to the French Revolution and witnessed a cultural movement called "humanism". Humanism stood for an overarching philosophy that all people should endeavour to be educated in everything from the arts to literature and science.

What was the Renaissance?

With the fall of the Roman Empire began the Middle Ages that were renamed the "dark ages" because a lot of which was learned and gained was soon lost. The Renaissance was in that sense a coming out of those dark ages into light. It was a rebirth of sorts where people's interest in all forms of arts, sciences and education in general, grew in prominence.

The Great Plague

The Renaissance emerged in Florence, Italy during the late fourteenth century, when there was a rebirth and a reawakening of philosophy, literature and particularly art. Prior to the Renaissance, Europe had witnessed the Great Plague from 1346 to 1353. That period was generally referred to as the "Dark Age" owing to the large number of lives (nearly fifty million) that were lost.

The movable type

The invention of the movable type by Johannes Gutenberg was one of the innovations that introduced printing technology to the world. By 1470 printing technology had spread far and wide and a system of distribution and spread of printed books began. It was during the Renaissance period that the concept of "sun revolving around the earth" by Ptolemy was debunked and Copernicus's claim of the reverse that the Earth and other planets revolved around the Sun emerged. Copernicus's argument was finally accepted despite widespread opposition from the Catholic Church. This was a few years after he was banned from teaching his concepts to students.

FUN FACT

Ptolemy was an Egyptian astronomer who promoted his earth -centred model also known as the "Ptolemaic system".

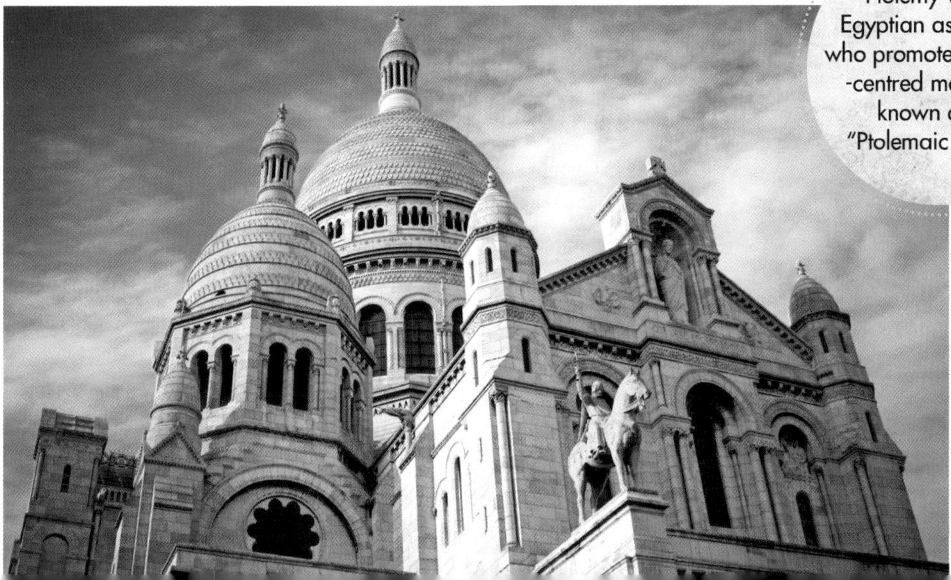

A building inspired by Renaissance architecture.

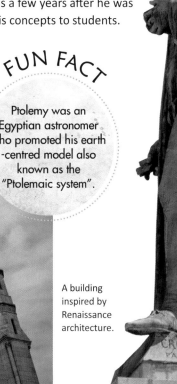

Statue of Johannes Gutenberg.

The Arts Movement

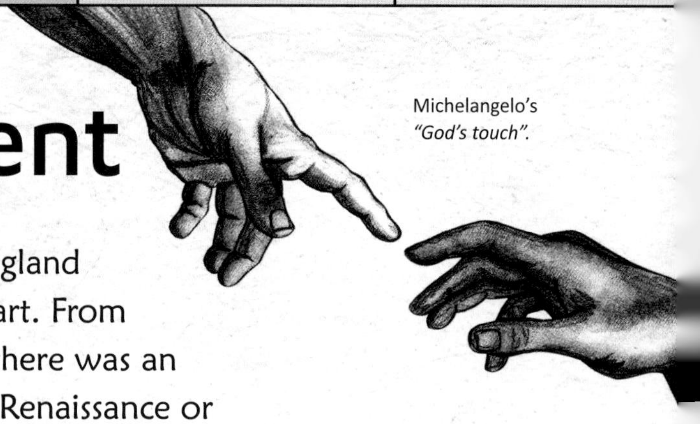

Michelangelo's *"God's touch".*

Post the aftermath of the 100 years' war between England and France, Europe was witness to a period of fine art. From drawing and painting to sculpture and architecture there was an unprecedented growth in the arts; hence, the name Renaissance or "Rebirth" of the arts. The Italian Renaissance art was as per the principles of Classical Greek Art. Therefore, the different forms of Ancient Greek and Roman art influenced Italian artists during this period. The decline of the Catholic Church is also seen as one of the reasons why the movement gained popularity.

FUN FACT

"The Renaissance" as it is known in French and, "Rinascimento" in Italian, was the after-effect of the growth of feudalism in cities like Italy and Southern Holland.

The humanist form

One of the most lasting features of the Renaissance is the humanist form of artwork. During this time, artwork was almost always inspired by religion and a lot of religious artwork was made for churches and chapels. However, artists also started getting inspired by Greek and Roman mythology and began painting and sculpting subjects. They also began developing portraits of real people.

Fountain di Trevi, Rome, Italy.

Ponte Sant'Angelo, Rome, Italy.

Concept of humanism

The Renaissance movement was based on the concept of humanism. It paid more attention to the worth of an individual as opposed to religious dogma. It was more concerned with the real and detailing of the real. Hence, the stress on real human faces and bodies. It was one of the reasons why Byzantine art became obsolete. This movement was at many levels similar to the Western age of discovery, wherein the urge to explore all elements of the world and nature at large remained. Similarly, during the Renaissance arts movement, artists had a greater desire to explore various facets of the arts.

The Madonna of the Meadow, painting created by the famous Renaissance artist Raphael (1483–1520) in 1505.

Humanism vs the Church Doctrine

Owing to the fact that sometimes the church opposed the works of certain writers, there was a certain amount of tension between progressive humanism and the Church doctrine. Giovanni Pico della Mirandola was declared a heretic (free thinker) because his works talked about how science and its findings, and humanism's philosophical dimensions were not matching with what the Church teaches and preaches.

Humanist movement

During the late 1300s, many European thinkers moved away from the Church and started to question and reason things out for themselves. They valued evidence-based judgments. The scholars promoted investigation and observation. This aspect soon began to be called as "humanism" owing to its insistence on human-based thinking and innovation.

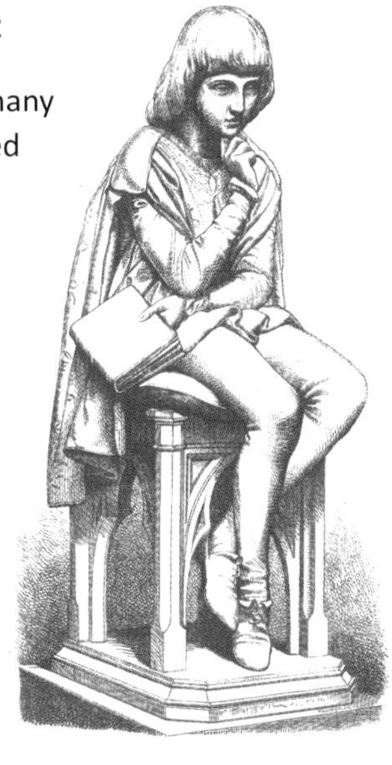

Pico published a collection of 900 philosophical theses.

Rise of the reformist movement

The dissent viewed in many works during this period became the primary argument and soon transformed into the central thought of the Protestant movement during the Reformation period.

Characteristics of Renaissance writings

The primary characteristics of Renaissance writings stemmed from an interest in the nature of life itself. It also became a background to rediscover the Greco-Roman culture and was all about understanding the world. Intrinsically, it had urban influences and celebrated an individual's thinking as opposed to dogma. English literature during this period focussed on poetry and drama. The lyric, elegy, tragedy and the pastoral forms of writing became popular forms that were adopted. John Milton composed his *Paradise Lost*, now noted as the greatest poem in English.

FUN FACT

It was during the Renaissance period that Dante wrote his "Divine Comedy", about death, religious faith and love. He wrote this play entirely in Italian rather than Latin, which was considered the language of scholars.

Statue of William Shakespeare (1874) in Leicester square, London, UK.

Writers of the Renaissance movement

Prominent writers during this period were Dante, Ariosto Ludovico, Boccaccio Giovanni, Baldassare, Cellini Benvenuto, Miguel de Cervantes, Chaucer, Donne John, Jonson Ben, Machiavelli, Marlowe Christopher, Michel Eyquem de Montaigne, Thomas, Petrarch Francesco, Rabelais François, Ronsard Pierre de, Sannazzaro Jacopo, Shakespeare William, Sidney Philip and Spenser Edmund among others.

The Renaissance movement had many celebrated artists including painters and artists like Michelangelo, Botticelli, Ghiberti and Raphael among many others.

Fresco of Raphael, Vatican, Rome.

Artists of the Renaissance Period

Renaissance art

Renaissance art is divided into two periods of early Renaissance from 1400 to 1475. During this period, artists tried to follow the classical artists and art forms that laid greater emphasis on symmetry. The popular artists from this period were Giotto, Masaccio and Donatello. The second period was that of High Renaissance, which was from 1475 to 1525 where there was an enhanced interest in viewpoints and realism became prominent. The artists of this period were Michelangelo, Leonardo da Vinci and Rafael. Although religious paintings also found favour among the Renaissance artists, it wasn't limited to the Church alone. Other subjects like Greek and Roman mythology also were used by artists to express themselves.

Sandro Botticelli *Madonna of the Magnificat*

Michelangelo: the artist par excellence

Michelangelo was thought to be the greatest artist during his lifetime, a painter, sculptor and an architect par excellence. His frescoed work on the ceiling of the Sistine Chapel is among his well-known works. He worked with marble sculptures during his lifetime and the Sistine ceiling as painted by him remains a great proof of his admirable art. He was one such artist around this time who was greatly documented. Many biographies are written about him spreading light upon his life.

Michelangelo's *David*, Piazza della Signoria, Firenze, Italy.

Botticelli and his works

Italian painter Sandro Botticelli's famous works include *Primavera, Pallas* and the *Centaur and The Birth of Venus*. His paintings were allegories on different aspects of love. A Florentine, his style was successful; however, he died in obscurity as his work remained unrecognised. His nickname actually means "little barrel", a name given to him by his elder brother.

Ghiberti and his works

Ghiberti, an Italian sculptor, became famous for his *Doors of Paradise*, for the Baptistery of the Florence Cathedral. Commissioned to make bronze doors for the Florence Baptistery, Lorenzo Ghiberti started with a trial piece on Abraham's sacrifice of Isaac. His set of doors contains 14-framed scenes from Christ's life. Ghiberti had implemented the fifteenth century Gothic style to the newer Renaissance style.

Ghiberti's *Doors of Paradise* at the Duomo Baptistery in Florence.

Raphael: the master painter

Raphael, the Italian master painter known for his Madonna paintings, is often referred to as the grand master of the Italian art Renaissance movement. He was exposed to the works of Leonardo da Vinci and Michelangelo, and soon he started work on a series of Madonna paintings. The Pope asked Raphael to paint frescoes. He was also the chief architect when the St. Peter's Basilica was rebuilt and was also named the guardian of the ancient ruins of Rome. He also designed tapestries for the Sistine Chapel. One of Raphael's famous painting is *The School of Athens*, where he depicted the eminent philosophers of history, Socrates, Plato, Aristotle and Pythagoras.

Raphael's *Conestabile Madonna*

Leonardo da Vinci

Leonardo da Vinci

Leonardo da Vinci, a great artist, was also known for his interest in research, particularly in anatomy, flying, animal and plant life. His celebrated art works include—*Mona Lisa*, *The Virgin of the Rocks* and *The Last Supper*. His *Vitruvian Man* sketch is still seen as one of the hallmarks of the Renaissance period. *The Last Supper* is a painting by Leonardo da Vinci that represents the scene of the last supper Jesus shared with his followers; it depicted Jesus while he made the announcement that one of his 12 disciples would go on to betray him.

This painting and many other works by Leonardo da Vinci are of great interest to symbologists around the world as they believe his paintings have many hidden secrets and messages. The novel *The Da Vinci Code* covered this belief in great detail with a plot line full of thrilling adventures.

Leonardo's Milan hippodrome statue.

Anatomy art by Leonardo da Vinci from 1492.

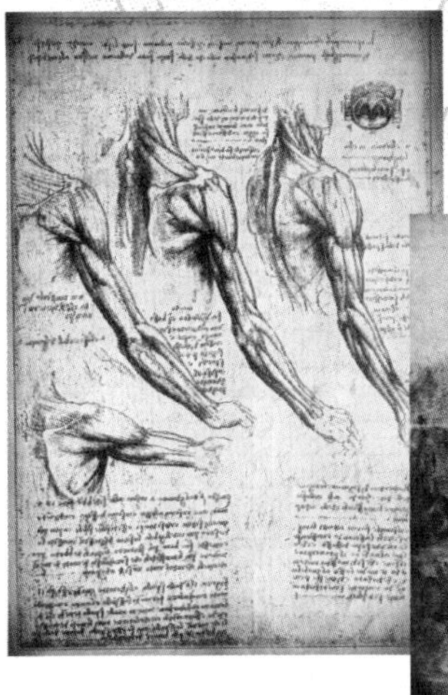

Leonardo da Vinci 's (1452–1519) *Mona Lisa* La Gioconda.

FUN FACT

Both Michelangelo and Leonardo, two accomplished artists, became rivals when Michelangelo mocked Leonardo da Vinci for not completing a statue of a horse.

Highlights of the Renaissance Period

FUN FACT

Christopher Columbus is said to have been in search of India. Instead he landed upon "the New World", which led to the discovery of the Americas.

The Renaissance Period is known as the era where there was a veritable "revival of learning" — a reawakening of the mind. From art to literature there seemed to have been an unquenchable thirst to attain more and acquire a new understanding. During this era, all individuals irrespective of their class began to think for themselves and there was an influx of people from the east after the fall of Constantinople in 1453.

Renaissance period and changes

During this period there was a considerable growth of cities. Soon, people were also taxed. Trade flourished between states and even countries. Cities in Italy grew into prominent trade centres and helped foster the soon to be brought about political and social changes. But Italy's position was put to test by other countries like England, France and Spain, who soon put in place measures to favour their trading middle class. This helped reduce the power of Italian traders. Furthermore, Portugal developed a direct sea route to Asia which reduced Italy's influence even more. As these countries began spreading their power and started establishing colonies in Asia, their power grew further.

Changes during this period

With the concept of humanism being the core of the era, more petty elements of human nature moved away and humankind itself became a subject that needed to be studied and observed. This period actually began in Florence, Italy and then spread across Europe around 1400 and further to England in the next 50 odd years. It was during this period that Columbus sailed across to the other side of the continent in search of India. It was also the time when Leonardo da Vinci painted the world's most famous painting — *The Mona Lisa*.

Christopher Columbus' first view of the New World on 12th October, 1492.

Final assault and the fall of Constantinople in 1453, by Mehmet.

Intellectual works during the Renaissance

This era witnessed unique and new approaches to the various sciences, medicine and philosophy. Copernicus observed that Earth and other planets revolved around the Sun. Galileo who was greatly impressed by Aristotelian science supported his view. It was also the period when the Gregorian Calendar came into being under Pope Gregory XIII, which differed from the Julian Calendar. Medical research saw a huge spike owing to Andreas Vesalius and William Harvey. During this time, Renaissance medical scholars studied different body parts. The uterine or fallopian tubes are named after Gabriele Fallopia.

Growth of local literature

Vernacular literature became vibrant and grew during the Renaissance period. Some governments also adopted vernacular language. Martin Luther published the German translation of the Bible and there were many translations that followed.

Renaissance period: the knowledge period

Many universities were established during this period. For instance, during the middle ages, the number of universities was around 29, but soon the number swelled to 46. Such demand for learning stemmed from the sheer numbers of men who were interested in learning. Soon, trained professionals emerged. During the sixteenth century there was a split in the Christian world when the Protestants rejected the overpowering authority of the Roman Catholic Church. The protestant movement was essentially a literary movement when it stressed on an individual reading the works of the Bible rather than passively receiving sermons from the priests. Martin Luther translated the works into German. It changed many habits followed by Christians across Europe from Scotland to England to Rome.

1400 AD: Revival of learning
1453 AD: Fall of Constantinople

Philosopher Plato (nineteenth century neoclassical statue) outside the Academy of Arts in Athens, Greece.

Martin Luther memorial in Erfurt, a town in Thuringia (Germany).

Literature During the Renaissance

During this period, literature flourished and found beautiful expression. Evidence of this was found in the poetry of Francesco Petrarch. A renewed interest in classical learning and values had a significant effect on English literature. Classical antiquity played an important role in shaping Renaissance literature.

FUN FACT

With the printing press, people began to translate and share great works for the education of the masses.

Renaissance writers

Giovanni Bocaccio wrote *Decameron*, a series of 100 stories set in Florence. Throughout *Decameron*, a mercantile ethic is prevalent. In this series, urban ideals of wit, sophistication and intelligence are treasured, while the vices of stupidity and dullness are cured or punished. The first book that was printed by the moveable type machine was the *Gutenberg Bible* from the Gutenberg Press which changed the course of book publishing across Europe. Humanist writers of Italy widely used the printing press during the Renaissance.

The Gutenberg printing press.

The Gutenberg Press was invented by Johannes Gutenberg who had fiddled around with such technology for a long time before finally creating the first movable printing press. However, the books were printed without colour. Any colour required was added manually by those publishing the books. This cost more money and more time.

Growth of writers and poets

This period witnessed the prolific growth of writers and their work, ensuring that literature became a part of everyone's lives and not just that of the elite, because printing made such literature more accessible to everyone. Giovanni Pico della Mirandola or Pico a member of Florence's Platonic Academy attempted to get together the teachings of Judaism, Christianity and Islam and published a collection of 900 philosophical treatises. Pico's *Oration on the Dignity of Man*, is about the people's free will and its affect to change their destinies. Niccolo Machiavelli rose to fame after Medici regained power in 1512, he retired from government and began to write and published *The Prince*, which was posed to be a handbook for rulers everywhere. Dante Alighieri became the first author to write in Italian when he penned *Divine Comedy* in Italian. Soon, other writers followed him and native languages replaced classical languages like Latin and Greek.

Statue of Francesco Petrarca in Uffizi Alley in Florence, Italy.

Emergence of Modern Europe

1500–1648

Similar to the Renaissance period, England had a golden period during the Elizabethan Age, when arts, painting and literature assumed great interest. This period saw the initial beginnings of Renaissance with the start of companies engaging in trade with countries like Russia and those in the Far East. The East India Company and the West India Company ensured deep benefits and profits for its investors.

The Elizabethan Era that existed from 1558 to 1603 was considered as the Golden Age in English history, because it was this period that finally saw some amount of peace and prosperity. This helped foster the arts in a big way. The period is named so after Queen Elizabeth I, who was the ruler of England at that time.

It was during the Elizabethan Age that William Shakespeare, famous poet and playwright, composed plays that brought about a unique style to theatre. It was also the period of relative calm before the English reformation and the protestant movement drew more battles.

Another battle that ensued later on was between the parliament and royalty. But England was in a much better position as compared to its European counterparts, whereas France was struggling with religious issues. During the Elizabethan period, the long standing duel between England and France remained in suspension.

Economy of Modern Europe

The sixteenth century remains an era of great economic growth, which brought about many changes in Europe. Even as population increased, commerce greatly began to occupy a big space in people's lives. Production increased and professionals like merchants, entrepreneurs and bankers became wealthy. A financial collapse prevailed with the Spanish king suffering bankruptcies one after another.

French bourgeois in traditional medieval clothes.

Rural life

Many Europeans were peasants and people who worked on land. Early modern Europe was a largely rural and agricultural society with most of the population living on farms. European peasants owed taxes to the local nobles, so most of them would rent their homes and would work on land owned by others. Wheat, rye, barley, peas and beans were the preferred crops that were grown in winter. Farmers close to the Mediterranean Sea grew olives and grapes. The people lived modestly and had a simple fare consisting of bread, beans, peas and vegetables.

Revolt against nobles

Tired of their poor economic situation, which was sometimes caused by bad harvests, the peasants revolted against the cruel and avaricious nobles. The peasants revolted in Hungary in 1514, in Germany around 1525 and later in England around 1549. These revolts did not bring in any change in the lives of the peasants because the nobles easily dampened these revolts.

City life

A new middle class began to be formed in the cities that consisted of merchants and bankers, who soon became powerful because of the abundant growth in their wealth. Guilds began to be formed. These guilds were institutions that looked at training, labour, wages, etc. and were managed by skilled craftsmen who owned their own establishments. They hired apprentices, who worked with unskilled workers. Unskilled workers comprised around 30 per cent of the cities' population. These unskilled workers became the lower classes and poverty became their constant companion.

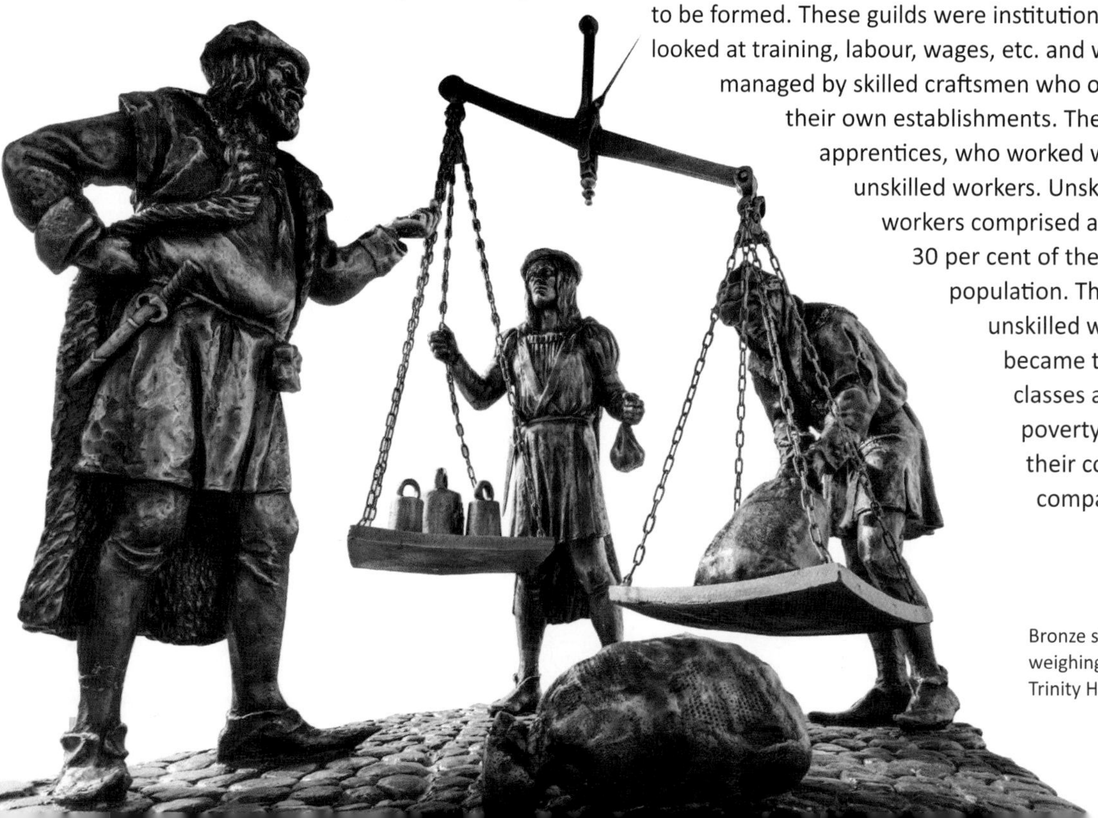

Bronze statue of trade merchants weighing wares and payment at Trinity Hill in district of Minsk.

Demography of Modern Europe

Europe's population grew unprecedented from 81.8 million in 1500 to 104.7 million in 1600. But by 1650, it fell once again, primarily because the population shifted to other countries like England. More Europeans began living in cities. Large cities were formed and became capital centres, such as Rome, Madrid, Paris Naples, etc. They also became centres for administration. It is infamously said that Naples had all the beginnings of a slum city during the sixteenth century.

Ancient city of Napoli (Naples).

The composition of people in Europe

From 1500 to 1750, the population of most countries in Europe grew steadily. But the plague and famine continued to haunt Europe. However, a new disease called Syphilis stalked the sixteenth century. Increased research in medicine showed results with diseases beginning to be identified. Religious wars also affected the demography and had an impact on the population figures. The 30 Years' War, one of the most destructive wars in Central Europe, had a considerable impact on the population, because of deaths on the battlefields and from those caused by famine and disease. It is said that thousands of villages in Germany were destroyed during the 30 Years' War and more than 20,000 died in the city of Magdeburg.

A European syphilis patient, being treated with Guayaco, a medicine made from wood of the Guaiacum tree (being prepared and cooked on the right).

European ports

Commercial ports turned into capitals and assumed identities as another set of cities. These include Venice, Lisbon, London, Hamburg and Antwerp among others. Antwerp became the main port and soon, it became the main market for spices that were being brought in from India. Urbanised settings grew rapidly.

FUN FACT

The Antwerp exchange was the biggest and most profitable money market, but the Low Countries' revolt changed tidings for Antwerp.

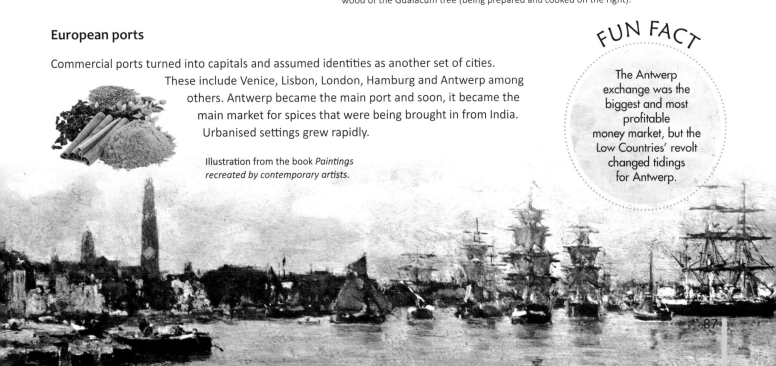

Illustration from the book *Paintings recreated by contemporary artists.*

Trade of Modern Europe

With increased population around cities, the opening up of maritime links between the East and newer techniques of shipbuilding, trade in the Baltic region was growing. In fact, maritime trade was at its peak. However, along with growing trade, urbanisation increased and the population steadily grew in cities. This led to the increased prices of food, especially wheat prices. In Germany, serfdom increased, where peasants for generations to come were bonded farm labourers under the feudal structure.

Vintage illustration of a market in Wales.

Development of new forms of trade

Cities soon saw people using the streets to sell their wares, which ranged from vegetables grown in kitchen gardens to other goods. Peddlers became a norm in cities. Soon, these peddlers grew in numbers and developed into larger markets across Europe. Different markets developed, from fish markets to grain markets to vegetable markets, all depending on the local fare. Shops joined the trade as well and products were sold from windows.

The rich grew richer

The nobles and people from the gentry managed to gather large pieces of land during the late fourteenth century, but they could not find labour to work on their land. They met with the governments and pushed for getting their way, even to export grain without paying extra duties. Some of the new laws further pushed for bonded serfdom all over Eastern Europe. In the West, however, capital was available and hence, landlords could hire labour and thereby gain profits. Peasants had to pay marriage and inheritance taxes, making them even poorer. Capitalism as a concept grew quite significantly in the feudal structure.

Landlords of Europe

With advancements in farming, the early sixteenth century saw France and Italy have systems like the sharecropping lease, which meant that a rich landlord would buy tracts of lands, bring it together, construct a house and rent the same. The tenant was supposed to give 50 per cent of the harvest as rent for the land.

1498: Vasco da Gama discovers trade route to India

1592: Japan introduces new foreign trade licenses

A depiction of scenes from the Forum market.

The beginning of slave trade in Africa

Between the period of the fourteenth and fifteenth centuries, Turk conquests stopped Europe's access to important markets, due to which European trade was affected. However, the Portuguese expeditions brought Europe in touch with Sub-Saharan Africa and they settled in the Cape Verde islands around 1460. They became the monopoly in slave trade. Africans were sent to different places from Madeira to Seville as slaves. These slaves were employed in weaving and dying industries. African trade of this sort led to the expansion of cotton, sugar and tobacco plantations in the Americas and Caribbean islands.

Captives were forced to march in a coffle from the African interiors, escorted by armed guards from East Africa.

Growth of transcontinental trade

Owing to better sea routes and increased sea traffic, trade across continents soared during the twelfth and thirteenth centuries. Venice became a trade centre and it was the place from where merchants like the Niccolo brothers departed for their journeys. More sea trade led to more expansion and Atlantic and European trade offered big returns.

Trade routes on land

The sea route along the Baltic and North Sea became a fast and cheap way to trade. Soon, cities like Vienna and Augsburg developed along the Danube River. Roads were developed from Poland to Bohemia to Frankfurt towards Cologne. The interconnectivity of roads near rivers and ports helped trade further.

FUN FACT

The early eighteenth century saw almost 36,000 slaves being exported each year, a number that grew to an alarming 80,000 per year by the 1780s.

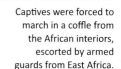

The discovery of newer, better sea routes led to an increase in trading.

Aspects of Modern Society

The concept of "nation-state" started with England and slowly moved towards other countries. While England decided on being a united nation ruled by a king with the parliament having a few powers, France was ruled by a monarch looking at further conquests even as internal feudal elements remained divided. Top positions in the army, government, civil service, church and judiciary were reserved for nobles.

French nobleman and noblewoman (1680–1700).

The Middle Ages and European society

There were two distinct classes in the European society during the Middle Ages; one remained the upper clergy of archbishops, cardinals, bishops, etc., and the other was the aristocrats, who were warlords with great military power. The aristocrats were constantly battling against the monarchs. A separate class called the "bourgeoisie" emerged during this time, consisting of people like mayors, merchants, etc., who opposed the oppression of the aristocrats. They were also hungry for political power. Another class included all the unskilled labourers, lawyers, teachers, as well as the unemployed.

Old engravings depicting the Catholic hierarchy.

Role of the Church

The Catholic church with the Pope at its helm was powerful during the Middle Ages. However, its power was slowly decreasing because it could not stem the corruption that ran within. It was very easy for the ward of an aristocrat to buy a position in the church and also be accommodated.

Economic system of Europe

Mercantilism was the principle that governed the European economic system. It meant that the state was as rich as the gold and silver bullion it had in its coffers. Import of goods was generally frowned upon because that would mean money going out. Agriculture remained the main source of trade in Europe, but it was impacted because of the severity of the climate during the fourteenth century, which had witnessed the "Little Ice Age". The Little Ice Age was a climatic condition where Europe suffered from a tremendously cold climate and an excess of rain, which greatly impacted the agricultural production.

FUN FACT

The word "bourgeoisie" denotes a world where the middle class was the dominant class in society. The term actually emerged during the Middle Ages from France, where it meant an inhabitant of a town.

An early spring picture of moorland and dry stone walls in the Yorkshire Dales National Park. Stripped of quality soil in the last Ice Age, these moors remained as poor quality grazing fields for the local sheep.

Navigation Acts

The Navigation Acts were a series of acts that curbed England from carrying trade to English ships in the seventeenth and eighteenth centuries. From 1651 to 1673, the English Parliament passed four Navigation Acts to balance mercantilists. These acts declared that only the English or English colonial ships could carry cargo between imperial ports. The trade of certain goods was also limited by these acts. Certain goods, including tobacco, rice and furs, could not be shipped to foreign nations unless they were being shipped through England or Scotland. It also mentioned that England would pay "bounties" to America for raw goods, but raised protectionist tariffs on the same goods produced by other countries.

Growth of mercantilism

Mercantilism was an economic theory that was in practice in Europe during the sixteenth century. It lasted till around the eighteenth century. It allowed the government to regulate the economy of the nation in such a way that it improved the power of the state at the expense of the power of its rival nations.

Mercantilism denoted that gold, silver and other such precious metals were vital elements that depicted the wealth of a nation. If a nation did not have gold mines or access to such mines, then they would procure the same metals through trade. However, the balance of trade had to remain in the favour of a nation, where the exports always exceeded the imports. However, this system received a lot of criticism, as people didn't feel that the only way for a nation to develop was at the expense of another nation.

Gold and silver rocks.

Development of higher learning

The latter part of the Middle Ages saw a number of establishments of high learning, such as schools and universities, emerging. The main areas of study remained the Bible and philosophy, but the institutions also offered other subjects.

Christ Church College, Oxford University, UK.

Discovery of the New World

The American Indians, also known as Red Indians, were believed to have moved to the North American continent via Siberia from Alaska. The chapter of discovery of the new world begins with Christopher Columbus, the explorer hailing from Italy, when he discovered a new land in 1492!

FUN FACT

Christopher Columbus actually miscalculated the distance between Europe and Asia. He thought Asia was just 2,400 miles away, when in reality, the distance was more than 10,000 miles with a huge continent separating them.

Christopher Columbus received by King Ferdinand and Queen Isabella on his return from the New World in 1493.

Age of exploration

The age of exploration started in the 1400s and continued right up till the 1600s. It was a time when European nations began exploring the world by travelling even further than the regular routes. It began by discovering new routes to India, then to the Far East, and finally, the Americas. Trade was one of the primary reasons behind the beginning of these explorations and expeditions. It started with the attempt to discover new routes to India and the Far East.

The age of exploration started with Henry the Navigator, who sent ships to map and discover the west coast of Africa. Soon, Portuguese explorer Bartolommeo Dias became the first European to sail around the southern tip of Africa and into the Indian Ocean.

Christopher Columbus: The explorer

Christopher Columbus was an explorer who wanted to prove that there was an easier route to Asia via the sea. Around 200 hundred years ago, Marco Polo travelled to the east and returned with spices and other goods. Columbus wanted to find a sea route to India, but he made it across the other side and discovered America instead.

Discovering new places

The King and Queen of Spain sponsored Columbus's journey. On 3rd August, 1492, he set sail from Palos with a crew of 87 men and travelled for over two months. He set foot on the Caribbean islands of Bahamas and named the island San Salvador. However, as he thought he had reached India, he called the natives "Indians".

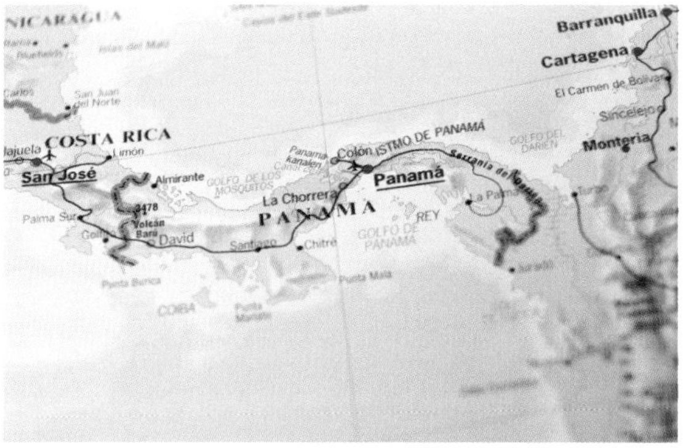

Map of Panama in Central America.

Discovery of Newfoundland and America

Columbus soon discovered that the new land was not anywhere close to Asia. In fact, another Italian explorer Amerigo Vespucci brought this to his knowledge. Vespucci set sail to the new land and, since he had realised that the new land was not Asia, German map maker Martin Waldseemuller decided to call the new region America after Vespucci's first name. Giovanni Cabot travelled to the north Atlantic Island and that region was called Newfoundland. Juan Ponce de Leon was the first explorer to land in North America in 1513.

Statue of Amerigo Vespucci at the Uffizi Loggia in Florence, Italy.

Discovery of Panama

Around the same time as the discovery of North America, another explorer named Vasco Nunez Balboa crossed the Central American Isthmus on foot and became the first European to see Panama at the Pacific Ocean. Panama was the first Spanish colony in the Pacific and was soon known as "the door to the seas and key to the universe".

The fact that there was more land to be explored and Earth was actually quite big was understood around this time. The job to assess the extent of Earth's expanse was first started by Ferdinand Magellan around 1519, but it was fully completed by Juan Sebastian around 1522. Columbus's next two expeditions proved to be rather unlucky for him. His popularity slowly began fading away and he returned to Spain in poor health, eventually dying in 1506.

Age of exploration

During these explorations, Europeans actually used the term "East Indies" for all of South East Asia, including India. Although Ferdinand Magellan was the first to begin the expedition around the world, he was unfortunately killed on the way and could not complete the voyage. Places like Australia, the complete African continent, as well as Antarctica and the Arctic region were discovered and mapped a long time after the age of exploration.

HERNANDO DE MAGALLANES
Cavallero Portugues, descubridor del Estrecho de su nombre.

Illustration of Ferdinand Magellan (1480–1521). He was the first to start the expedition around the world.

1492: Christopher Columbus discovers the world

1513: First explorer lands in North America

FUN FACT

Did you know that Magellan had given Pacific Ocean its name? After he sailed through bad weather and storms in South America, he entered the Strait of Magellan, which was a calmer ocean. Hence, he called it "Mar Pacifico", meaning Peaceful Sea in Portuguese.

Europe during the Age of Monarchy

Hugo Grotius was a poet and jurist.

Even as battles and wars were fought in Europe during the sixteenth century, a certain level of unity existed in the continent. Hugo Grotius's work *De Jure Belli ac Pacis* (on the law of war and peace) was an appeal towards creating and honouring the spirit and law of international relations. Europe became the wider public audience; for instance, French philosopher Descartes' work was for all of Europe, just like his German counterpart Leibniz. Descartes was a mathematician, philosopher and writer who became popular for his philosophical take, "I think, therefore I am".

Bust of Rene Descartes, a French philosopher from the seventeenth century.

Prominent European royals and politicians

Richelieu, the chief minister of France, dominated the country from 1624 and earned himself the title of one of the great politicians of France. During his tenure, he attacked the Huguenots, brought about changes in the armed and naval forces, and managed to remove all rebellions. Cardinal Jules Mazarin, who managed to establish France's supremacy among the other European powers and suppress all rebellions against the monarchy, completed his work.

King Henry of Valois

Henry of Valois was the king of France from 1574 and was one of the kings under whom the Wars of Religion deteriorated, because he was the last male heir to the Valois dynasty. James I became the King of Scotland and England opposed the idea of an independent Parliament with no interference from royalty. Peter I, also known as Peter the Great, was the Tsar of Russia and jointly reigned over Russia with his half brother Ivan.

Old engraving of sixteenth century of King Henri III of France in a Polish costume.

Russian emperor Peter the Great, was also known as The Bronze Horseman.

Ruins of the Ogrodzieniec Castle, Poland, Europe.

1618: Beginning of the 30 Years' War

1648: Peace of Westphalia was signed

Problems for the monarchs

The 30 Years' War started around 1618 and lasted until 1648. It started when Roman Emperor Ferdinand II of Bohemia tried to curtail the religious activities of his people. That brought about fierce opposition from the Protestants. Others joined the war; for instance, Sweden, France, Spain and Austria were fighting on German land. The war finally ended with a treaty known as the Peace of Westphalia.

Peace of Westphalia

The Peace of Westphalia was signed between May and October 1648, and it brought an end to the 30 Year's War. The treaty was first negotiated in the Westphalian towns of Munster and Osnabruck, thereby earning its name. The first to sign the treaty were the Spanish and Dutch, followed by the Roman Emperor, then Germany, France and Sweden. The wars started in 1618 when Austria's Habsburg attempted to impose Roman Catholicism upon Protestants in Bohemia. This led to a revolt against the Catholics, Romans against the French and France against the Habsburg of Spain.

A stamp printed in Germany shows the Peace of Westphalia and the end of the 30 Years' War.

Participants of the war

Everyone from the Swedes to the Danes, from the Poles to the Russians to the Dutch and the Swiss were pulled into this conflict. The royals who were part of this war included the King of Bohemia, emperors Ferdinand II and III, Christian IV of Denmark, Gustavus II, Adolphus and Queen Christina of Sweden, Philip IV of Spain and his brother Cardinal Infante, Louis XIII of France, Cardinals Richelieu and Mazarin, several popes and many others.

Fought largely on German soil, the 30 Years' War brought about utter misery as various groups of mercenaries lived off the land and plundered the villages. The Peace treaty was signed by more than 194 states, from the biggest to the smallest. They were represented by 179 plenipotentiaries and had many diplomats in attendance too.
Papal Nuncio, Fabio Chigi (the future Pope Alexander VII) and the Venetian ambassador presided over the peace treaty conference. The treaty managed to make the Swiss independent of Austria and Holland from Spain, even as Germany managed to secure its autonomy. The treaty also brought an end to the Eighty Years' War between Spain and the Dutch Republic.

FUN FACT

The Eighty Years' War was fought from 1568 to 1648 and finally came to an end with the signing of the Peace of Westphalia, where Spain acknowledged the independence of the Dutch Republic.

Turkey and Eastern Europe (Ottoman Empire)

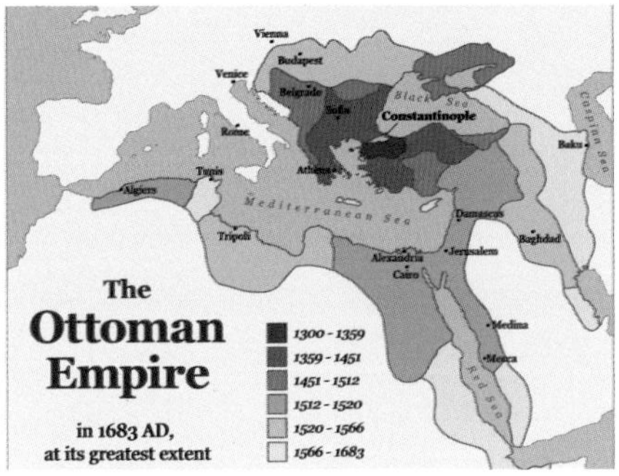

The Ottoman Empire was created by Turkish tribes and became one of the most dominant states during the fifteenth and sixteenth centuries. It lasted for 600 years, ending in 1922. At its peak, it had taken over the gates to Vienna from South Western Europe, from Hungary to Serbia and Bosnia, from Romania to Greece and Ukraine. It had taken over Iraq, Syria, Egypt, Israel and Africa, including Algeria.

Expansion of the Ottoman Empire

The Ottomans were essentially Muslim Turks who fought against the lessening Christian state. They were nomads from the Kayı Tribe, who had fled from the Mongols of Genghis Khan in the twelfth century. After the defeat of the Mongols in 1293, Osman became the prince of Byzantine Bithynia in North Western Anatolia, close to Bursa. His successors focussed their attacks on Byzantine territories near Bosporus and the Sea of Marmara to the west. The Ottomans attracted masses of unemployed nomads from the Middle East who were from the Islam faith. The Ottomans' successors Orhan (or Orkhan, ruled from 1324–1360) and Murad I (1360–1389) won the Byzantine territories.

The Ottoman Empire's quest for power

In the next 150 years, the Ottoman Empire expanded and its quest to be the most powerful led to the capture of Constantinople by Mehmet II, who converted Constantinople into his capital and called it Istanbul. After the capture of Constantinople, many scholars and artists fled to Italy, and began the European Renaissance. It was also one of the reasons that prompted Europe to explore newer trade routes to the Far East, leading to the age of exploration.

An illustration of a port in early Constantinople.

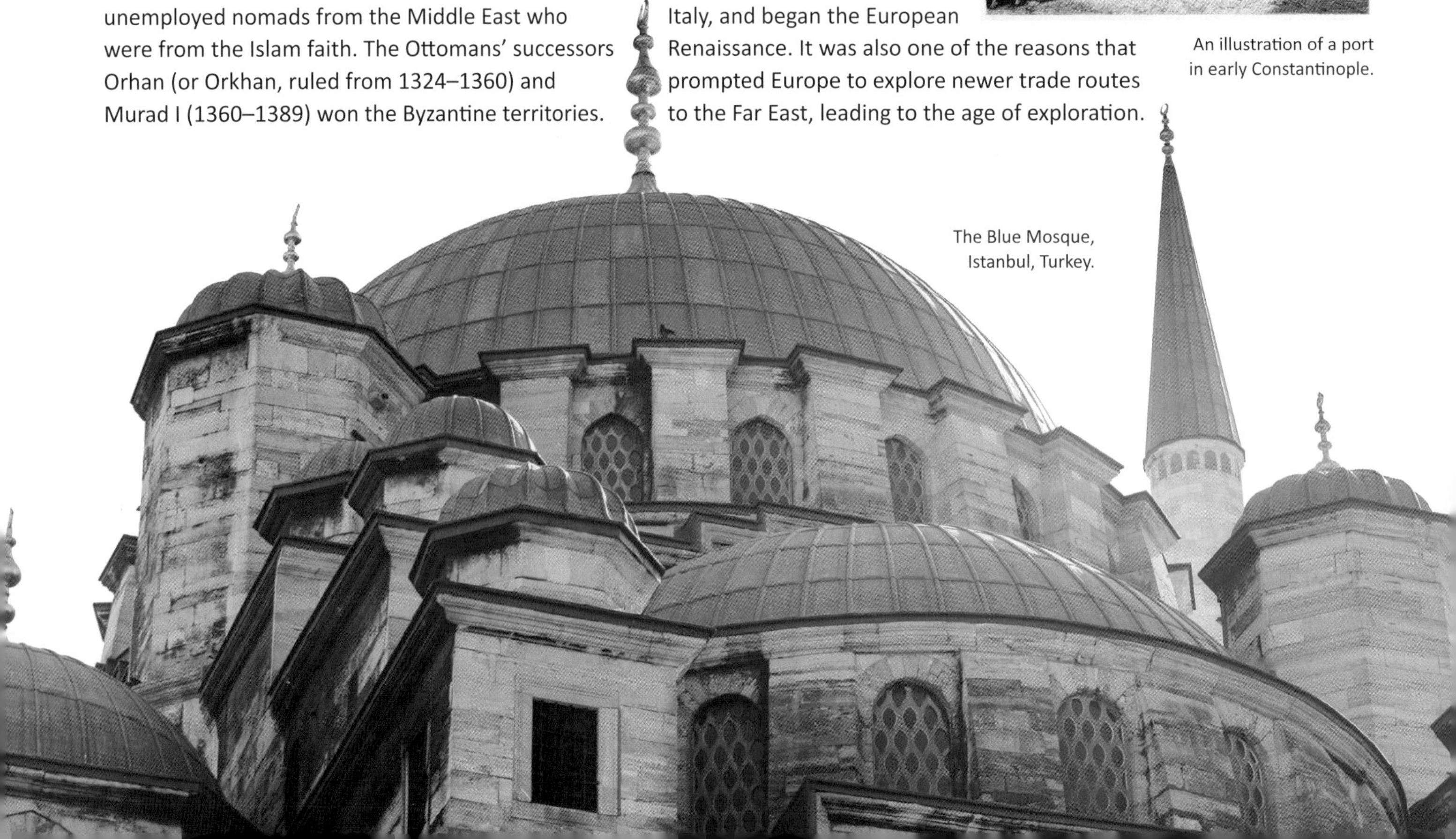

The Blue Mosque, Istanbul, Turkey.

The Ottoman Empire

It was during the reign of Suleiman the Magnificent, that the Ottoman Empire was said to have been at its peak. It was due to Suleiman's superior military planning that he could invade more territories and conquer new lands. He was a magnificent ruler and was also the caliph—the religious leader of his people. He put in place a big bureaucratic set up that was led by a vizier who followed Suleiman's commands.

Suleiman the Magnificent also had a supreme army who were called "janissaries". The janissaries were soldiers who had received training in every kind of military warfare and were also in tune with their religious faith. The janissaries had unwavering faith and loyalty towards their sultan.

Suleiman ruled from 1520 to 1566 and it was under his reign that the empire had included a small part of Eastern Europe with both Greece and Hungary.

Statue of Suleiman the Magnificent at Edirnekapi, Istanbul, Turkey.

FUN FACT

Did you know that the Sultan had many wives and they lived in the Topkapi Palace in Istanbul? The Sultan moved to a different room in the palace every night, owing to a fear of being killed!

Decline of the Empire

Even while the Ottoman Empire was at its magnificent best under the rule of Suleiman, it showed a few signs of weakness that eventually led to its slow but steady decline. It is said that one of the main reasons for the fall of the Ottoman Empire was the lack of abilities of the rulers themselves. Suleiman himself grew tired of his administrative duties at some point and chose to spend more time devoted to the pleasures of harem instead of focussing on the betterment of his people. The grand vizier stood in for the sultan at various events, but he was only second in command to the sultan and did not have enough power or even the loyalty of all the Ottoman subjects, which brought about a lot of division within the empire itself.

In 1683, Polish King John III Sobieski defeated the Ottomans in Vienna and it was this battle that brought an end to the expansion of the Ottoman Empire. The Ottoman Empire ceased to expand and began its steady decline in the late 1600s.

Battle of Mohacs, 1526, Ottoman victory over Hungary, led by Suleiman the Magnificent, Askeri Military Museum in Istanbul, Turkey.

The empire also began to face economic competition from India and Europe. Internal corruption and poor leadership led to its decline until it was abolished and Turkey was declared a republic in 1923.

FUN FACT

Did you know that the leader of the Ottoman Empire was known as the Sultan and the title was given to the eldest son? When the new Sultan took over the reign of the Empire, he would imprison his male siblings! When he had his own son, the Sultan would then kill his brothers!

Statues of an Ottoman Pasha and Janissary, Istanbul, Turkey.

Reformation

FUN FACT

People started to feel that the Catholic church's practices were inconsistent with the Bible's teachings and therein emerged a dissent, which transformed into a movement called the Protestant Reformation.

Martin Luther

Reformation was the religious revolution that occurred during the sixteenth century, led by Martin Luther and John Calvin, among others. It had multiple effects in all spheres, from political to economic to social and became the foundation of the Protestant movement. The Renaissance brought out an increased awareness of the written word across Europe and the number of people reading the Bible increased. With this awareness, many disapproved of the Catholic Church's unnecessary extravagance.

Beginning of the Protestant Reformation

During the Middle Ages, not many people other than priests knew the written word. With the Renaissance, however, many people learned to read and write. With the invention of the printing press, new ideas could be spread quickly and scriptures like the Bible were printed and distributed easily to people. Additionally, as the standard of living improved among the Europeans, they could afford to give their children a formal and thorough education.

It was during this time that a monk by the name of Martin Luther began to question the Catholic Church and its various practices. He made a list of 95 points, where he listed the teachings of the Catholic church that differed from the Bible's written word and he highlighted where the Church had gone wrong. He published his writings as the *95 Theses* in 1517 and nailed it to the door of a Catholic Church.

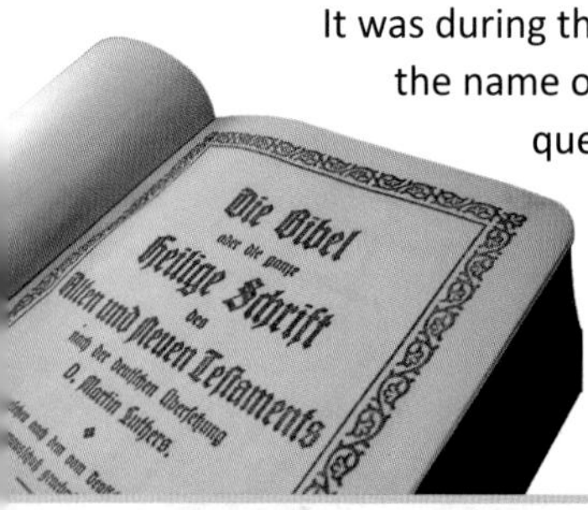

Martin Luther's translation of the Bible into German.

The 95 Theses

The 95 points or theses were written by Martin Luther, a pastor at the University of Wittenberg. He was a monk and scholar who wrote a document that questioned the methods of the Church and asked for an explanation behind the "indulgences" of the Church, which told people that they would be forgiven if they paid money to the Church. The 95 theses stated that the Bible was the central authority when it came to religion and that people attained salvation through their faith, not their deeds. This was the basis for the Protestant Reformation.

Lutheran Church Dresden Frauenkirche in Dresden, Germany.

Reformation Movement, St. Peter's Basilica, Vatican City, Italy.

Criticising the church

95 Theses said that God wanted his believers to ask for repentance through faith and not deeds, leading to their salvation. Another criticism was why the Pope, who was wealthier than most princes, could not build the basilica of St Peter with his own money instead of the money taken from poor believers. The document was distributed throughout Germany; it even reached Rome. In 1518, Martin Luther was called to Augsburg, South Germany, to defend his views to the imperial assembly. Even after three days of debate with Cardinal Thomas Cajetan, there was no resolution in sight.

Lutheran Church of the Redeemer in Jerusalem.

1519: Swiss Reformation began

1555: Peace of Augsburg signed in Germany

Reformation wall in Parc Des Bastions, Geneva, Switzerland. Sculptures of the four great figures of the Geneva protestant movement: Guillaume Farel, Jean Calvin, Theodore de Beze and John Knox.

Beginning of the Reformation movement

Quite a few people started agreeing with his views that the Catholic Church had become corrupt and many from North Europe began to separate from the Catholic Church. Many new churches were established and were called the Lutheran Church and the Reformed Church. In Switzerland, John Calvin also spoke out against the Catholic Church's corrupt practices. King Henry VIII split from the Catholic Church. The Church of England split because he wanted to divorce his wife, but the Catholic Church would not let him, so he decided to create the Church of England.

The Reformation movement led to an outbreak of wars, where a few rulers converted to Protestantism, while some continued to support the Catholic Church. This religious divide led to the 30 Years' War that was fought in Germany, which also involved most of Europe.

King Henry VIII statue.

Counter Reformation

Chiesa del Gesu Church built in the late sixteenth century by the Jesuits in Rome, Italy.

The Counter Reformation, also known as the Catholic Reformation or Catholic Revival, was the result of the efforts of the Roman Catholics against the Protestant Reformation, which started in the sixteenth and seventeenth centuries. It occurred around the same time as the Protestant Reformation.

Internal calls for reform

Even within the Catholic Church, the reformation movement had brought about different views and new religious orders. Other groups were established and brought about another level of religious renewal; for instance, the Ursulines, Jesuits and Carmelite order. Pope Paul III was the first Pope to actually show some reaction to the Protestant movement. He called for the Council of Trent, where he tried to normalise the training of priests and requested for the prohibition of the luxurious living of the clergy. The Jesuits were founded in 1540 by St. Ignatius Loyola and were disbanded in 1773 by Pope Clement XIV. They were known for their role in education, missionary work and theology. Pope John Paul II constantly clashed with the Jesuits. He believed that they had become too political and leftist in their views.

Portrait of Pope Paul III.

The Roman inquisition

The Roman inquisition started in 1542 to counter dissent and could, to some extent, control the Protestant movement. It involved the army and political leaders against the protestant movement. In fact, the policies of Emperor Charles V and his son Philip II clearly reflect this. They were linked to the Spanish inquisition. The elements that came under direct attack due to the target of these inquisitions were the Virgin Mary, St. Peter, etc.

After-effects of Counter Reformation

The Counter Reformation brought about the standardisation of worship. Laws of the Church were reorganised and the life of clergies was brought under scrutiny. The movement brought many people back to the Catholic Church in Austria, Poland, Holland, Germany and Hungary. However, in England, the Counter Reformation movement took longer to be effective. The main players of this movement were Caesar Baronius, St. Robert Bellarmine, Pedro Calderón de la Barca, Richard Crashaw, St. Francis Borgia, Robert Southwell and Torquato Tasso.

FUN FACT

The Sack of Rome in 1527 by the troops of Charles V was enough to convince even the most confident of cardinals that it was dangerous to get involved in political gambles.

Statue of Saint Peter in the Vatican city, Italy.

Pope Clement XIV.

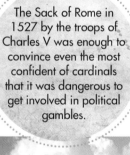

The French Revolution

1789

The French Revolution, also known as the Revolution of 1789, dramatically changed France and brought the old regime to an end. The reasons for the revolution were different from the resentment amongst the bourgeoisie, who felt excluded from the power. The antipathy continued with the peasants who wanted to change the feudal setup, and philosophers who wanted to reform the political and social scene. The other reasons included France's involvement in the American Revolution that brought about huge economical problems, which also played an important role in the revolution.

The population of France comprised 98 per cent of common people, but, they did not have any say. They wanted equal representation, so they debated over the voting process and, soon, the third estate unofficially took over the title of national assembly. When clerical deputies and liberal nobles joined them, Louis XVI took all three orders into his new assembly.

The National Assembly of 1789 was a revolutionary assembly with all its representatives from the third estate. On 14th July, they stormed into the Bastille Fortress. The hysteria brought peasants to the streets, who looted and burned the homes of tax collectors and landlords, and thereby ensured that feudalism would be abolished.

Aristocratic Revolt in France

Towards the end of the eighteenth century, King Louis XVI's investment towards the American Revolution left France's economy in shambles. The royal treasure was empty. For more than 20 years the country had suffered bad harvests. Inflation was at an all time high. This led to a feeling of great discontent among the peasants. Some resorted to rioting and looting. Others took to the streets and decided to revolt.

March of the women to Versailles, 1789.

Fiscal reforms

Around the time of the French Revolution, France was already going through a financial crisis. However, one of the triggers of the revolution actually occurred when Charles-Alexandre de Calonne, the controller general of finances, wanted to tax the privileged in order to deal with the budget shortage. He called for an assembly that consisted of the estates general, clergy and aristocracy, with very few representatives of the bourgeoisie and proposed his reforms to them. However, the assembly did not want to take responsibility of this. They suggested calling the Estates-General, who represented the clergy, the aristocracy and the Third Estate, which consisted of the commoners. This assembly had not met since 1614. However, this did not stop Calonne or his successors from trying to enforce their fiscal reforms, despite protests from different classes, which ultimately led to the aristocratic revolt.

A portrait of the Peasant War that called for the abolishment of the feudal system.

Freedom of press

A lot had changed for France from 1614. There was a call for equal representation and the removal of the noble veto, which meant that everyone could vote, not just the nobility. This displeased the nobles. A public debate followed, but a stalemate stalled the proceedings.

Louis XVI reappointed Jacques Necker as the finance minister. The king also granted freedom to the press and there was printing material all over France regarding the rebuilding of the French State. On 26th August, 1789, the Declaration of the Rights of Man and of the Citizen was introduced, which claimed liberty, equality, inviolability of property and the right to resist oppression. On 5th October, 1789, Parisians marched to Versailles and brought the royal family back to Paris.

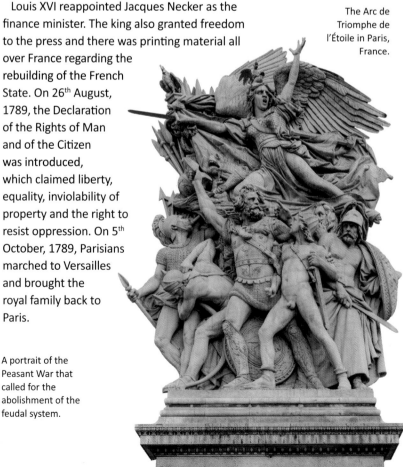

The Arc de Triomphe de l'Étoile in Paris, France.

Tax payment

Louis XVI appointed Charles de Calonne as the controller general of finances in 1783. The French government approached various European banks for a loan, but because of its bad financial crisis it found no credibility and got no loan. Calonne saw taxation as a measure to save the country from financial disaster. He came up with an idea to extend taxation not just for peasants but also for the nobles and the members of the parliaments. At the Assembly of Notables, Calonne urged the nobles to either agree to the new taxes or to surrender their exemption to the already existing ones. The nobles refused both and opposed Calonne, who was dismissed shortly thereafter. The wealthy commoners or the bourgeoisie were hardworking, educated men who did not have titles like the elite and were, therefore, subjected to the same taxation as the poor peasants. The bourgeoisie would soon become the catalyst for the Revolution.

Alexandre de Calonne (1734–1802).

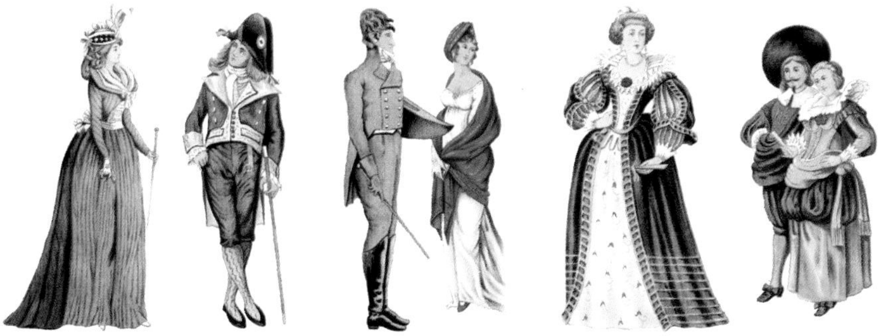

Aristocrates of France.

FUN FACT

The guillotine was a popular method of punishment during the French Revolution. It remained a legal form of execution in France right up till 1981!

Absolute rule

For many years prior to the French Revolution, the French royalty was corrupt and had a system of absolute rule. The local parliaments (provincial judicial boards), guilds or religious groups enforced laws. The royalty of the Bourbon dynasty, French nobles and clergy abused power during the late 1700s and the poor French peasantry were forced into feudal obligations. Heavy taxes were imposed on the working class in order to pay for the extravagances of the royalty. However, the peasants, who were a majority of the population, grew tired of being exploited. They were well aware of the situation and the unfairness of it all. Soon, they refused to pay taxes.

Empty treasury

The economic situation in France during the late 1700s had considerably worsened. It didn't help that the country was already suffering from a famine and cattle diseases, which made the agricultural yields poor, a condition that didn't bode well for France's large population.

Furthermore, France's prolonged involvement in the Seven Years' War of 1756-1763 and its participation in the American Revolution of 1775-1783 had brought the country to the brink of bankruptcy. To make matters worse, King Louis XVI lived an extravagant lifestyle that was funded by the people's taxes and Queen Marie Antoinette had frivolous spending habits, which only put more pressure on an already empty treasury. The people were frustrated by their conditions and it was this unrest that caused the great French Revolution.

Statues of King Louis XVI and Marie Antoinette from Saint Denis Basilica.

Events of 1789

Years of feudal oppression and economic problems led to the French Revolution. King Louis XVI's financial advisors reviewed the almost empty treasury and tried to increase the taxes. But this advice was not accepted and a controller general of finance, Charles de Calonne, was brought in. Calonne called for taxing the nobles. He suggested that, among other things, France begin taxing the previously exempt nobility. The nobility refused, even after Calonne pleaded with them during the Assembly of Notables in 1787. Financial ruin, thus, seemed imminent.

The voting process

The Estates General met in Versailles on 5th May, 1789. They wondered how the voting should progress by giving advantage to the majority of the population. The Third Estate was larger than the nobility and clergy but the Parlement of Paris ruled that each estate would receive only one vote irrespective of its size. This way, the Third Estate's vote was eventually overruled. This led to feuds that were incompatible and the Third Estate, which recognised the majority it enjoyed, unofficially declared itself as the sovereign National Assembly on June 17 of the same year. Just days after this announcement, quite a few members from the other two estates quickly shifted their loyalties over to the new revolutionary assembly.

Declaration of Rights, 1793.

The royal officials were not happy with this revolutionary assembly and chose to ban the deputies from attending their meeting by locking the hall on June 20. But that didn't stop the assembly, which gathered at the king's indoor tennis court and refused to leave until they were given the right to choose a new constitution for France. This was the first time that the French citizens publicly revolted against their king. Due to this event, the king eventually gave in and asked the nobles and the rest of the clergy to join the assembly. This new formation was officially named the National Constituent Assembly on July 9.

The insurrection of the slaves of Santo Domingo in Paris. Free men entered the Convention and called for the abolition of slavery.

Formation of a new constitution

In the countryside, peasants and farmers who were struggling against the feudal system, attacked the manors and big estates of landlords. These attacks were called the "Great Fear". The assembly released the declaration of the rights of citizens that put an appropriate judicial code in place to protect the autonomy of the French citizens.

Declaration of Pillnitz of 1791.

The short-lived peace

Although the national assembly managed to draft a constitution, the peace of the moment was temporary, because differences between the moderates and radical assembly members slowly arose. Shortly, the common folk, including workers and labourers, started feeling ignored and their opinions were not being considered. Thus, while a few wanted constitutional monarchies to continue, there were others who wanted the monarchy out of the country. The Hapsburgs feared that a similar revolution would spark off in Prussia and they announced the Declaration of Pillnitz, which was brought out by the Hapsburg Holy Roman Emperor Leopold II and Frederick William II of Prussia. This declared that both the Roman Empire and Prussian King were against the French Revolution.

Failure of the National Convention

The National Convention abolished the monarchy and declared France as a republic. The convention executed Louis XVI for treason in January 1793. The Committee of Public Safety's performance was poor and it did not help that the war with Austria and Prussia did not end well for France. The Montagnards and Girondins opposed each other, and that took centre stage in the first phase of the Convention, which was from September 1792 to May 1793. The Montagnards were in favour of granting the poor class some political power, but were opposed by the Girondins, who wanted a more bourgeoisie representation. Soon, the Montagnards controlled the Convention's second phase. Unhappy with the Girondins, angry French citizens led the convention and the Jacobins under Maximilien de Robespierre took over.

Attempt for a stable economy

Robespierre tried to implement laws to stabilise the economy, but somewhere, the fear of counter-revolutionary forces made him a little obsessed and he started a reign of terror. There was a time from 1793 to 1794 when he executed more than 15,000 people at the guillotine.

Maximilien de Robespierre

1789: Formation of the National Assembly

1793: Execution of Louis XVI

FUN FACT

Did you know that while the peasants had to pay taxes to the nobles, the Church and the king, the nobles themselves didn't have to pay taxes at all?

Execution of King Louis XVI in January 1793 during the French Revolution.

New French Regime

On 4th August, the Assembly adopted the Declaration of the Rights of Man and of the Citizen, also known as the *Déclaration des droits de l'homme et du citoyen*, which was a statement of democratic principles based on the philosophical and political ideas of Renaissance thinkers, such as Jean-Jacques Rousseau. It was committed to the replacement of the ancient regime with one that focussed on equal opportunity, freedom of speech, sovereignty and, most importantly, a representative government.

Declaration of the Rights of Man and of the Citizen in 1789.

Attack on monarchy

The Declaration was an open attack on the monarchy and strongly opposed their regime. It wanted to base the element of equality before the law and aimed to replace the system that existed under the monarchy. Despite limitations in the aims of the declaration, this Declaration of the Rights of Man and of the Citizen was recognised as the "credo of the new age" by famous historian Jules Michelet.

Menus-Plaisirs hotel, Versailles, France—seat of French National Constituent Assembly in 1789.

Formation of the formal constitution

Drafting a formal constitution was quite a demanding task for the National Constituent Assembly, which was already reeling under the pressure of the adverse economic times that the country had been facing.

For many months, the Assembly argued on questions such as who would be accountable for electing delegates. Would the clergy owe loyalty to the Roman Catholic Church or the French government? How much authority would continue to remain with the king? The first written constitution went with the moderate voices of the assembly and put a constitutional monarchy in place. According to this, the monarch would get royal veto power and would also be allowed to appoint ministers.

This negotiation, with its moderate thinking, could not be accepted by radical leaders like Maximilien de Robespierre, Camille Desmoulins and Georges Danton, who started advocating public opinion towards a republican form of government and the trial of Louis XVI.

A 1789 cover page from Robespierre´s book.

Reign of terror

The execution of the king was not the most violent phase of the revolution. After the divisions in the National Convention, the most violent phase of French history was only just beginning. In 1793, the Jacobins seized control of the National Convention and brought in radical measures, including putting a new calendar in place and abolishing Christianity. Noting the chaos and disorder in and around France, Jacobin, the foremost political party, were steadfast in their approach to squash any resistance. Neighbourhood watches were made to seek the people who were not loyal to the Jacobin stance. The 10-month period was the reign of terror; it was supervised and directed by the Committee of Public Safety, a committee of 12 leaders that also included Maximilien de Robespierre. Alleged enemies of the revolution were guillotined under the draconian Committee of Public Safety. During this period, thousands of innocent people were tortured and put to death, sometimes solely for having a diverse political opinion.

The Jacobin's Fountain in Lyon, France.

A guillotine used during the executions.

1795: France's first bicameral legislature

1799: Napoleon Bonaparte is France's first consul

First bicameral legislature

The National Convention, which comprised the Girondins, approved a new constitution in August, 1795, thus creating France's first bicameral legislature. The creation of this legislature meant that the executive power would lie in the hands of a five-member directory or the "directoire". This directory was appointed by the Parliament.

Royalists and Jacobins protested the new regime, but were rapidly silenced by the army that was led by a young general named Napoleon Bonaparte.

The Directory

The Directory went through a host of problems in its four years of power. It faced financial disasters, popular discontent, incompetence and political corruption. By the 1790s, the directors were relying heavily on the army to sustain their power.

On 9th November, 1799, a young general by the name of Napoleon Bonaparte staged a coup and abolished the Directory. He appointed himself France's "first consul" and went on to become one of the most famous leaders in the history of France.

Napoleon Bonaparte

Monnet's illustrations of the night of privilege abolition.

FUN FACT

Before the revolutionaries took over the country of France, both Protestant and Jewish religions were illegal in France!

French Reign of Terror

Bataille of Fleurus 1794.

Other countries looked upon the French revolution with renewed hope. Switzerland, the United Provinces and Belgium in particular were impressed with the French Revolution. But counter revolutionaries comprising nobles left the struggle, abandoned their country and moved away. The "émigrés", as they were called, formed armed or unarmed groups and asked for support from European leaders.

France declares war on Austria

The war between France and Austria was a pure political move made by the rulers of France in order to "exploit the revolution". The King, Louis XVI, his supporting monarchs and other officials wanted to start a war so that it would increase the popularity of the king among the people. Although some people in his court felt that at the time France was too weak to win a war. They were worried that an unwanted war would increase the intensity of the revolution brewing between the people. Some believed that the revolution would increase the influence of the military and the monarchy but anger the people of Austria and other European countries. Upon the death of the Austrian Emperor, Leopold I!, France declared a war against Austria on 20th April, 1972. Prussia joined Austria in the war. France won the war against Austria by defeating the Prussian and Austrian army. This gave them the confidence to wage more wars against European powers.

Statue on top of the Monument aux Girondins on Place des Quinconces, Bordeaux, France.

With Austria's defeat, France was able to take over the Austrian Netherlands. This upset Britain and the Dutch Republic who did not want Netherlands to come into the hands of France. France also waged a war with Belgium and Rhineland in 1792. Meanwhile the French Revolution was still brewing and the people of France believed King Louis XVI to be weak and indecisive. He was beheaded in 1973 and Marie Antoinette, his wife, was executed a few months after that. Meanwhile, Britain, Austria and Prussia formed a coalition known as the "First Coalition". Spain and some other European powers joined in and they waged a war on France. As a result, the French faced many defeats and the troops stationed in the newly conquered territories were forced to make a hasty retreat. Within France, its people were conducting revolts against the republican regime of France.

An illustration showing Marie Antoinette before her execution.

Ronot Charles, the last of the Montagnards.

The Montagnards vs Girondins

In the Legislative Assembly, the Girondists were the voice of the democratic revolution and were useful in furthering it. They managed to get the king to agree to a ministry comprising Roland, Dumouriez and Servan who supported the revolution. Shortly after, a war was declared against Austria. The Montagnards and Girondists were opposed to the monarchy. Both sides had monarchs, republicans and democrats who did not want to break the unity of France. When the First Coalition made matters worse, the Montagnards who had the support of workers, craftsmen and shopkeepers seized power and brought in liberal, economic and social policies to appease their support base. These policies ensured that the rich were heavily taxed. They provided assistance to the needy and disabled. Education was to be compulsory and free for all.

Wars of Vendee

One of the policies was to sell the properties of the émigré. Such policies saw stiff opposition and aggressive reactions. The wars in Vendee and other uprisings in Provence, Normandy, Lyon and Bordeaux served as a response to these policies. The reign of terror managed to change things around with the arrest of more than 300,000 suspects. This brought the uprisings to a halt, with more than 17,000 executions, some without a trial.

The Battle of Le Mans was a battle in the Wars of Vendee.

The government in place raised an army of a million men and fought with the Austrians to regain Belgium. The victory made the restrictions seem futile and Robespierre was overthrown and executed in 1794. The Maximum Policy was eliminated. The idea of economic equality was abandoned and the National Convention discussed if a new constitution was required. In 1795, Napoleon Bonaparte crushed another attempt by royalists to seize power and detached the National Convention.

1792: France declares a war on Austria

1795: National Convention is detached

A Girondins monument from 1902 in the city of Bordeaux.

FUN FACT

The agitators of the revolution began to spread a false tale about Marie Antoinette. In this tale, when Marie Antoinette was told that people had no bread, she remarked, "Let them eat cake!"

Napoleon Bonaparte

Napoleon Bonaparte, also known as the "Little Corporal", became the French general, first consul (1799–1804) and also the emperor of the French (1804–1814/15). He became an important personality in the country's history. Being from the army, his major interests lay in strengthening the army and that's just what he did. He managed to transform the French military. He initiated the Napoleonic Code, a great example of the civil-law code. He also rationalised education.

Napoleon Bonaparte becomes a national hero

While fighting against Austria in 1796, Napoleon took over the command of the French army. Upon his arrival in Italy, he realised that the French army was losing to the Austrian army as most of them had died, were wounded or sick. He re-organised the army and ordered the troops. He was an efficient leader. He wanted to have more soldiers than the enemy. He called for help when needed and kept the spirit of the troops up. Soon the Austrians were forced to leave Italy. When the victory was announced back home, Napoleon was hailed as a national hero. Napoleon became first consul at the age of 30. In December 1799, his plea for peace with Britain and Austria was rejected. During the 1800s, he launched a surprise attack on Austria in the Battle of Marengo. The Austrian army was defeated and the Austrian Emperor, Francis II, had to agree to sign the Treaty of Luneville in 1801. England too fell in line and signed a peace agreement with France called the "Peace of Amiens".

Napoleon crossing the Alps.

First consul

In 1802, Napoleon proclaimed himself "First Consul for Life", which stood for a legislated succession to rule for his son. Despite the fact that he had no sons and being the first consul, he was the most powerful, yet he was very wary. To keep the charade of a republic, he set up imaginary representatives, including a legislative body and council of notables, which in reality were powerless. Napoleon sold the French territory of Louisiana to the newly independent USA in 1803 for 80 million francs, which was referred to as the "Louisiana Purchase".

Louisiana state quarter coin and old French coins used in 1856.

Battle of Marengo.

Napoleon the leader

He demonstrated great prowess in restoring peace and order after the French Revolution. He had worked very hard to gain the support of the Royalist faction. He tried to improve relations with the Catholic Church as Catholicism remained the religion of the majority. He signed a Concordat with Pope Pius VII, as per which the Church officially recognised the French Republic and returned the property that it had taken during the Revolution. In return, Napoleon announced that Catholicism was the official religion of the Republic of France.

Pope Pius VII

The Napoleonic code

There was a demand for such a code in France during the time of the French Revolution. Napoleon already had the base of the code, he simply needed to add details. Under the Napoleonic Code, all male citizens were perceived to be equal whether rich or poor. The previous French traditions of class over mass, privileges to the rich and hereditary nobility were removed. All male citizens had freedom to property, person and contract. They were able to enjoy civil rights. The dissolution of marriage by terms of divorce or annulment was also discussed. However, such rights of women were granted to the father or husband, or the male that controlled the property.

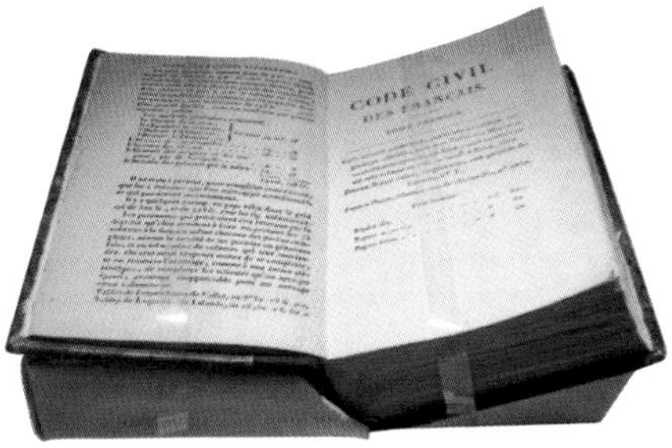

The Napoleonic Code in Speyer, Historical Museum of the Palatinate.

1799: Napoleon is a national hero

1803: Napoleon sells the territory of Louisiana

FUN FACT

"Napoleon complex" is a psychological condition where short people become defensive due to their height. It was named after Napoleon because he was incorrectly believed to be 5 feet 2 inches when actually he was 5 feet 6 inches.

The Napoleonic Era

Napoleon wanted to establish a French-dominated empire in Europe and ruled for 15 years. His family was wealthy and he received an excellent education. He later attended a military academy in France and became the second lieutenant in an artillery regiment. He returned to Corsica (captured by France) when his father died. He soon consolidated his power and gave himself the title of Emperor. He was always at war with Prussia, Austria and Britain. Until 1812, France won all the wars under his leadership as he had great tact and could turn the fate of a losing battle. Napoleon's strategy was to annex territories and set up smaller kingdoms in parts of Germany, Italy, Poland and Spain.

Napoleon abdicates

Napoleon's regime brought about many changes in the country that included everyone being equal before the law; he made the bureaucracy very strict by having able bureaucrats to handle those duties. The educational institutions that Napoleon started gave specialised technical training.
Despite the fact that he made certain announcements on accord of the Roman Catholic Church, but overall during his period religious freedom survived. During his era, he managed to destroy the old regime in Belgium, western Germany and northern Italy.

The era of Napoleon

Napoleon won many battles against Austria and Italy. He wanted to take over the world and fought many battles for France. He would collect tax from the territories he conquered in other nations.
This tax money was used to repair France's failing economy. Therefore, Napoleon focussed on winning the battles he fought against Italy and Austria. He sent money and gold back to France. In 1798, he tried to find passage to India through Egypt but was defeated by Admiral Nelson of Britain.

Napoleon went on to become one of the most important figures in the history of France due to his dedication towards his country.

Napoleon on the battlefield at Borodino.

Napoleon Bonaparte

Monogram of
Napoleon of France.

Battle of Waterloo 1815.

Napoleon is abdicated

In the period between 1803 and 1815, France was engaged in several wars, called "Napoleonic Wars", with many European nations like Britain, Austria and Russia. He then began to wage a large-scale economic war against Britain in 1806 called the "Continental System". Russia backed out of this system and Napoleon decided to attack Russia. Instead of responding, the Russian troops kept retreating and Napoleon's soldiers were forced to trek deeper into Russia with diminishing resources. Russia then invaded France during the Peninsular War. Thus, Napoleon's army lost many battles at the same time against Prussia, Britain, Russia, Sweden and Austria. Napoleon was forced to abdicate and was exiled to a coast of Italy.

Hundred Days campaign

On 6th April, 1814, Napoleon was exiled to Elba, a Mediterranean island. It was a small island and Napoleon was allowed to rule over it. His wife and son were sent to Austria. Napoleon, now in his mid-40s, was as determined now as when he first became the Emperor of France. With support from more than one thousand people, Napoleon escaped from Elba to return to Paris. Here, his loyal supporters and citizens welcomed him back. The new king, Louis XVIII, fled in fear. Napoleon began his Hundred Days campaign. He groomed a new army. Meanwhile, the leaders of Britain, Prussia, Russia and Austria prepared to get rid of Napoleon once and for all. Napoleon started the campaign in 1815 by invading Belgium. The British and Prussian armies were present here. The Battle of Ligny in Prussia saw Napoleon defeat the troops. The next battle, the Battle of Waterloo, was fought in Brussels where Napoleon was defeated and forced to abdicate once again.

After the Napoleonic Era

After Napoleon was exiled, the allied powers and remaining leaders of the French republic came together to try and restore Europe to what it was before Napoleon. However, some nations took advantage by trying to invade and conquer territories. Prussia invaded new territories in western Germany. Russia took over Poland and Britain took over the French, Spanish and Dutch colonies. A new monarchy was put into place.

FUN FACT

Napoleon was first married to Josephine de Beauharnais, a widow who was six years older. A childless marriage resulted in the marriage being annulled. Napoleon had many illegitimate children.

Congress of Vienna, conference to organise Europe after the defeat of Napoleon, 1815.

Industrial Revolution

The Industrial Revolution altered the procedure of manufacturing different items. New machines were invented around the 1700s and by the 1800s, it was possible to mass produce certain items with the use of machinery. Starting in Britain, this revolution quickly spread to Europe and North America bringing about an age of urbanisation with it.

About the revolution

The Industrial Revolution took place between the eighteenth and nineteenth centuries. At the beginning of the revolution, the European nations practiced agriculture. All nations had predominantly rural societies. It was during this revolution that the US and the nations of Europe developed urban and industrial practices. Then it spread to the rest of the world. A historian named Arnold Toynbee first used the term "Industrial Revolution" to show England's economic development.

Technological revolution

The use of iron and steel as raw materials, the discovery of new sources of energy such as fuel and coal as well as improved transportation such as with the steam engine kick-started the industrialisation of Europe. The invention of machines like the spinning jenny and power loom allowed for mass production which took less time than manual labour. The factory system came into existence. Means of communication also improved with the introduction of the radio and telegraph. Industries began to use scientific knowledge to improve their products and come up with more uses for raw materials.

Other changes in society

The earliest effects of such technological changes were seen in the production of agricultural materials. This allowed people to make more money all round which ensured a wider distribution of wealth. Now, man stopped looking at agricultural land as a source of wealth and began to think of other ways to earn. It helped develop the working class who were free to think of other things besides work and money.

The Industrial Revolution was a time of invention.

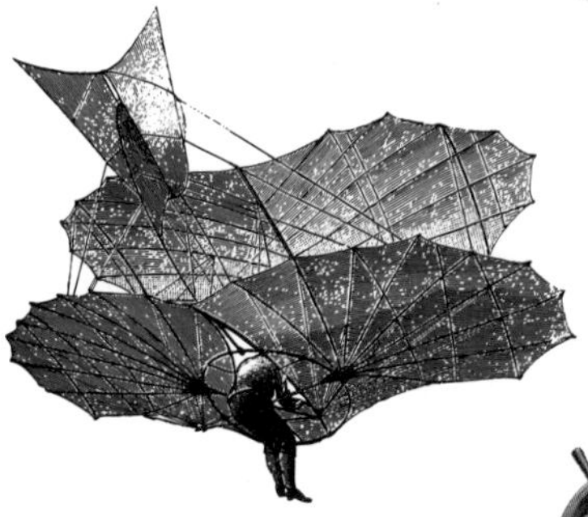

FUN FACT

Two men named William Cooke and Charles Wheatstone introduced the first commercial electrical telegraph. Now, to communicate with each other, people could use the telegraph.

First Industrial Revolution

The Industrial Revolution first began in Britain in 1760 and was contained there until 1830. This gave the British an edge they wanted to preserve. So, they banned the export of skilled labourers, machinery or techniques of manufacture. Also, wealthy men from other countries hoped to bring the big secret to their countries. As a result, the Industrial Revolution moved to Belgium thanks to two Englishmen, William and John Cockerill, who started machine shops there. Then came the Agricultural Revolution where farmers were replaced by machines and had to find jobs in towns.

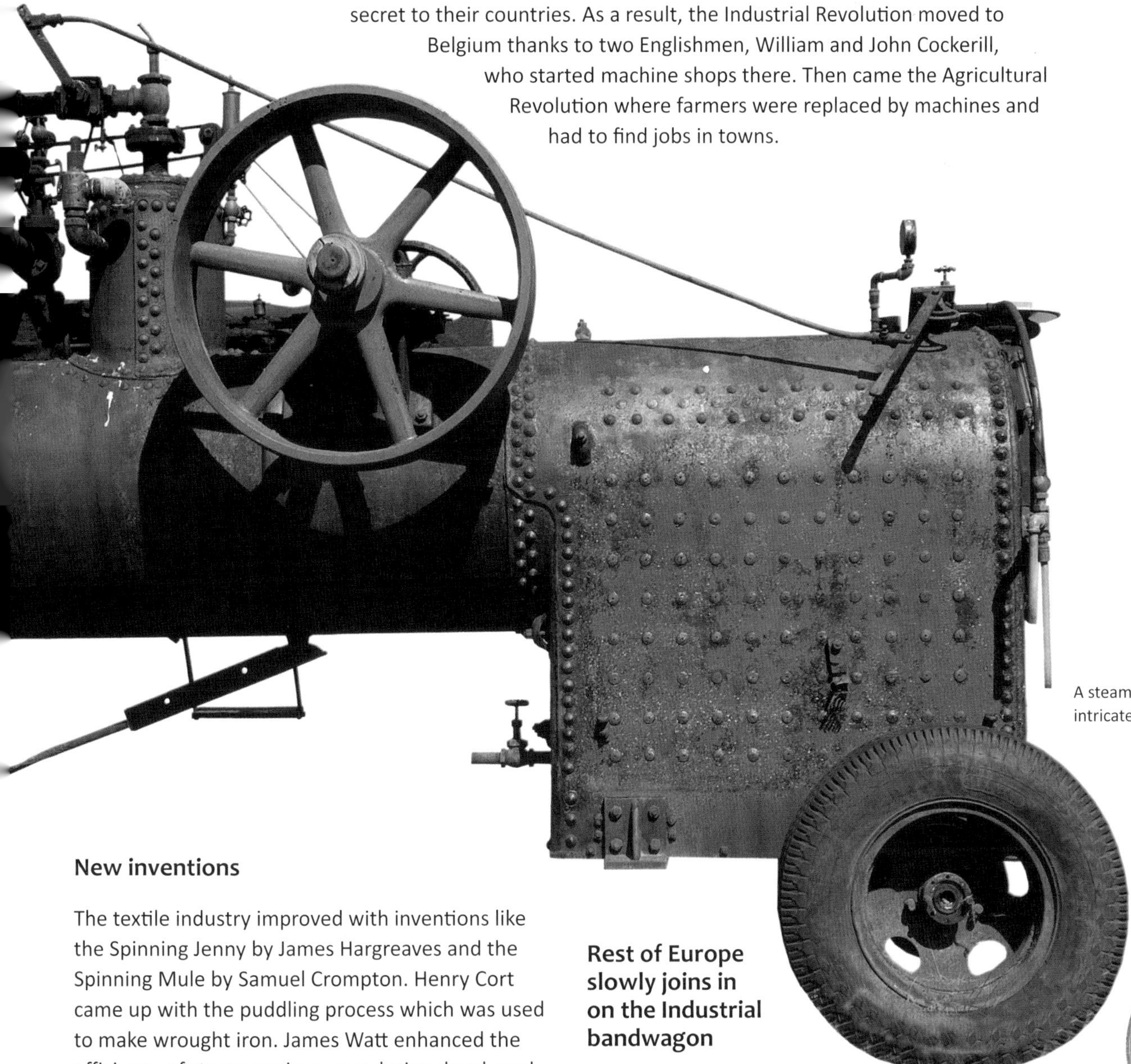

1760: Start of the Industrial Revolution in Britain

1807: Industrial Revolution comes to Belgium

A steam engine with the intricate parts below.

New inventions

The textile industry improved with inventions like the Spinning Jenny by James Hargreaves and the Spinning Mule by Samuel Crompton. Henry Cort came up with the puddling process which was used to make wrought iron. James Watt enhanced the efficiency of steam engines on a design developed by Thomas Savery and Thomas Newcomen.

A cotton mill in Lancashire, England using power looms in 1835.

Rest of Europe slowly joins in on the Industrial bandwagon

When Britain was undergoing vast industrial developments, France was immersed in the Revolution and its indecisive political situation discouraged people from making large investments towards industrial developments. It was only in 1840s that France joined in and despite having had great developments it lagged behind England. Germany started its industrial development only after 1870 and it grew so rapidly that it became the world leader in many industries. In Asia, Japan joined in this revolution. Soon, Soviet Union, China and India also became industrialised by the mid twentieth century.

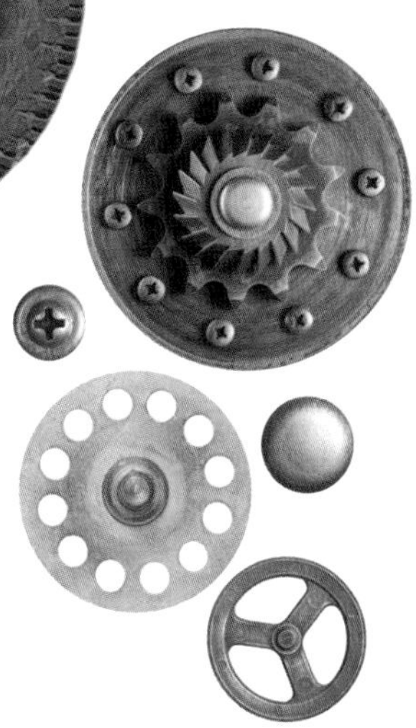

Effects of Industrial Revolution

The Industrial Revolution radically altered the social structure of England. People from all classes gained education and became literate. With better living conditions, life expectancy improved and the population began to grow. The roles of men and women began to change as women entered factories as workers. At the beginning though, women were urged to stay home and men were paid higher wages than female workers.

A typical family scene in eighteenth century Britain.

Growing population

The population in the industrial nations began to grow faster than ever. This was the result of various reasons. Firstly, there was a sharp drop in the death rate as more food became available. Also, fewer plagues and epidemics broke out as people began to eat healthier diets. The birth rate also increased. Younger generations earned higher wages and were able to marry and produce children earlier.

The Industrial Revolution saw an improvement in the medicines available.

Growth of the working class

The literacy rate increased due to an increase in the number of private schools. Also books, newspapers and journals were now mass produced at a quicker rate. This was because printing presses began to use machines like the Gutenberg Press. With the use of machines, work was done faster which gave people leisure time. Higher wages meant money for hobbies. So, people began to read newspapers and books. As a result, they began to think and form opinions about the society. Workers became aware of their conditions. Rural workers started moving towards cities to get jobs and earn more money.

Gender bias

Prior to the Industrial Revolution, gender roles were different, because both men and women worked together in the cottage industries. Businesses were mostly home run. Farmers involved their entire families, thus making it a "family business". Women were deprived of any social, political or economic rights outside their home. Women could not vote or even own property. The "rule of thumb" was a cruel law that found tacit support by the courts and referred to the rule that a man could beat his wife, with a stick so long as the stick was not bigger than the width of his thumb.

FUN FACT

The mid-1700s saw England producing cotton cloth. The spinning of cotton into thread on a spinning wheel was the first thing that launched England into the Industrial Revolution. Since such spinning and weaving were done in homes, they were called cottage industries.

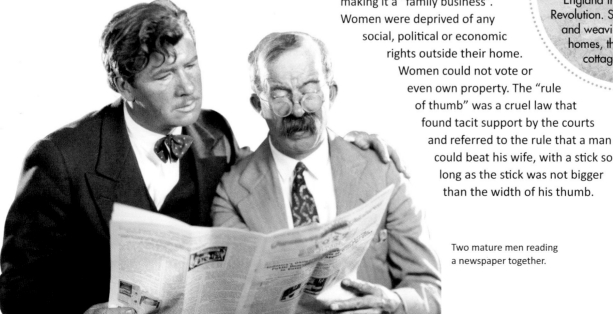

Two mature men reading a newspaper together.

FUN FACT

"Assembly line", the brainchild of Henry Ford, improved the manufacturing process in which workers stood in lines next to conveyor belts which moved parts that were to be added in a sequence.

Metal factories mostly employed men as they were believed to be stronger.

Change in gender roles

As most businesses were run from homes, there was no difference between work and home life. This changed with the Industrial Revolution where men, women and even children worked in factories or mills. Men were paid more than women and children. The working hours were long. After many years, the government tried to eradicate child labour, even as the working hours for women were reduced. Many women left the workforce to take care of their homes and children. Men became the breadwinners of the family. The roles formed by the Industrial Revolution came to dictate the perceptions of men and women, as these gender roles remained the same for the next generations.

Female labourers working in a factory.

Transformation of transportation

With the mass production of goods and raw materials came the need for better modes of transport. The Industrial Revolution saw stronger and more reliable roads, the building of canals and the introduction of railway lines. Raw materials were now transported using faster means. Manufacturers were also able to find and travel to new markets. This not only helped spread wealth to other parts, but also helped introduce the industrial revolution to faraway places.

The Industrial Revolution saw the invention of steamboats, cars and aeroplanes.

A costly affair

With rapid industrialisation and urbanisation, heavy, bulky raw materials like iron and coal were required, but transporting them was a costly affair. The demand for coal also increased. Its transportation was difficult and it was a very expensive resource. Goods were earlier transported by water. With the construction of canals, waterways were expanded and improved and more places could be reached by water. With steam engines and locomotives, the use of horse-drawn carriages was limited to private use and for short distances.

Social Impact of the Industrial Revolution

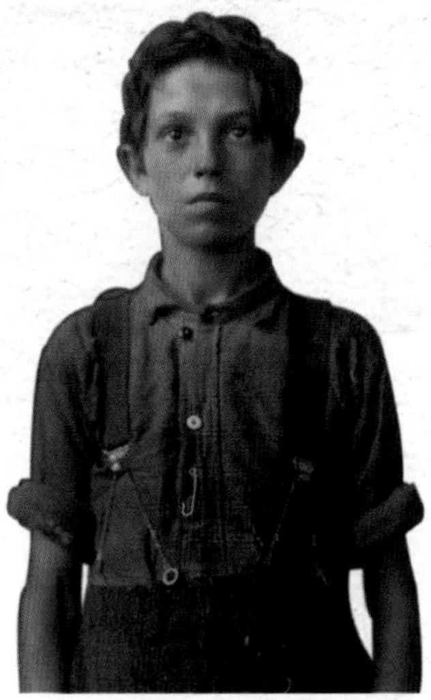

With the introduction of factories, people's lives slowly changed. People moved from rural areas to cities in search of work. Cities grew and expanded while villages were deserted. Urbanisation set in. Workers spent hours at factories and were closely supervised by their foremen. Disagreements between workers and supervisors arose. Many social evils were introduced.

A photo of a city in Britain in the early nineteenth century.

Britain gains economical supremacy

Many technological innovations took place in Britain during the Industrial Revolution. Thus, it became the epicentre of industrialisation. It also helped that Britain had a greater supply of coal which increased the production of iron. Although France had plenty of wood, it had very little coal. Holland was able to produce peat but needed every other material to carry out a large-scale production of iron. Being an island country, Britain also had water transportation that aided in its trading with the market overseas.

So, while it is said that in the eighteenth century, both France and Britain were at par with each other, the French revolution gave Britain the chance to supersede France and become the new leader of Europe. It also helped that they had a huge head start.

FUN FACT

In the 1860s, around one-fifth of the workers in British factories were under the age of 15. They worked long hours in highly dangerous conditions.

Employment of cheap labour

Owners of industries were looking at the best way to maximise their profits. Machines were doing everything, so factories employed unskilled workers. Children were employed for this reason. In fact, an entire family worked in the same factory, especially a poor family. Most factories had 15-hour working days which was not suitable for children. These conditions led to many people falling sick or dying. Housing conditions were yet to be improved and would see improvement nearly half a century later.

1760: Start of the Industrial Revolution

20th century: USA is leading in industrialisation

Factories would release a lot of harmful gases into the environment.

Introduction of Laws

Around the 1700s, the conditions of workers were exposed and the British Parliament introduced laws that limited working hours and prohibited the employment of children, especially very young children. It was around the same time that Charles Dickens published his novels on the suffering of child labourers. People began to fight for child rights and protested against factories. Workers also joined these protests and spoke about their conditions.

Oliver Twist was one such novel where a child is employed in a workshop.

Photo of a workshop with young boys.

Migration to cities

With the Industrial Revolution, Britain saw an increase in cities and big towns which had factories, both big and small. The population increased from 8 million in 1801 to over 40 million in 1901. Cities expanded and people migrated from villages in search of work. They mostly ended up working in factories. Men, women and children began to work in factories and even in the hot, unhealthy work environment of coal mines. The cost of labour for factories was now very cheap. Owners of such establishments grew rich fast, while the labourers were very poor and lived in slums.

Battersea Power Station, London, UK.

Social and economic thoughts during the mercantilism

The Industrial Revolution dominantly followed mercantilism which believed that resources were limited and one had to control these resources. Economists and thinkers like Adam Smith and Jeremy Bentham came up with many theories and ways to promote and follow mercantilism. Bentham proposed that all the models be it social, economic or political should ultimately be only about bringing happiness for people.

FUN FACT

Even though the Industrial Revolution came to the US much later than it came to Britain, by the twentieth century the US became the world's leading industrial nation.

Revolutions of 1848

1848, French revolutionaries burning the royal carriages at the Chateau d'Eu.

There were a series of revolutions that began against royalty and monarchs, but particularly against the monarchies in Europe. The revolutions of 1848 commenced with Sicily and soon spread to Germany, France, Italy and even Austria. These revolutions were mostly unsuccessful.

Poor economic conditions

Between 1845 and 1846, all of Europe was facing economic crises. Poor grain harvests, constant battles, high death rates and other such factors contributed to the poor and depressing economic conditions. There was a shortage of food, so food prices were high. The rate of employment and opportunities for labour were less. People began to resent the monarchs and nobles for their high status and comfortable lives. All this led to terrible unrest which ended up creating the Revolutions of 1848 across Europe, except for Russia.

Guardhouse students of 1848 were the springs of the revolutionary movement.

Revolts galore

The Italian revolution started around 1848 in Sicily. The idea of holding revolts soon moved to France. However, it did not spread to Russia, Spain and Scandinavia. In England, there were some protests and demonstrations held in Ireland but it did not manifest to anything more than that. Revolts also broke out in Holland, Belgium and Denmark, but they ended with peaceful negotiations and useful reforms.

The Working Class Revolts

The revolution seemed to gain attention and victories in France. There were many differences of opinions. This led to the "Workers' Insurrection" in June, 1848. The Austrian monarchy braved the protests, while in Prussia King William IV led a movement for the unification of Germany. But France did not lend its support to the revolutionaries in Europe.

Statue of King William IV, Greenwich.

Use of Force to Suppress Revolutions

A picture depicting the three types of revolutionaries of 1848.

The Revolution of 1848 was a liberal, nationalist movement that had taken over pretty much the whole of Europe. It was seen as the first protest against capitalism. Soon, countries from other nations followed suit. In Europe, these revolutions were called the "Spirit of 1848". Constitution-led governments were formed in unified Germany and Italy, and much later in all of Europe.

1848: Start of the European revolutions

1852: Napoleon III takes over France

Napoleon III and empress Eugenie entrance in Saint-Malo through triumphal arch, 1858.

Repression

Monarchs and other rulers used the nation's armies to repress the revolts and the insurgents. This was seen in France, then was followed by the Czechs in Prague and also by the Austrian army in Lombardy and Vienna. The Berlin and Prussian armies followed later. In fact, the French intervened to set things in order while this was done in Rome. The King of Prussia tried to unite Germany via a union of the German Princes. Austria and Russia, asked him to discard this idea and the same was discussed at the Convention of Olmütz in 1850.

FUN FACT

"Prussia" refers to areas of eastern and central Europe, respectively, which came under the Polish and German rule during the Middle Ages.

Results of the clampdown of revolts

The results of such shutting down of revolts were that the liberal democratic concessions that were granted earlier were withdrawn. Now, absolute monarchy was re-established in countries like Italy, Germany and Austria. The governments in agreement with the middle class and clergy, who felt threatened by the socialist ideology, strengthened their police forces. The freedom of press was restricted. In France, there was a coup against the assembly, when in 1852 Napoleon III took over the reins. The uprisings spread to the parliamentary governments. Austria came back to power over Hungary and drove the Sardinians away from Lombardy and Venice. Liberals, republicans and socialists across Europe either sought refuge in the US or went into hiding.

The Bundestag in Frankfurt.

Romanticism

The word "romance" stood for many things. During the Middle Ages, romance was a style of writing found in stories, prose and poems which was used to refer to the heroic deeds of knights and soldiers. This changed with time, when it referred to a type of narrative in prose which had a unique, imaginative and unrealistic manner. "Romanticism" was a cultural movement that started in Europe. It was a reaction to the Industrial Revolution.

The House of the Seven Gables in Massachusetts is a 1668 colonial mansion. It was made famous by the American author, Nathaniel Hawthorne.

Spread to other fields

Hawthorne's "House of Seven Gables" is often referred to as an example of romance. Romanticism was actually a movement that started in the eighteenth century and continued to the nineteenth century. It had its traces in the fields of art, philosophy, religion, literature and even politics. This was a popular technique of art and method of writing.

Characteristics of Romanticism

The many characteristic elements of Romanticism include a deep admiration for natural beauty, an emphasis on emotion over logic and feelings over common sense and an internalising of the self. It was the largest artistic movement of the late 1700s and it influenced artists and writers across the continents. Poets and artists fostered individualism and idealism. It was also about actual emotion and passion. There was awareness towards mysticism and the supernatural.

Poets of this movement

Many poets embraced the Romantic Movement. Fredrich Schiller and Johann Wolfgang von Goethe being two examples. Wordsworth, Coleridge, Shelley, Keats and Lord Byron from England took the movement forward. Noted poet and writer Victor Hugo also contributed to the movement. Among the American poets, Walt Whitman and Edgar Allan Poe became the faces of the Romantic Movement in the US.

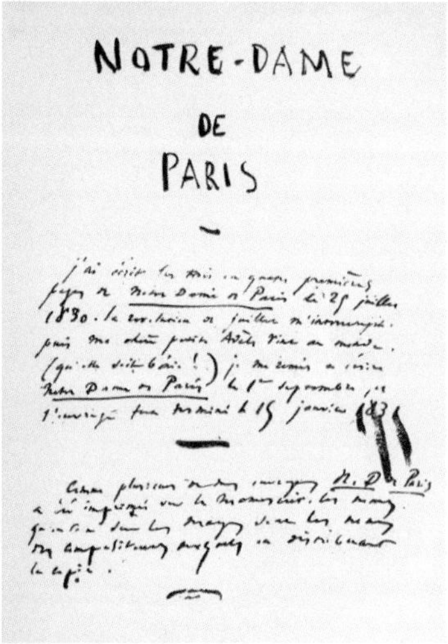
NOTRE-DAME
DE
PARIS

Notre-Dame de Paris, by Victor Hugo. Title of the original manuscript, 1829.

A monument of Victor Hugo in Paris, France.

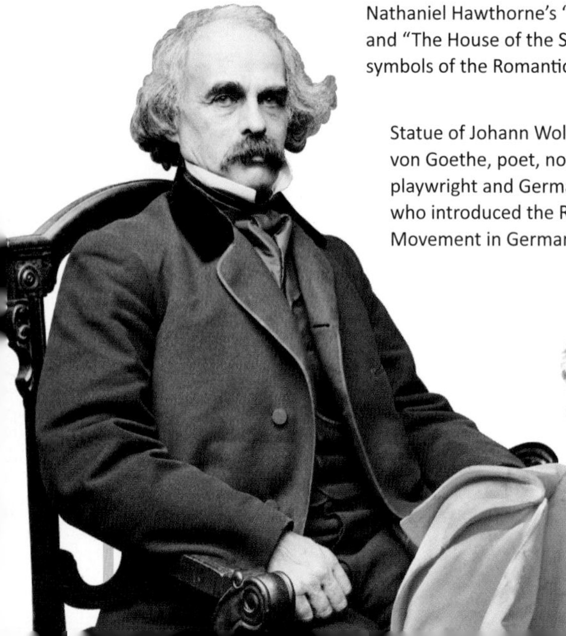

Nathaniel Hawthorne's "The Scarlett Letter," and "The House of the Seven Gables" became symbols of the Romantic Movement.

Statue of Johann Wolfgang von Goethe, poet, novelist, playwright and German scientist who introduced the Romantic Movement in Germany.

FUN FACT

Did you know that the famous composer Ludwid van Beethoven gained his popularity during the Romantic period?

Romanticism and the Writers and Poets

An illustration from a Goethe poem, along with a line from one of his works.

The characteristic attitude of Romantic Age consisted of a heightened appreciation of natural beauty, a preference of emotion over reason and of feelings over intellect. By the eighteenth century, the words "romantique" and "romantic" came to be used in French and English, respectively, and meant magical, dramatic and astonishing. German poets and critics August Wilhelm and Friedrich Schlegel named this movement.

Celebration of creativity

The writers of the Romantic Movement, as it is sometimes referred to, celebrated imagination, followed their intuition and were spontaneous. They believed in subjectivity, revolutionary thought, individualism and democracy. This was visible in the work done by Goethe, a German writer. Friedrich Hölderlin, Jean Paul, Novalis, Ludwig Tieck, Friedrich Schlegel, Wilhelm Heinrich Wackenroder and Friedrich Schelling were some other popular German writers. Poets like Vicomte de Chateaubriand, Charles Baudelaire and Rainer Maria Rilke, though not actively participating in this movement, were influenced by its ideologies. This was obvious from their work. Also, the ballads composed by English lyrical writers showed traces of this ideology.

Second phase

The second phase of Romanticism started in 1805 and lasted until the 1830s. It inspired cultural nationalism and a renewed reflection to national identity. It celebrated folklore, folk ballads, poetry, folk dance and folk music.

Sir Walter Scott (1771-1832), a Scottish author who wrote narrative poetry early in his career, before historical novels became his primary genre.

Romantic writers and poets

Sir Walter Scott was one of the first writers to have been interested in German Romanticism. He translated the works of some German poets and authors. He later moved on to historical novels and is said to be the inventor of them. Lord Byron, Shelley and Keats popularised the romantic poems. Authors also wrote on supernatural and grotesque themes. Mary Shelley's *Frankenstein* is a popular work of this period. Poets like William Wordsworth and Samuel Taylor Coleridge, poet and painter William Blake became examples of Romantic sensibility in Britain. German artists such as Caspar David and Friedrich Johann were celebrated for their works.

Hermann and Dorothea, characters of a Goethe poem.

Romanticism in the Arts

Venice - The Dogana and San Giorgio Maggiore by J. M. W. Turner

FUN FACT

Did you know that it was during the Romantic Movement that landscapes attained some significance among artists and art history students?

1800: Beginning of the Romantic Era

1850: Decline of the Romantic Era

The Romanticists believed that every person had a right to life, liberty and equal opportunity. These ideas found their way to the American Declaration of Independence. The Romantic Movement was innately against industrialisation due to its social and ecological impacts. Romanticism revived peoples' concern for nature. Interest in old legends and folk ballads soon grew and writers used these elements in their writings as well.

Emotions on canvas

The Romantic Age inspired artists to display their emotions on the canvas. Artists began to depict a scene based on their feelings towards a theme or a subject. This brought mood to an art piece. The movement gave wings to the imagination of the artists. It motivated the artist to delve into the spiritual world. The themes ranged from landscapes to religion. It was not about brush strokes, but about what feeling the art evoked. Precision was not the key, but emotion was.

Romanticism and the artwork

Caspar Friedrich's, *The Wanderer above the Sea of Fog* is one of the paintings that belonged to the realm of the Romantic Movement. The image of a man standing at a precipice of a hill with his back to the viewer is a great metaphor on man and the meaning of his existence in nature. Francisco Goya's *Third of May 1808* depicted the emotions of the Spanish resistance against Napoleon's army. The painting was among the first on war and its devastation.

The Wanderer above the Sea of Fog by Caspar Friedrich.

Other artists of the Romantic Movement

Other artists who contributed to the Romantic Era include Thomas Cole, the American artist who was known for his painting of landscapes. He was also the founder of the art movement in Hudson River School. Among the English artists were John Constable, Henry Fuseli and J.M.W. Turner. Their works represented the elements of romanticism. The other European Romantic artists were Eugene Delacroix, Thomas Gainsborough, Caspar Friedrich and Goya.

Eugene Delacroix's painting depicting Henri IV conferring the regency upon Marie de' Medici.

Art movement at the Hudson River School

The American Romantic artists were all about meticulous and romanticised landscapes. Most of them came from the Hudson River School. They were guided by Thomas Cole, who painted his first landscape at the Catskill Mountains. The Hudson River School was America's first artistic fraternity and it identified a group of city-based landscape painters from New York. In 1848 after Cole's death, Asher B. Durand led this movement. He soon became the president of the National Academy of Design.

Neoclassicism

Neoclassicism was an artistic style that began in the late eighteenth and early nineteenth centuries. The Neoclassical Movement was often described as a counterpart opposing Romanticism. It focussed on reviving the old forms of classical art used in Greece and Rome. It started from Rome and then spread to England, Sweden and Russia. The famous neoclassical painters of that time included Jacques-Louis David, Angelica Kauffmann, Jean-Auguste-Dominique Ingres and Anton Raphael Mengs.
The noteworthy sculptors and architects of the neoclassical movement included Houdon, Canova, Mansart, Soufflot and John Nash among others. Neoclassicism is appreciated even today.

An example of Neoclassical art.

Jacques-Louis David's Portrait of Mrs Serizy.

Reaction to art

Neoclassicism was seen as a reaction to the Baroque and Rococo form of art and brought back the old formal architectural styles. France had a great influence on this art movement which then spread to England and Germany. This form of decorative art was popularised by kings and soon the styles came to known as Jacobean, Charles II, William and Mary, Queen Anne and Georgian. Robert Adam, an architect was someone who also used this form for his furniture, carpets and other accessories. Towards the end of the movement, Neoclassicism became a topic exploited by political, economic, spiritual and social reformists. It was seen as a cure to religious fanaticism.

Designed by Robert Adam in 1774 in the Palladian style, Pulteney Bridge crosses the River Avon in Bath, England, UK.

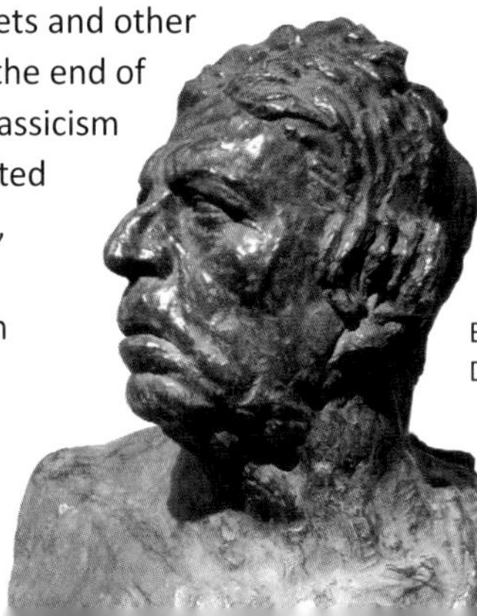

Bust of Jean Auguste Dominique Ingres.

Realism

Realism was an artistic technique which looked at a subject or theme in a straight and realistic manner, without the rules of artistic theory. Realism was a reaction to the over-the-top nature of Romanticism. Some paintings that depicted realism can be found in Copley and Goya's works. Realism started as a movement in France with artists like Camille Corot and Jean Millet. American painters like Eakins and Ossawa Tanner were also influenced by realism, which was clearly reflected in their works.

Madonna of Loreto and Pilgrims by Caravaggio is now in Basilica di Sant Agostino.

Work on realism

The movement started with the work of the French author Stendhal. Honore de Balzac was seen as the father of realism with his Le Comédie Humaine, a multi-volumed interlinked collection of novels. This was followed by Gustave Flaubert's novel, *Madame Bovary*, which reflected Bourgeois ambience of its times. Guy de Maupassant, Joris Karl Huysmans, George Eliot, Thomas Hardy and Henry James were other authors whose works represented realism.

Realism in the ages

Realism, in a way, is about seeing things as they are, with little or no use of one's imagination. Realism, as an approach, can be found in Hellenistic structures, which accurately depicted certain elements of normal life.
Caravaggio, Francisco de Zurbaran and Jose de Ribera were painters who were influenced by the Realism Movement.

Gustave Courbet, a French painter of the Realism Movement, opposed the academic neoclassical ideals and used mythological subjects.

Realism in literature

English writers like Daniel Defoe and Henry Fielding are great examples of authors who wrote on realistic themes. Balzac was another such writer who was influenced by the Realism Movement. In the book, *Le Comédie Humaine* or *The Human Comedy*, he spoke of real French problems like money, power, social status, patriarchy and matriarchy. Gustave Flaubert was another proponent of the realistic movement.
His book, *Madame Bovary* was in fact an incisive account of the mentality of the French people.

A USSR postcard showing a painting by Jose de Ribera.

A postcard printed in the USSR of the painting, *The Lute Player* by Caravaggio.

A monument of Honore de Balzac in Berdychiv, Ukraine.

Scientific Positivism

The term "positivism" is all about a focus on positive sciences. It is something that can be tested and experienced. Auguste Comte was seen as the key supporter of positivism and he divided human history into three levels—religious, metaphysical and scientific. He stated that for the first two levels, humans tried to understand and explain things using personal feelings. In the third level, they focussed on observing and experimenting. These levels added to the development of humankind.

A monument of Auguste Comte, a French philosopher.

Emergence of sociology

In 1838, Comte came up with the term, "sociology". He used this term to describe a new way of looking at the society and promoted it as a different branch of study. His three-stage model of human knowledge explained the phases of religious and metaphysical world views that preceded the scientific approach to knowledge. His model also linked the data that he accumulated to form his theories.

New scientific foundation

Comte felt that everything from law to politics and religion should be rebuilt with a view of the newly formed scientific foundation. For example, according to Comte, religion needed to be about humanity and reason. It needed to have customs and symbols that were based on the new way of thinking. Herbert Spencer and Thomas Huxley not only agreed with his thought but also propagated and studied sociology.

FUN FACT

The German biologist Emil du Bois-Reymond had only one thing to say of the metaphysical studies—"We are and shall be ignorant".

Twentieth century positivism

During the twentieth century, positivism gained a new avatar. It was known as logical positivism so that people do not confuse it with philosophy and its branches of study. It was also known as logical empiricism. It held that rationalism within the modern viewpoint was important. There are temples in Rio de Janeiro, Porto Alegre and Curitiba in Brazil and Paris that were built by nineteenth century Comtean positivists. In fact, even today London has a society of positivists.

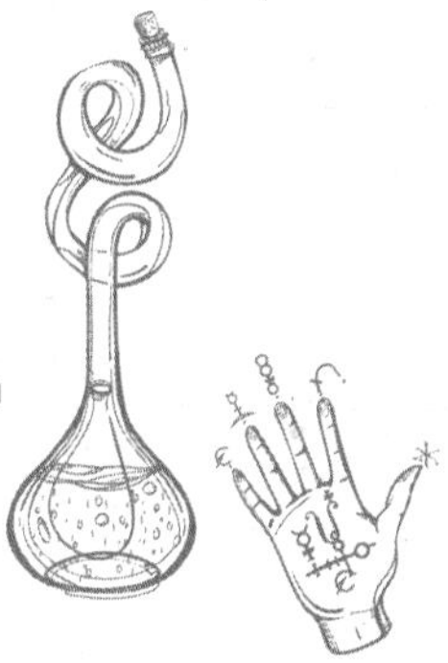

Cesare Lombroso, an Italian psychiatrist and criminologist, was one of Comte's major supporters. Paul-Emile Littre and Louis Weber also studied from his ideas. John Stuart Mill would disagree with some points put forth by Comte, but also would agree with most. He wrote *System of Logic* in 1843, which expanded upon subjects like positivism, scientific reasoning and considered logic and mathematics to be empirical sciences. Herbert Spencer was considered second to him.

Thomas Huxley

Logical Positivism

Logical positivism was a movement which started in Vienna, Austria in the 1920s. People by now had started to focus on the scientific reasoning behind certain occurrences in nature. Also, scientific knowledge became popular because of its factual approach. A.J. Ayer's work first popularised logical positivism. It became extremely significant in the philosophy of science, logic and language. The movement believed that philosophy must avoid dogmatism, as done by science.

Statue of Sir Karl Popper at Vienna University.

Characteristics of logical positivism

Logical positivism is also referred to as "logical empiricism". It believed in rejecting metaphysical doctrines for their meaninglessness. It also promoted the opinion that the only factual knowledge is scientific knowledge. Unlike the previous movements of a similar nature, which believed that one could gain knowledge by personal experience only, logical positivism believed that knowledge comes from experiments, verifications and attempts to confirm an idea. It does not believe that metaphysical doctrines are false, saying that there is some credibility to them. However, it believes that they are without meaning. It believed that questions about God and freedom cannot be answered as they are not meaningful questions.

Vienna Circle

The Vienna Circle is a group that founded logical positivism. It first came into action in 1929. It consisted mainly of physicists and mathematicians who would discuss common subjects before World War I. The group was displeased by the explanations provided about subjects like logical truths and natural sciences. Hans Hahn, a leader of the Vienna Circle, first presented his work *Logisch-philosophische Abhandlung*, in 1921 before his students of the University of Vienna. Positivism, an idea propagated by this movement, believes that knowledge on any subject is a positive data of experience and that a fact should be based purely on logic and mathematics. This train of thought was proposed by the Scottish thinker, David Hume in the eighteenth century. However, he classified this view under formal sciences.

FUN FACT

A. J. Ayer's views shocked and upset those who followed metaphysical and aesthetic philosophies. They refused to take him seriously and considered his views as an expression of his tastes.

Statue of David Hume.

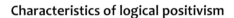

Mid-Nineteenth Century

1801–1900

In the mid-nineteenth century, different issues began competing and gaining prominence over each other. For instance, many revolutionaries across Europe dreamt of voting rights for all, a "fourth estate" or press that had freedom of printing stories, an elected legislative body and a functioning constitution. Although there were many attempts towards this, they were successfully destroyed under Metternich's rule. Metternich was Austria's minister of foreign affairs. He formed a successful alliance against Napoleon I. He helped bring back Austria as a leading European power.

However, the defeats only strengthened the revolutionaries to fight, especially in Germany. Italy struggled for liberalism and nationalism converged into an unstoppable struggle which drew everyone (including intellectuals) into the movement. In France and England, there was a renewed vigour towards making radical changes, which found form in strikes, trade unions and charters that demanded a complete democratic parliament. Nonetheless, many parts of Europe experienced great losses.

Advance of Democracy

Even as the quest for greater freedom from monarchy continued through different struggles, it seemed as though the collective thinking was that democracy was predestined. But in 1830, Prime Minister Arthur Wellesley of Wellington, opposed parliamentary reform. With increasing support, some changes began in his own party. When the new government under Earl Grey came into power, he promised parliamentary reforms and managed to get the royal assent at the third attempt in the passing of the reform bills in 1832.

Women suffrage in Wyoming Territory–women voting at the polls in Cheyenne, Wyoming, 24th November, 1888.

Reform acts

The first Reform Act, also known as the Representation of the People Act of 1832, created 67 new constituencies, including small owners of land, farmers and shopkeepers. It formed a uniform franchise in the boroughs. It managed to give the right to vote to all householders who paid a rental of more than 10 pounds. These were limited efforts. Many from the labour force could not vote. The Reform Act of 1867 managed to give voting rights to the labour forces in cities.

Changes to electoral franchise

The British Reform Act of 1832 brought forth the first changes to electoral franchise legislation in more than 50 years. To carry forward these changes, William IV needed to support them for them to be passed. The act also provided voting rights to the middle class. This increased the size of the electorate from a mere 435,000 to 652,000. This enabled the middle class to also have some amount of influence in politics. Pressure from popular groups led to these changes. The act increased constitutional rights.

William IV (1765-1837)

Big Ben and House of Parliament from Westminster Bridge, London, UK.

The Wellington Monument in Hyde Park, was built in honour of the first Duke of Wellington, Arthur Wellesley, and his triumph in the Peninsular and Napoleonic wars.

1830: Arthur Wellesley opposes parliamentary reform

1832: The Reform Act of 1832 is proposed

Wars of the Mid-Nineteenth Century

A Crimean War monument.

Wars of the mid-nineteenth century mirrored the changing nature of the European society, politics and economy. The Napoleonic Wars had taught the major European powers that a general European conflict must be evaded. In fact, the principles of the Congress of Vienna formed the base of nineteenth-century diplomacy.

Movement to unite Italy

Revolts and revolutionaries were seen as the biggest hazard to European peace. There were plenty of army-led interventions that limited and blocked the spread of revolutions. The Crimean War became the major conflict in the region. It had the potential to grow into a large-scale European war. The House of Savoy rejected the "Risorgimento" or the movement to unite all of Italy. The rulers of the Piedmont-Sardinia turned against the Italian rulers and attempted to conquer Austria, an Italian possession.

Italian unification

The Italian unification was a series of wars that were fought to consolidate the different Italian territories in Europe. The First Italian War of Independence was fought between 1848 and 1849 between the Kingdom of Sardinia and the Empire of Austria. The battles of the war took place in Custoza and Novara.

Austrian Uhlans charge Italian Bersaglieri during the Battle of Custoza.

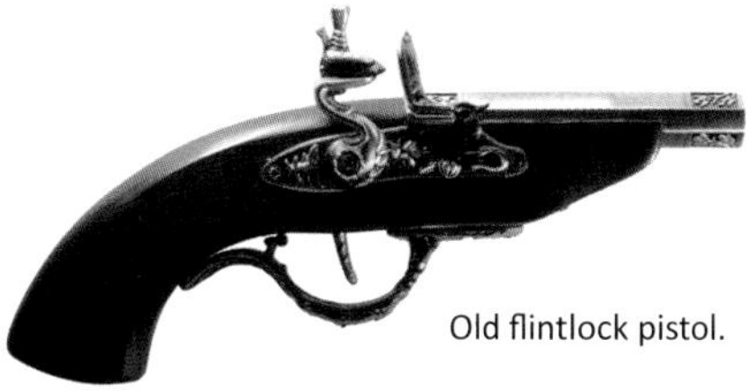
Old flintlock pistol.

The Austrian Empire emerged victorious at the end of this war. After this the Second French Empire joined the side of the Kingdom of Sardinia to fight against the Austrian Empire. This war was also known as the Franco-Austrian War. It was fought in 1859 and proved to be an important war for the Italian Unification. Thanks to the fierce support offered from France, the Franco-Sardinian side won the war. Austria entered into an armistice. In the Third Italian War of Independence, the Kingdom of Italy fought with the Austrian Empire. The Prussian Wars taking place parallelly turned favourable for Italy which was able to gain the unification of its territories with the capture of Rome.

FUN FACT

The wars of the mid-nineteenth century used the products of the Industrial Revolution including trains, steam-powered navy, telegraph and rifles.

Statue of Giuseppe Garibaldi.

Literature During the Mid-Nineteenth Century

The nineteenth century is known to be one of the greatest periods for literature. Romanticism was the main literary movement during the early nineteenth century. In English poetry, the romanticism element began around 1798 with the works of Wordsworth and Coleridge, who wrote lyrical ballads. The French revolution as well as the Industrial Revolution had its impact on the literature of this period. The French writer Jean-Jacques Rousseau, and the German writers Friedrich Holderlin and Ludwig Tieck were famous during this period.

A gypsy character from a poem by John Keats.

Prominent poets and authors of this period

This period saw poets using simple language in their works, particularly Wordsworth. So, even the common man could enjoy poetry. John Keats and Lord Byron also gained popularity for their poems. *Crime and Punishment* was published in 1866 in the literary journal, *The Russian Messenger*. It was written and published in installments. It was written by the Russian novelist Fyodor Dostoyevsky, who was sent to jail in Siberia in 1849 for this book. He was sentenced to death. However, his sentence was reduced to four years of hard labour. During his time in prison, he wrote *The Brothers Karamazov* and *The Idiot*. Fyodor Dostoyevsky, the Spanish poet, Espronceda and the Italian writer Giacomo Leopardi expressed their nationalistic fervour in their works.

Emergence of realism in literature

Authors like Flaubert, Dostoyevsky, Tolstoy, Maupassant and Ibsen practiced realism. They wanted to portray contemporary life objectively. One of the most known writers during this period was Charles Baudelaire, who used "symbolism" in his writing.

Jean-Jacques Rousseau

Herman Melville

Edgar Allan Poe

Leo Nikolayevich Tolstoy

Henrik Ibsen

Giacomo Leopardi

Ralph Waldo Emerson

1830s: Romanticism begins in the US

1870s: Romanticism comes to an end in England

American writers of this age

Works of James Fenimore Cooper and Edgar Allan Poe as well as the poems of Walt Whitman and Longfellow were popular in the US. Thoreau and Emerson were important writers of this time. Their theories provided different insights. Henry David Thoreau was a pencil maker, teacher and carpenter besides being a writer. His teaching profession at the Concord School ended in a few weeks because of a disagreement with his superintendent over disciplining his students.

FUN FACT

Did you know that Walt Whitman wrote a poem about Abraham Lincoln's struggles as a president in his "O Captain! My Captain!".

Works of other Americans

Works of Herman Melville, Emily Dickinson and Edgar Allan Poe had instances of different current issues of USA including slavery and the American Civil War. In his short life, Edgar Allan Poe became one of the most influential writers in the history of literature. He led the way towards the creation of the form of the short story and also helped develop different genres including horror stories and detective tales.

Slow decline of the Romantic Movement

By the late eighteenth century, France and Germany saw literature move away from classical forms. A new concept of romanticism was formed. Different styles, themes and types of content emerged during the Romantic Movement in the eighteenth and nineteenth centuries. Different philosophies, agendas and points of interest were sometimes competing and working with each other. In England, Romanticism continued until the mid-nineteenth century. While in the US, it came in late. It commenced in the 1830s and continued until the beginning of the Civil War. There were different styles of writing and literature in both the countries but certain factors were common in all forms.

Gustave Dore's illustration of Edgar Allan Poe's *The Raven*; the poem's narrator with visions of angels surrounding the beloved departed Lenore, 1883.

Edouard Manet, al-Bar delle follies bergere

Arts of the Mid-Nineteenth Century

A new style of art emerged around 1862, with Edouard Manet. It was perhaps the first wave of sorts in the sphere. It was termed "modern art"—the term only came into use in 1883. For the first time, Theodore Duret used the term "avant garde" to explain the work of young artists. Modernity soon became a theme among artists, but the people did not embrace this art form as they did with others.

Meaning of avant garde

The word "avant garde" comes from the French word, "vanguard", meaning an artist or style. It is used to describe the exploration of new artistic methods. It also means experimenting with new methods with the intention of producing better art. The Museum of Modern Art in New York City was founded in 1929.

Art and artists of this period

As the century began, realists changed the focus to everyday subjects. Impressionists focussed on painting effects of light. A new generation of artists emerged who wanted to express their personal opinions in their works of art. For more than 200 years, official exhibitions had dominated art and the artists' mind space.

Manet, Pissarro, Cézanne and Renoir were the important artists of this time. Post 1860, Manet experimented with a style that came to be known as the impressionistic style.

Impressionism soon began to be seen as the fitting end to the realism that was found at the end of the nineteenth century. Monticelli was another French painter whose work affected Cezanne. Others who also seemed to be slightly influenced with the impressionistic style included English artist Sargent and American artist Whistler.

Paul Cézanne's, *The Hermitage at Pontoise.*

Pierre-Auguste Renoir's *oarsmen at Chatou.*

Pierre Auguste Renoir's *Girl with a Fan.*

A bust of Edouard Manet, the impressionist's painter.

The Realism–Romanticism Divide

Delacroix and Marees were essentially artists who were inspired by the Romantic Movement. Leibl and Hans Thoma were artists who were more comfortable with realism. In America, Thomas Eakins brought forth a new realist style that came to be known as expressionistic. Monet and Pissarro were other significant artists of this time.

Three Tahitian Women by Paul Gauguin.

Impressionism movement

Impressionism was a movement that was started in France by a group of young artists who rebelled against the French Salon. They wanted to bring about a new style of painting which put their impressions of the subject or theme on the canvas. This movement began in the 1860s and became famous in 1870. The impressionists played with colours and light rather than physical objects or places. So, they did not focus on the other physical details of the painting. Often, an outdoor area was chosen as the setting as impressionists often chose sunlight or moonlight to paint in. They used rapid brush strokes and pure, untempered colours to save time. They used unusual visual angles and common everyday subjects.

Post-Impressionism

Towards the end of the nineteenth century, and in the early twentieth century, another movement was started. Here, people rebelled against impressionism and were interested in creating personal and emotive art. The contributors of this style of painting were Vincent van Gogh and Paul Gauguin. It was called "Post-Impressionism" and it included many distinct artistic styles used in different contexts as that of the art created during the Impressionist Movement. With the impressionist and post-impressionist movements, art once again became a reflection of the world and moved away from being a means for the artist to express his personal expression and thoughts.

Self portrait - Eugène Ferdinand Victor Delacroix.

Vincent Van Gogh's *The Sea at Saint-Marie.*

FUN FACT

Impressionism was a style developed in France during the late nineteenth century, where artists attempted to capture a visual reading of their subjects by using colours and not lines. Artists like Claude Monet and Pierre Auguste Renoir were inspired by this style of painting.

Second Industrial Revolution

The late nineteenth century and the early twentieth century saw modern industry take root everywhere. New materials came to be used. The machines that were used in the eighteenth and early nineteenth centuries were classified as simple machines used for small tasks. Mechanical machines and advanced machines were soon to follow. Hence, the period after 1860 was called the "Second Industrial Revolution".

Old illustration of an iron factory in La Houilles foundry, France.

The use of electricity

The Second Industrial Revolution witnessed the replacement of steam, as the main source of energy, with electricity. Soon, electricity came to be used for both transportation and communication. This further increased production and enhanced the manufacturing processes. With progress came other social problems including the unsolved and unattended problem of unemployment. New world leaders emerged in the US and Germany.

Aspects of the Second Industrial Revolution

The Second Industrial Revolution brought forth newer inventions and products. It opened new markets. Larger factories came into existence. New market leaders began to appear as the industry started to become more competitive. The Second Industrial Revolution replaced iron with steel and more effective machines and engines. Germany soon caught on and gained a lead with England's prowess of producing steel. They also started producing elements required to make soap, paper and dyes. Electricity was the new form of energy that was used. The first electrical generator was built in 1832 and soon the electric light bulb became a common commodity. Electricity was largely used in countries like Germany and USA. By 1837, the first electric telegraph was invented where messages were sent using needles and wires to a remote receiver. Then the Morse code was developed by Samuel Morse which became an effective method of communication. In 1876, Alexander Bell invented the telephone by a way of transmitting and receiving sounds across long distances.

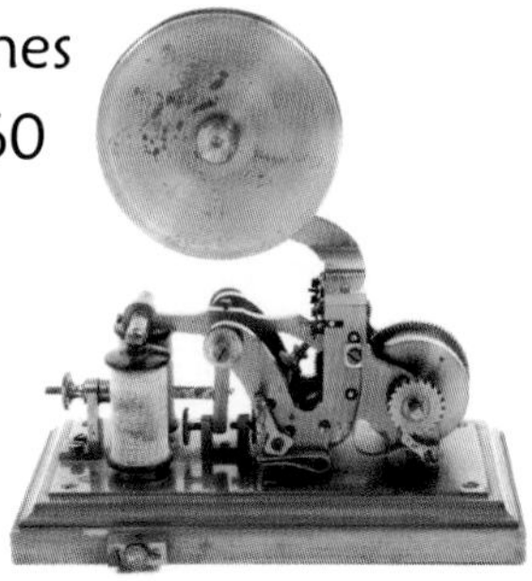

The inner parts of the telephone.

Electric machine (magno electric).

With an increase in the production of steel, it was now used to make railway lines at a lower cost. Steel was more durable than iron. Its strength, larger size, longer length and durability along with its cost made steel the best material to build railway lines. Robert Forester Mushet was the first man to make railway lines from steel. He worked for the Darkhill Ironworks Company in Gloucestershire.

FUN FACT

Britain, the leader of the First Industrial Revolution, now lost its edge to Germany which became the leader of the Second Industrial Revolution.

A modern suburban electric train.

Elements of the Second Industrial Revolution

A woman sending Morse Code.

Despite the general improvement in health care and the standard of living, the social problems remained the same. Unemployment still existed and the gap between the rich and poor continued to grow wider.

1870: Second Industrial Revolution begins

1914: End of the Second Industrial Revolution

Development of power stations

The period between 1870 and 1914 was known as the period of the Second Industrial Revolution. During the Second Industrial Revolution, society saw the growth of the usage of electricity, petroleum and steel. Iron began to be replaced by steel which was used for construction, making machines for industrial use, as well as for building rail lines and ships. Candles and gas lamps were replaced by the electric light bulbs. Britain's first power station opened in 1881. By 1919, blocks of residential areas received electricity from the power station.

Sources of energy during the Second Industrial Revolution

Besides electricity, gas was another fuel used to produce energy. Coal gas was used to allow factories to work for longer hours. A kind of electrical boom took place first in America and then in Germany where more and more people began to light their houses and factories with electricity. Gradually, electricity influenced the development of better means of transport and communication.

Inventions of the Second Industrial Revolution

Telegraphs began to be used regularly in 1837. The Morse Code became an efficient tool for communication. USA and the prosperous nations of Europe, like Britain, laid down telegraph lines. This made long-distance communication quicker and clearer. The telephone was another technological breakthrough that helped transmit and receive sounds across long distances. Its popularity grew very quickly. Guglielmo Marconi's radio also successfully brought about a change in the society.

Antique Morse Code Inker as used to mark or record Morse Code signals on paper.

Voice sounds were transmitted for the first time on 3rd June, 1875 over this instrument invented by Alexander Graham Bell.

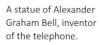

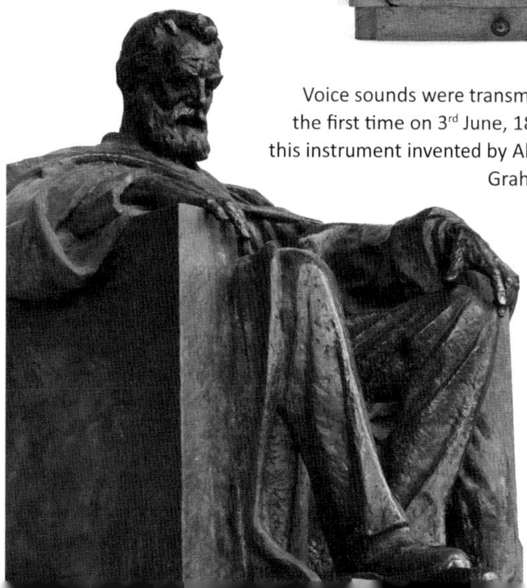

A statue of Alexander Graham Bell, inventor of the telephone.

Rise of Organised Labour and Mass Protests

Class conflicts were slowly creeping into society as the labour force was unhappy with the management that was only interested in efficiency and costs. Protests against such bosses rose amongst workers in the later part of the nineteenth century. Unions and strikes became the norm with these unions often clashing against the government. People lived in cities and worked for employers who treated them like machines. All that they were interested in was in ensuring that their factories functioned properly.

New Model Unionism in England

Though the 1848 revolutions failed, they managed to bring the working class together. Skilled workers came together to form a conventional union movement called the "New Model Unionism", which asked workers to approach trade managements and settle differences through non-violent negotiations. Many workers disagreed with this type of protest which led to the formation of several trade unions. From miners to factory workers different trade unions held strikes.

Rise of Mass Unionism

The depression of the 1870s led to many agitations across Europe. Mass unions formed in Europe, especially Western Europe by 1890.

A monument of the worker and farmer in Moscow.

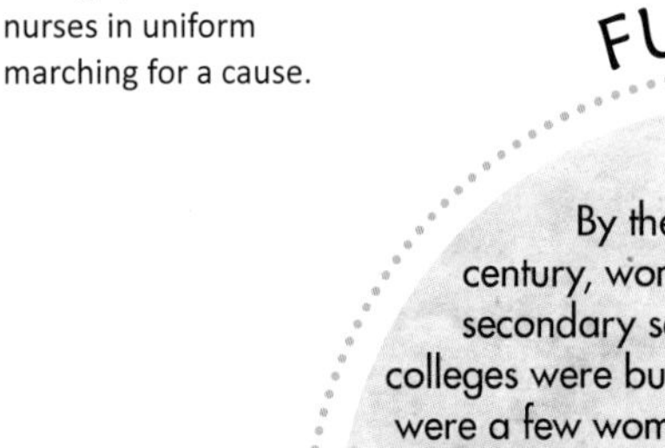

Vintage photo of nurses in uniform marching for a cause.

FUN FACT

By the late nineteenth century, women began enrolling in secondary schools. Many women's colleges were built. Despite resistance, there were a few women who studied to become doctors and lawyers. Europe also saw a larger number of women working in the service sector as nurses, telephone operators and teachers.

Annual assembly of the Dupont printing workers in Clichy, France.

The agitations pick up

In 1892, over 200 workers started agitations in France. By 1904, more than four lakh workers conducted strikes. These agitations and strikes were also seen in Britain and Germany. The British Trades Union Congress across Europe came forward to revolt against the system. The French and Italian general confederations of labour held similar protests. France saw the formation of a unique alternative syndicalist ideology. Organisations, both new and old, now tried to make conditions friendlier for their workers.

There were some differences between the First and Second Industrial Revolution. There was a direct effect on wages and standards of living.
The geographical focus of the revolution shifted from Britain to other parts of the Western world.
The relation between knowledge of nature and how it affected technological practices irreversibly changed the way technological changes occurred.

FUN FACT

Did you know that the modern Bicycle was invented in the second Industrial Revolution by Harry John Lawson? John Kemp Starley introduced the first safety bicycle a few years later.

Socio-economic impacts

There was rapid economic growth between the period of 1870 and 1890. The prices of goods were lower than ever due to the techniques of mass production being used. The standard of living improved all round. However, the flipside was that the machines replaced human labourers which created large-scale unemployment. Farmers who failed to produce enough crops, did not have to worry about food shortage as food could be quickly imported from other places. Many public health initiatives came into place so that health and sanitation improved all round. The London Sewage System was constructed in the 1860s.

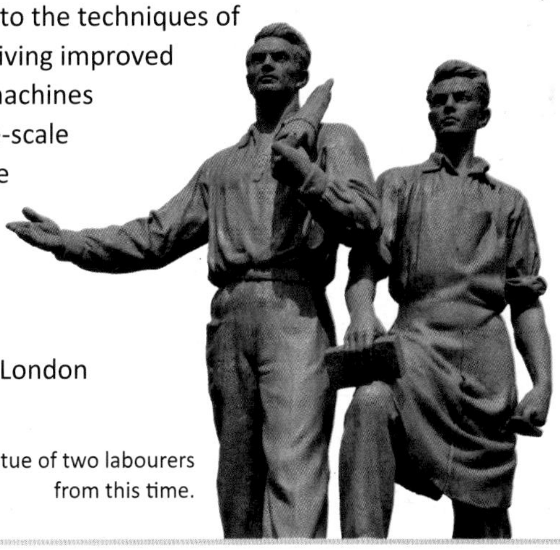

A statue of two labourers from this time.

Workers' resistance poster (hands holding hammer and sickle).

People and agitations

Industrialisation had taken its toll on people, where a lot of them began to blame machines for loss of jobs. Labour unions became the most effective means to stand up against manufacturers. Unions or organisations of workers came together to bargain with an employer for better wages, lesser working hours and better working conditions. At the time, a large group of workers had a better chance of having their demands met than a single person standing against the manufacturer or owner. Business owners disliked unions and their demands as most of them meant an increase in costs and less profits. They opposed the unions. They fired workers who became part of unions and banned them in their factories.

Vintage photo of workers at an oil rig.

Eastern Europe

The term "Balkans" refers to the huge peninsula between the four seas—Black, Mediterranean, Adriatic and Aegean, which run through Greece, Serbia, Bulgaria, Macedonia and Bosnia. The Balkans, with its limited resources, became a region that big empires like Ottoman, Russia and Austro-Hungaria were interested in, for its strategic location close to the waterways.

Political map of the central Balkans formed by Albania, Bosnia and Herzegovina, Serbia, Kosovo, Montenegro and Macedonia. The map includes capitals, cities, national borders, lakes and rivers.

A poster of the Serbian Relief Committee of America.

Change in Eastern Europe

Late nineteenth century nations like Greece, Serbia, Montenegro and Bulgaria freed themselves from the Ottoman rule. Other European nations like England, Britain, France, Germany and Russia showed interest in the region. Russia wanted to expand its territory into the Balkans and wanted to take control of the Bosporus, which gave access to the Mediterranean Sea.

Western powers struggle to acquire the Balkans

Many Balkan nations, under Russia's insistence, became party to a military alliance known as the Balkan League. It was an alliance consisting of the states of Bulgaria, Serbia, Greece and Montenegro which had fought the First Balkan War together against the Turkish Ottoman Empire. The league was formed to keep the Austrian authority in check at Russia's insistence. This league was created due to Russia's growing fear of the ever-expanding Austrian territory and the spread of the Ottoman Empire. The league was looking at completely removing the Ottomans out of Europe.

Declaration of war

The Balkan League declared war against the Ottomans in 1912. They were successful in ousting the Ottomans from this territory. In June 1913, Greeks, Serbians and Romanians together defeated Bulgaria's attempt in wanting to win some part of the Balkan territory. Bulgaria was penalised under the Treaty of Bucharest. Even as the league succeeded in its attempt to defeat Bulgaria, its members had disagreements over the territorial division of Macedonia after the war.

FUN FACT

Did you know that Montenegro was left devastated after the first and second Balkan Wars but still entered WWI? However, they entered WWI in a politically and militarily devastated state.

An ancient tower and lighthouse in the Straageit of Bosporus.

The Foreign Policy by the Western European Powers

Serbia won both Balkan Wars and the size of the nation increased with the acquirement of Kosovo and some parts of Albania and Macedonia. This made the bigger powers sit up and take note, and review their foreign policy.

Serbian nationalism

Serbs had settled around the Balkan Peninsula during the sixth and seventh centuries. They adopted Christianity in the ninth century. Around 1166, Stefan Nemanja, a Serbian warrior and chief, became the founder of the Serbian state. In the fourteenth century, the Serbian state came under the rule of Stefan Dusan and emerged as a powerful state in the Balkans. However, the battle of Kosovo of 1389 ensured that the state became a part of the expanding Ottoman Empire. In the nineteenth century, the state saw many struggles for freedom from the Ottomans. Many Serb nationalist groups were formed around the 1900s.

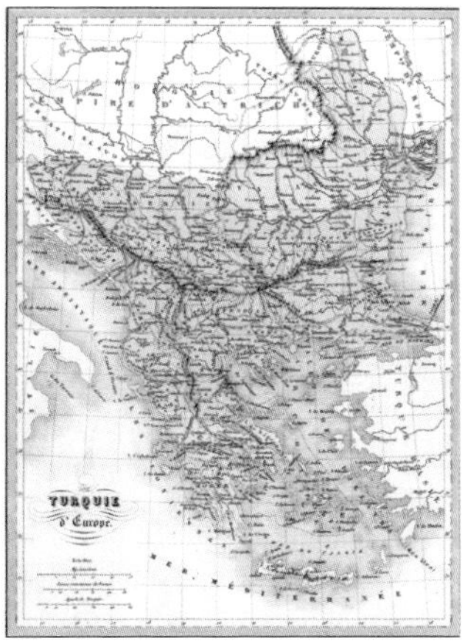

Map of Greece and the Balkans 1860.

The objective of these nationalist groups was to free Serbia from any external control and set up a national government as an independent state. The nationalist movements got more fervour owing to the annexation of Bosnia and Herzegovina.

Serbian defence

Austria–Hungary controlled Bosnia and Herzegovina while Turkey controlled Old Serbia and Macedonia. The Serb nationalists thought of these territories as theirs. They believed that Belgrade had the right to control all the territories, not Vienna or Constantinople. In Old Serbia and Macedonia, volunteers from Serbia fought alongside the Serbs from the two regions who were in conflict with Bulgarians. In 1870, Bulgarians had been given effective authority over the two regions. Serbia even created a secret organisation called "Serbian Defence" which sent trained volunteers to help the Serbian nationals. They were ultimately successful as in 1912 and 1913, both Old Serbia and Macedonia were returned to Serbia after the Bulgarians had been defeated.

1912: The Balkan League declares war

1913: Bulgaria is defeated by the Serbs

FUN FACT

Zindan Gate is the middle south eastern gate of the Belgrad Fortresss. It lies between two round towers. The Ottoman Empire used the towers' basement as a dungeon.

The Zindan Gate.

Crimean War

A map showing the crisis in Ukraine, the pro-Russian protests in the east, the riots reported in Kharkiv, Luhansk, Sloviansk, Donetsk and Mariupol.

The Crimean War took place between 1853 and 1856. It got its name from the Crimean Peninsula on which it was fought. The Crimean Peninsula is located to the south of Ukraine near the Black Sea. Britain, France, Sardinia and the Ottoman Empire defeated Russia in this war. The primary reason for the war was to settle the conflict between the Middle Eastern powers. These conflicts were caused by the demands of the Russian leaders and nationals to control the orthodox subjects of the Ottoman Sultan. The dispute between Russia and France grew due to the privileges of the Russian orthodox and Roman Catholic churches in the holy places in Palestine.

Expansionist Russia

There was unrest for many years up until the Congress of Vienna came into power, which brought some much needed peace to Europe. For around 40 years there was peace. Then all of the conflicts lead to the Crimean War. It all began when Russia, who wanted to control the Black sea ports, first conquered the Ukrainian Cossacks and then the Crimean Tatars. This brought them in direct confrontation with the Ottoman Turks.

Escalating tensions

Russia regarded itself as one of the guardians of orthodox Christians. It viewed the Ottoman Empire, as Tsar Nicholas I had put it, "as the sick man of Europe", because of the slowly declining territorial boundaries and finances in the continent.

France was interested in enforcing Catholicism on the holy places in Palestine, which escalated tensions between Russia and France.

An old illustration of a commemorative medal of the battle of Alma, the first battle fought in the Crimean War.

Austria joins Britain and France as allies

The Crimean War was fought from 1853 to 1856 between Russia and an alliance of Britain, France, the Ottoman Empire and Sardinia. The conflict occurred near the Crimean Peninsula on the Black Sea. When Russia invaded Danubian, to exert pressure on Constantinople and the Ottoman Empire, upset Austrians joined Britain and France. It was in October 1853 that the allies declared war on Russia.

The ruins of the Genoese Fortress in the Bay of Balaclava, Crimea.

An old illustration showing the conquest of Malakoff by the French army.

FUN FACT

During the Crimean War, the total number of fatalities exceeded 250,000 and that is where nurses like Florence Nightingale and Mary Seacole played a major role. They nursed and cared for the wounded soldiers of the war.

Control of the Baltic Sea

Britain and France gave an ultimatum to Russia asking to stop the conflict with the Ottoman Empire. But Russia did not budge. In 1854, the Anglo-French fleet took control of the Baltic Sea with their modern metal ships. They demolished the Bomarsund fortress to the north. The allies crossed the Black Sea and entered Crimea. It took a year for them to seize the naval base at Sevastopol and tear down the fleet and dockyard. At the battle of Alma, the British and French managed to defeat the Russian army at Sevastopol, but could not take advantage of this situation. At the Battle of Balaclava, the legendary "Charge of the Light Brigade" took place where both sides suffered many casualties. In 1856, the nations met at the Congress of Paris where the Treaty of Paris finally ended the Crimean War.

Modern nursing methods

Both sides lost many soldiers during the Crimean War. Nearly 16,50,000 soldiers lost their lives. Many of these soldiers died from diseases rather than wounds acquired during the war. This was because they faced horrible living conditions that exposed them to disease-carrying germs and surroundings. Florence Nightingale not only helped the soldiers and treated them, but also brought the attention of world leaders to their plight.

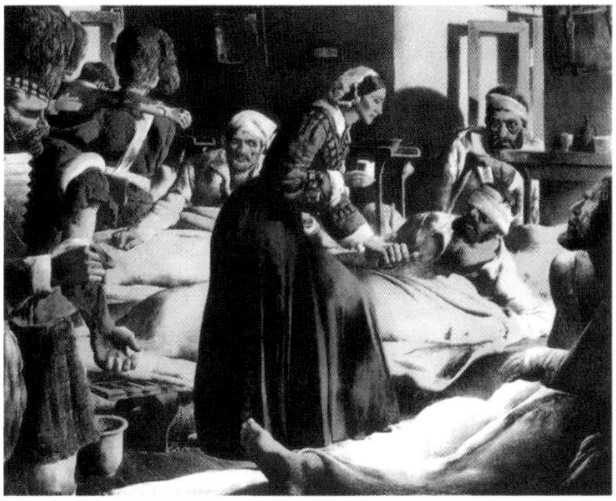

Florence Nightingale treating soldiers at Scutari, a suburb of Istanbul, in the Crimean War.

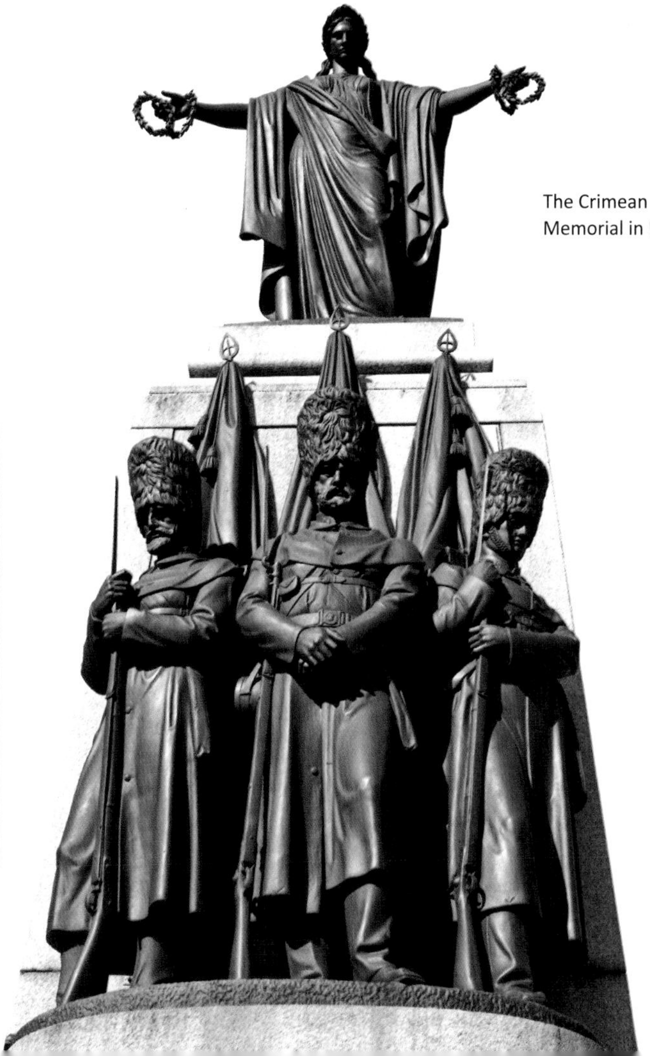

The Crimean War Memorial in London.

End of the Nineteenth Century

The Industrial Revolution changed lives and the way of living in England, Europe and North America. Life was slowly changing for men as well as for women. By the late nineteenth century, 80 percent of the population was from the working class. Many women joined the working class. When they were old enough, they married and had children.

A horse drawn float declares National American Woman Suffrage Association's support for the Bristow-Mondell Resolution drafted by Susan B. Anthony in 1874.

Education of women

Women on a phone bank.

Many things changed for women in the nineteenth century. New laws were introduced which banned women and children (under 10) from working underground. Also, the Factory Act stated that women and children were not to work more than 10 hours a day in textile factories. Another law stated that women were not allowed to work in factories for more than 56 hours a week. In the nineteenth century, women received sufficient education and joined the working class.

Women's Rights National Historical Park statues.

Empowerment of women

Divorce was made legal by 1857. However, women were still unable to file for divorce without facing judgment from society. Women were employed in secretarial positions where they learned how to use the typewriter, the telephone and the intercom. Life became much more comfortable for women during the nineteenth century. In 1884, Wimbledon allowed women to play in the matches for the first time. Women steadily gained more rights in the nineteenth century. In 1849, an American woman named Elizabeth Blackwell became the first woman to gain a medical degree. In 1869, Britain allowed women to vote in the local elections. New Zealand was the first country to allow women to vote in the national elections. Susan B. Anthony and Elizabeth Cady Stanton led the campaign for women's rights in America in the nineteenth century.

Susan B. Anthony American civil rights leader.

Twentieth Century

1901–2000

The world history saw many inspiring inventions, movements and changes in the twentieth century. The field of medicine expanded so that treatment was available for many more diseases and ailments. As a result, the average life expectancy increased by 30 years. Trains became the fastest means of travel. The Wright brothers' flight also opened a whole new avenue for the future. The Lumiere brothers invented colour photography in the 1900s and around this time Edison invented the light bulb.

The twentieth century brought about technological, medical, social and international innovations, but this also led to war and genocide. Increased mechanisation and enhanced global communication were the hallmarks of the twentieth century.

While England focussed on coal, iron and textiles industries at the start of this period, she later moved on to the service industries. Around 15 per cent of her population was poor. During this time, it is estimated that nearly 1,106,000 people died in the wars of England.

Germany's Rapid Industrial Surge

The beginning of the twentieth century saw Germany working on a large navy fleet. Germany was steadily growing as an imperialist power and this made France suspicious and wary as she was on the lookout to acquire more states. Germany did not renew its alliance with Russia. Russia joined Germany and France, forming an unlikely alliance.

Nine men in suits dwarfed by two massive dynamos (electric generators) in a factory.

The Steamship Russian MNCCYPN.

In Britain's footsteps

By 1850, Belgium, France and Germany had begun to follow the Industrial Revolution lead from Britain. With inventions came changes and soon steam pumps and engines made their entry into Germany. The demand for mass production of iron increased and the demand for coke and coal followed.

Establishment of railways

The first German railway was setup in 1835 connecting Dresden and Leipzig. It was an overnight success. By the 1850s, Germany was well-connected. She had constructed half the amount of railway lines as Britain and twice the amount of France. The decade was called "railway mania" in Germany. Railway construction boosted the production of steel. Mechanical engineering emerged as a new field. Soon Germany became a leader in chemical and electro-technical industries.

Germany's railway network

Germany was undergoing significant changes and the most prominent among them was the rise of large-scale industries. The ones of note were textile mills and coal mines. The construction of railroads, steamships and motorable roads made transportation easier. A new section of society called "middle class" came about. This section soon sought some leverage within the political arena. With these changes, urbanisation became an important phenomenon that gained momentum in Germany post the Congress of Vienna.

Alfred Krupp

The cannon king

Towards the end of the nineteenth century, Alfred Krupp had earned himself the name "the cannon king" owing to his development of the cast-steel cannon. He was a German industrialist who manufactured various armaments and weapons for warfare. His firm, "Krupp Works", was famous for its high-quality cast steel. This firm developed with the advent and growth of the railway industries. Starting out with the manufacture of railway axles and springs, his firm later introduced seamless steel railway tires. His was one of the first firms to provide burn and accident funds to its workers.

FUN FACT

The first Krupp factory focussed on field gun manufacture. It supplied guns to many different countries.

Zollverein and the development of Germany

Zollverein was a German customs union which was formed in 1834 under Prussian leadership. Its aim was to establish a free-trade zone in Germany. This union aided in the re-unification of German territories. Zollverein was formed in order to initiate better trade flow and bring down internal competition. Most of Prussia's neighbouring countries and regions joined in the Zollverein. However, Hamburg and Bremen (protected regions of Austria) were excluded from this pact. This led to the Austro-Prussian conflict.

Leaders of industry

With industrialists like Alfred Krupp and inventors like Ernest Werner von Siemens, Germany was able to gain great ground in wars and conflicts. The manufacture of armaments, steel and improvement of railway networks benefitted the people of Germany. With Siemens' invention of the electric generator, Germany became a leader in the electrical industry. The design of electric machines greatly benefitted from this invention. Previous designs were ignored and designs from Siemens were given importance. He produced about 50 such devices for the Bavarian railways.

Ernest Werner von Siemens.

Leaders of communication

Siemens also laid underground telegraph lines for the army. He set up the firm "Telegraphenbauanstalt Siemens and Halske" which specialised in telegraphic projects. He became the pioneer of the electric industry. His work brought about enormous technological advancement. He earned many awards for his great achievements in science and technology. He also expanded the scope of electrical engineering and was named the founding father of electrical engineering in Germany. In 1880, he was credited to designing the first electric elevator. Carl Siemens established telegraph factories in London, Vienna and Paris. He was also in charge of establishing telegraph cables across the Mediterranean Sea right up to India.

In the early-twentieth century, the cannon became one of the most useful and necessary weapons of war.

1882 poster for the railroad shows passengers waiting for their train.

Russo-Japanese War in 1904–1905

Defence of Port Arthur (Lushun, China) in Russo-Japanese War.

Both Russia and Japan were looking to gain control of Manchuria and Korea. Japan resented the fact that a European power wanted to gain control over Asian territories. With this war, it wanted to put an end to Russia's expansionist policy in the Far East. It became the first Asian power to have defeated a European power.

1904: Japan declares war on Russia

1905: Russia signs the Treaty of Portsmouth with Japan

Russia's expansionist policies

Russia was seeking a port that could be operational all year round. The port of Vladivostok, which they controlled, was only operational during the summer. Russia turned to Port Arthur along China, but faced opposition from Japan as this port was controlled by the Japanese government. Japan was displeased by Russia's ambition to control Korea and Manchuria. Both countries held negotiations. Confident of victory, Russia was not very willing to accept points laid across by the Japanese government. Hence, when Japan decided to drop their interests in Manchuria in return for Russia's cooperation and support for their own acquisition of Korea, Russia refused.

The Russo-Japanese War started in early 1904 when the Japanese attacked the Russian naval fleet at Port Arthur following Russia's lack of cooperation during the negotiations. By March, they landed in Korea and soon cut-off the fleet from the mainland. The Russians received reinforcements from the Trans-Siberian Railroad but eventually, Japan was more successful in crushing Russia.

FUN FACT

The war started out with 330,000 soldiers from Russia and 270,000 soldiers from Japan.

Russia, Saint Petersburg - 12th July, 2014: Russian 6-inch (152.4 mm) heavy siege gun model 1877 utilised in Russo-Japanese War, World War I, Russian Civil War at the Artillery Museum in St Petersburg.

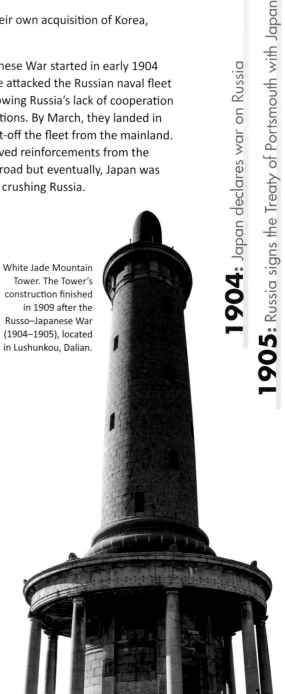

White Jade Mountain Tower. The Tower's construction finished in 1909 after the Russo–Japanese War (1904–1905), located in Lushunkou, Dalian.

The Treaty of Portsmouth

In 1905, General A. N. Kuropatkin, the Russian commander, surrendered to Japan and withdrew the troops from Mukden. The commander did not consult his superior officers while taking this decision. He surrendered despite having provisions for food and ammunition for 90 days.

Depiction of Theodore Roosevelt leading the Rough Riders in the charge at San Juan Hill, Cuba, 1898.

The final battle of Mukden

The war against Japan was greatly challenging for Russia from the very beginning. Despite Russia having a larger army, she lost the final battle of Mukden in March 1905. Over 89,000 Russian soldiers lost their lives or suffered injuries. On the Japanese side, about 71,000 soldiers were left dead or injured. In the Battle of Tsushima Japan shattered the Russian fleet which carried the relief army. Japan was nearly bankrupt due to the war by this point. Back in Russia, people were protesting against the war, which they never wanted. As a result, Japan was able to coerce Russia to enter the peace treaty with them.

Role of USA in the Treaty of Portsmouth

The US President, Theodore Roosevelt, was the mediator for the peace conference held at Portsmouth, USA in 1905. The treaty proved fruitful for Japan who gained control of Liaotung Peninsula and the South Manchurian railroad as well as half of the Sakhalin Island. Russia gave up southern Manchuria and China regained its control.

The Guard Tower in Port Arthur Historic Site.

Post treaty changes

The people of Japan had expected more from the treaty and demanded for Sakhalin along with some monetary benefit as well. Frustration among the masses led to the Hibiya riots and eventually led to the collapse of Katsura Taro's cabinet.
The Treaty of Portsmouth brought about better Russo-Japanese relations.

Postcard celebrating the signing of the Portsmouth Peace Treaty. President Theodore Roosevelt won the Nobel Peace Prize for his efforts in bringing Japan and Russia to the peace table.

The US President Theodore Roosevelt, 1905.

The Balkan Wars

The Balkan Wars were two wars which almost wiped out the power of the Ottoman Empire from Europe. They were fought between Serbia, Greece, Montenegro and Bulgaria, who were the members of the Balkan League formed by Russia in 1912. The Balkan league also wanted the territories of Albania, Macedonia and Thrace. Montenegro initiated the wars by first declaring war against Turkey in 1912.

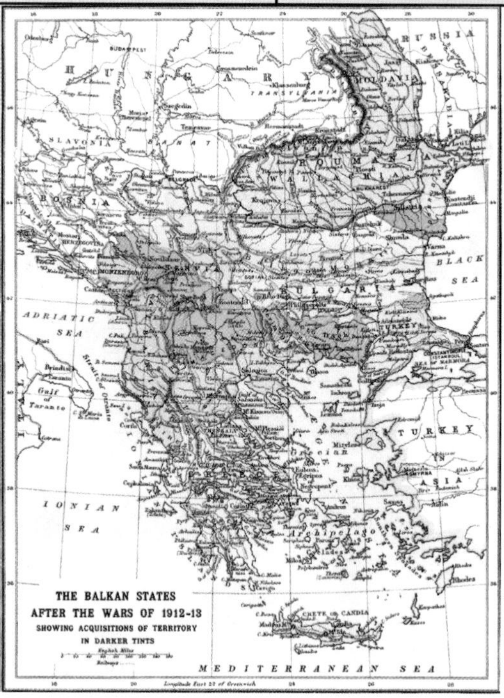

Map showing Balkan states after the wars of 1912–1913.

The first Balkan war

The Ottomans decided to strike before the Balkan League formed more allies. So, they declared war against the Balkan League on 17th October, 1912. The Bulgarian army managed to seize the Ottoman forests at Adrianople and defeat the Ottoman armies at Kirk Kilisse and Buni Hisar. The Serbian army reached the Adriatic coast, crushing the Ottoman defences along the way. The Greek army curbed all attempts by the Ottomans to send reinforcements from Salonika. Montenegrin armies seized Scutari, a town of Albania. Thoroughly defeated, the Ottomans signed an armistice with the Balkan League. They were left with a handful of small territories at the end of the first Balkan war as the major ones were taken by the Balkan powers.

Young Turk Movement

Austria and Italy supported Albania in declaring its independence after the fall of the Ottoman Empire. The Great Powers met at London to ensure that their interests remained untouched in the Ottoman. In 1913, a Young Turk government began protests and riots in Constantinople, determined to continue the war and bring victory, and regain their territories.

FUN FACT

The Young Turks led several political reform movements and initially started out as a secret society of students studying in the fields of military and medicine.

Tensions between Serbia, Montenegro and Austria

Negotiations between the Balkan League and the Ottomans were centered upon the division of territories. Scutari was seized by the powers. However, as the population largely consisted of Albanians, Austria demanded that it be merged with the newly independent Albania. Due to pressure from other forces, Serbia and Montenegro withdrew from the territory. In London, a peace treaty was signed between the Balkan League and the Ottomans. In this treaty, the influence of the Ottomans was limited to a strip of land in Thrace which was marked by the Aegean port of Enos to the Black Sea port of Midya.

Running through the Balkan Mountains in Bulgaria is the scenic Shipka Pass. Shipka Memorial represents the victory of Serbians over the Ottoman forces.

The second Balkan war

Serbia expressed its wish to occupy Macedonia, a territory that Bulgaria was fighting for. Greece and Serbia had shared interests in Macedonia and were struggling to remove Bulgarian ambitions. However, the fight was so hostile that even Russian efforts to mediate and bring peace failed. In 1913, Bulgarian soldiers kick-started the second Balkan war by attacking the Greek and Serbian positions in Macedonia. Greece and Serbia then formed an alliance against Bulgaria. Montenegro, being a part of the Balkan League, decided to side against Bulgaria. Greece and Serbia counter-attacked and defeated Bulgaria. On the other hand, for their own reasons, Romanian and Ottoman soldiers attacked Bulgaria. Bulgaria agreed to cease the attacks. The Treaty of Bucharest was signed where Greece and Serbia took over Macedonia while Romania acquired Dobrudzha. The Treaty of Constantinople removed Bulgarian hold from Adrinople for the Ottomans.

Statue of a Turk soldier at Gallipoli, Turkey.

Participants in the Bucharest Peace Treaty negotiations, 1913.

Growing tensions

At the end of the second Balkan war, Greece gained southern Macedonia, Serbia gained central and northern Macedonia and Bulgaria was given a small part of it. Greece also gained the Crete Island while Serbia acquired Kosovo. Albania was able to retain its independence. A defeated Bulgaria turned to Austria for support. This further angered Serbia who were forced to give up Albania due to Austrian efforts. They in turn attacked and seized Vienna.

Impact of the Balkan Wars

Both Balkan Wars created many casualties. The Bulgarian army lost around 65,000 soldiers. The Serbian army lost around 36,000 soldiers, while Montenegro and Greece together lost 12,000 soldiers. The most damage was done to the Ottoman Empire, which was completely disintegrated. They lost 125,000 people, including soldiers and civilians. These deaths were caused by war, disease and lack of resources.

Austria–Hungarian impact

Before 1913, Russia looked at Bulgaria as a valuable ally. Bulgaria became displeased with Russia's mediation in the Bulgarian–Serbian dispute. They also blamed Russia for their role in the war as well as the Bucharest Peace Treaty. As a result, Russia remained with only Serbia as an ally.

The Serbians, in turn, were displeased with the Austro–Hungarian powers as they came in the way of their acquisition of Albania. A war in Bosnia further aggravated the Serbian and Austrian tensions. As a result, the Austrians decided to enter into a war against the Serbians. The two Balkan wars and the growing tensions between the powers led to the First World War.

1912: Montenegro declares war against Turkey

1913: The Treaty of Bucharest is signed

Painting showing Bulgarians overrun the Turkish positions.

Assassination of the Austrian Archduke

Illustration showing the assassination of Archduke Franz and his wife Sophie.

The tensions in the Balkan region reached its peak with the assassination of Archduke Franz Ferdinand by a Serb in Sarajevo, Bosnia, on 28th June, 1914. A Bosnian Serb nationalist shot the Archduke Franz and his wife Sophie to death. He was on an official visit to the Bosnian capital of Sarajevo. The killings caused a severe outburst, leading to the outbreak of World War I.

Heir to the throne

Archduke Franz Ferdinand came to be the heir to the Austro–Hungarian throne after the death of his cousin. Bosnia was one of the territories controlled by the Austro–Hungarian powers. However, it wanted to be independent. Serbia worked with Bosnia so they could attain their freedom. Serbia formed an alliance with Russia, while Austria and Hungary formed one with Germany. Bosnian nationalists working for their independence saw an opportunity to make people notice their struggle when Archduke Ferdinand announced his intention to visit Sarajevo, the Bosnian capital.

Konopiste Castle, former domain of Archduke Franz Ferdinand.

The assassination

Archduke Franz Ferdinand

On 28th June, 1914 Franz Ferdinand and his wife were travelling through Sarajevo to the Town Hall. Gavrilo Princip and his associates planned to assassinate the Archduke. They first threw a bomb at his car which bounced away and exploded beneath the car that followed. Later, Franz Ferdinand and Sophie made a visit to an officer who was injured by the bomb. On the way, they were shot to death by Gavrilo Princip. It was later revealed that Princip had wanted to aim for Franz Ferdinand and General Oskar Potiorek, the military governor of Bosnia and not Sophie.

The arrest of Gavrilo Princip, assassin of Austrian Archduke Franz Ferdinand.

It was on the day of his wedding anniversary that Archduke Franz Ferdinand was killed, when he was supposed to have been inspecting the army in Sarajevo with his wife Sophie. Austrian Emperor Franz Josef had prohibited him to appear in public with his wife, especially on state occasions as Sophie was a commoner.

WORLD WAR I

1914–1918

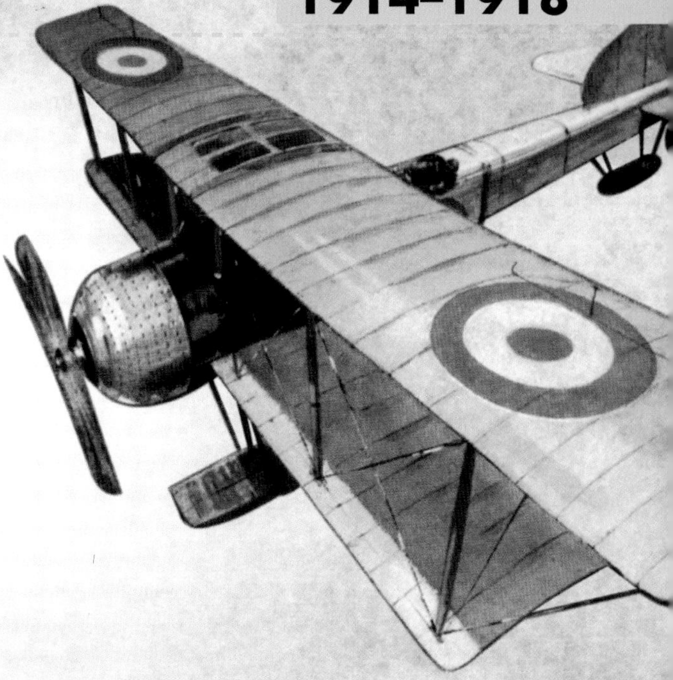

The Austro-Hungarian Empire was ruled by the Hapsburg dynasty. Serbia, a country south of the Austria–Hungary border, was an ally of the Russia Empire . The Austro-Hungarian powers were looking for an excuse to enter into a war with Serbia. The assassination of Archduke Ferdinand was looked upon as a personal offence and as an attack made to the entire country. It was soon believed that Serbia was behind the attack, even if it was the work of Serbian nationalists acting independently. The Austro-Hungarian powers declared an unreasonable ultimatum to Serbia. They agreed to most of the points but refused two: that unnamed Serbian officials should be dismissed as per the request of Austro-Hungarian military and that there should be Austro-Hungarian participation in movements against them in the Serbian soil.

An event that had begun as a local European war soon gathered momentum and became a global war that extended for four long years from 1914 to 1918. World War I became the first war wherein 28 nation states from around the world were involved. It was no wonder then that it gained the name The Great War or the war to end all wars.

World War I: The Beginning

The immediate cause of World War I was the assassination of Franz Ferdinand, the archduke of Austria-Hungary in Sarajevo,Bosnia. His death at the hands of Gavrilo Princip – a Serbian nationalist with ties to the secretive military group known as the Black Hand – propelled the major European military powers towards war. Tensions spiralled in the Balkan region and led to different nation states taking different sides. Austria-Hungary declared war on Serbia, Russia supported Serbia, and Germany joined Austria and Hungary. France allied with Russia and so Germany declared war on France as it wanted to acquire France. Thus began the first World War in 1914 which revealed the imperialist tendencies of the nations involved.

Austria-Hungary asserts its authority

Post the assassination of Archduke Ferdinand, Austria-Hungary wanted to assert its authority in Europe. Russia intervened and offered support to Serbia. This made Austria reach out for Germany's support. Emperor Franz Josef wrote a letter to Kaiser Wilhelm. German Chancellor Theobald Hollweg offered unconditional support to Austria.

Serbia refuses Austria-Hungary's conditions

The Austro-Hungarian ambassador forwarded the region's demands to Serbia on taking steps to eliminate terrorist organisations within its borders and contain anti-Austrian propaganda. It also included an Austrian-Hungary autonomous enquiry into Franz Ferdinand's assassination. The message also indicated that Serbia should be ready to face military action in case the conditions laid down by Austria could not be met. Serbia rejected these difficult demands and urged Russia to come to their assistance against Austria.

FUN FACT

During the World War I, many soldiers suffered injuries and shrapnel wounds to the face. Harold Gillies, a pioneer in the field of plastic surgery made dedicated attempts to improve and develop the procedure of facial reconstruction.

A French military helmet donated by the French Republic to the solders of Serbian army during World War I.

French helmet of World War I.

German army advancing on the Russian Steppes in World War I.

Old engraving of 16th century of King Henri III of France in Polish costume.

Austrian atrocities in Serbia. A long line of blindfolded and kneeling Serbian men near the Austrian lines were ruthlessly shot on command. One in five Serbians died during the World War I.

World War I commences

On 29th July, Austro-Hungarian military started bombarding Belgrade. Russia asked for partial mobilisation (assembling at the war zone and preparing supplies) against Austria-Hungary. The war was to take place at the Russian frontier, even though Germany hoped for it to move to the Balkans. They requested France to take a neutral stand in the war and Russia to halt mobilisation. When France and Russia ignored the request, Germany declared war against Russia and France.

Impact of World War I

World War I soon involved many other nations including Italy, Japan and nations of the Middle East. USA also joined in the World War I and had many casualties with the death of around 20 million soldiers and an equal number of wounded people.

Technological destruction

With World War I, the world was able to witness the destructive side of technology. Nations fell and new nations were born. New boundaries and maps were made. While some prospered in the aftermath, others had to bear the brunt of terrible economic crises.

Effects of World War I on Germany

Germany particularly suffered following the war since under the Treaty of Versailles, it had to pay heavy reparations to the Allies. It did not help that the country was itself facing severe economic depression. Unemployment and inflation were at its highest and its currency, the Reichsmarks, was devalued to a large extent. World War I changed many things even socially. It created an impact on culture, literature and had far-reaching political, economic and diverse social effects. By mid-1920 after the American stock market crash, the world suffered from the Great Depression, which affected Germany on a large scale.

Soldiers firing a French 37 mm artillery gun in second-line trench. This World War I cannon had a maximum range of a mile and a half. Dieffmatten, Germany. 26th June, 1918.

1914: World War I begins

1918: End of World War I

FUN FACT

In USA, World War I was at an all-time high, where everything German was looked upon with suspicion. Even German food names were changed. For instance, frankfurters were re-named to hot dogs.

Central Powers vs Allied Forces

Czar Nicholas II and French General Joffre at Joint Maneuvers in August 1913. The Triple Entente allies threatened Germany with a two front war in the tense years before World War I.

Germany, Austria-Hungary and Turkey formed the Central Powers and opposing them were the Allied Forces comprised of Britain, France and Russia. The other nations included in the Allied Forces were Portugal, Japan, Italy and finally USA. After USA entered into this alliance, it was called "Associated Powers" at the behest of Woodrow Wilson, the then President of USA.

Two sides of the World War I

Germany had the largest army and guided the Central Powers. Its military strategy was known as the Schlieffen Plan, which was basically about the central powers taking over France and Western Europe, which would then mean that Germany could focus on Eastern Europe and Russia. The Ottoman Empire got dragged into the war because of its economic ties with Germany. A military alliance was signed between Germany and the Ottoman Empire in 1914. Bulgaria joined in late, but its interests were clearly to expand its territory and invade Serbia.

Triple Entente Powers

During the late nineteenth century, Russia and Britain were rivals since both the nation states were interested in matters concerning Asia, particularly countries like Persia, Afghanistan, China and India. With Russia's defeat in the Russo-Japanese War, Britain and Russia formulated the Anglo-Russian entente of 1907. The Anglo-French Entente Cordiale of 1904, the World War I Triple Entente comprising Britain, France and Russia was established in opposition to the Triple Alliance also known as the Central Powers that comprised Germany, Austria-Hungary and Italy.

Russia was the early entrant into the war. The Russian Empire included Poland and Finland as well. USA wanted to remain neutral during World War I, but it entered the war along with the Allied powers in 1917, when it mobilised some 44 million soldiers for the war.

FUN FACT

At the start of the war in 1914, all of the nations involved believed the war would end in 1914 itself. None of them imagined that the war would drag on for four long years!

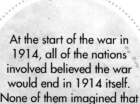

Czar Nicholas II reviewing Russian troops. When Russia entered World War I, its army was the largest, but least modern of the major European powers.

Leaders of World War I

Kaiser Wilhelm II from Germany, Emperor Franz Josef from Austria, Mehmed V the Sultan from the Ottoman Empire and Tsar Ferdinand I from Bulgaria were the main leaders of the nations fighting from the Central Powers. The Allied Forces had leaders like French Prime Minister Georges Clemenceau, British Prime Minister David Lloyd George, King George V of Britain and US President Woodrow Wilson. Nicholas II, the last Tsar of Russia, the titular King of Poland and the Grand Duke of Finland was also an Allied leader. The other leaders included Count Karl von Stürgkh, the minister-president of Austria, Count István Tisza, the minister-president of Austro-Hungary, Sultan Mehmed V the sultan and caliph of the Ottoman Empire.

Kaiser Wilhelm II, Hohenzollern Bridge, Cologne

Bust of the Emperor Franz Josef I

Tsar Nicholas II

President Woodrow Wilson

General Ferdinand Foch

A statue of former French Prime Minister George Benjamin Clemenceau.

Clemenceau's quote about the war

It is said that Clemenceau reinstated France's self-confidence when he famously said, "The Germans may take Paris, but that will not prevent me from going on with the war. We will fight on the Loire, we will fight on the Garonne and we will fight even on the Pyrenees. And if at last we are driven off the Pyrenees, we will continue the war at sea. But as for asking for peace, never!"

The Great War

In 1914, a popular magazine published the thought, "Some wars name themselves. This is one such war and it has come to be known as "The Great War" between the years of 1918 and 1939. The term "First World War" was used by Ernst Haeckel, a German philosopher who predicted that this war would be a world war involving nations from around the world, as opposed to a "European war" which only involved the European nations.

Austrian detachments holding trenches in Galicia dug await an attack from Russian troops.

1914: The Ottoman Empire enters World War I

1915: Italy ends its alliance with the Central Powers

World War I Technologies

An old machine gun on a tripod.

New weapons and artillery came to be used in World War I. Almost all the nations involved began to train their armies in the new weapons and warfare techniques. Germany especially focussed on training its soldiers to the newer techniques for a guaranteed victory.

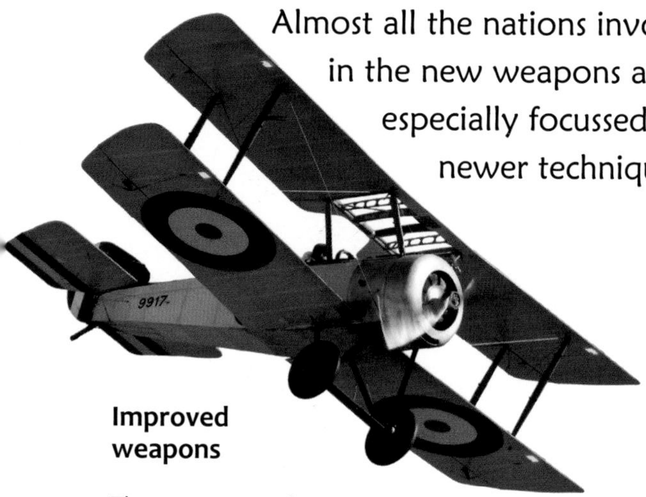

Improved weapons

The weapons and technologies available to the Allies and the Central Power were more sophisticated and powerful than those available even during the previous Balkan Wars. This influenced planning and warfare conduct. The machine gun and the rapid-fire artillery gun, developed between the 1800s and the 1900s were the most important weapons in use during the beginning of the war. The rapid-fire artillery gun could fire about 600 bullets a minute and had a range of 900 m. Improved brakes also helped save time in reloading and aiming the guns.

German's plan

Alfred Graf von Schlieffen was the chief of the German General staff. Under his leadership, the German troops decided to avoid frontal attacks. Instead, they looked at using machine guns, fortifications and barbed wires. Schlieffen was of the view that Germany should focus on western France as this was a crucial area which could make entry into other territories difficult.

Technological advantages in warfare

An army that was able to use machine guns, rapid-fire artillery guns, barbed wires, brakes and trenches in their strategy had an advantage over the other side as such a strategy could blow away their frontal attacks as these were made by cavalry or infantry. Tanks were another major advantage of the war.

1900s: Introduction of machine guns

1914: Germany trains its soldiers on new technologies

Troops ride on World War I tanks going forward to the battle line in the Forest of Argonne, France.

World War I Artillery

Old engraving depicting Gatling Machine Gun.

The World War I artillery was used against the trench warfare. Artillery became one of the most important requirements on a battlefield. In fact, during World War I, the artillery used around the world improved greatly to produce guns that shot more bullets in less time and spread to a farther range. Hence, trench warfare became unsafe and unreliable as the soldiers in trenches were left open to attacks.

Artillery barrages

An artillery barrage was a means to distract the enemy forces. Here, an artillery barrage would be used before an enemy infantry to distract them from the place of attack. This would reduce the number of troops on the enemy side so that by the time of the attack, there would be fewer troops to fight. Germany made use of mortars as they could shoot at an angle of more than 45 degrees, which meant it could land in the enemy trench before exploding.

Use of poison gas and the U-boat

Germany first used poisonous gases in the Battle of Second Ypres in 1915. It became a significant psychological weapon during World War I. The first military submarine, or U-boat, was put to use during the American Revolution. Submarines made a great impact during this time with Germany launching fleets of U-boats. These U-boats attacked ships with torpedoes causing heavy losses for the allies.

The main targets of the U-boats were the merchant trips that were involved in bringing supplies from USA into Europe.

World War 1 RMS Lusitania, off Kinsale Head, Ireland, as a second torpedo hits 7th May, 1915.

Along with trench warfare, infantry warfare was also slowly being countered by the modern-day weapons available to the troops. Infantry support guns were invented as a response. These weapons were introduced as a means to effectively increase the firepower of infantry guns. They were used by the commanding officer in order to increase response of the unit. They were light and easily managed on the battlefield. Field artillery was also greatly improved during the First World War.

Submariners hoisting a torpedo during World War I.

A gas mask was first used by soldiers when the poisonous gas was first used as a weapon in the Battle of Ypres in 1915.

FUN FACT

The term U-boat came from the German word **Unterseeboot** or undersea boat. Winston Churchill famously called the U-boat the "dastardly villains who sink our ships!"

Strategy of the Western Allies

German infantry advancing during manoeuvres.

France decided to take on the offensive strategy and attack Germany before it was completely ready for it. Hence, General J Joffre, the chief of General Staff came up with the Plan XVII. This was a mobilisation plan. But it underrated the German force and wrongly undervalued the German army deployment thinking that the Germans would deploy only 68 infantry divisions, when in reality the Germans actually deployed 83 infantry divisions.

Plan XVII

According to Plan XVII, the French would attack from different places and await the response of the German troops. They would defend themselves and continue to resist the attack until their ally Russia could join and support their side of the attacks. The plan included the segregation of troops in different regions. The first army was supposed to have attacked from Alsace, while the second army would attack the German troops in Lorraine.

Attack via Belgium

Joseph Joffre, one of the men behind Plan XVII, did not take into the account the possibility of a German invasion of France via Belgium. They realised this only some time before the declaration of the war but it was too late to re-strategise. The French believed that Germany would want to avoid British involvement. So they believed that Germany would not invade via Belgium, especially since Britain had a neutrality treaty with Belgium at the time. Even after the French were able to correctly estimate the German armies' strength, they lacked faith in their own troops.

Defeat of the French armies

The attack of the German troops in Alsace-Lorraine by the French failed miserably. There were heavy losses caused by miscalculation and lack of proper available weapons. The same was the case in Belgium where the preparedness and available artillery for warfare was lesser than in Lorraine. The French suffered massive losses and were pushed back to their starting points. Germany managed to move into Belgium and the northern part of France to a point only a few kilometres from Paris. However, they were unable to do much here as by this point the German troops were losing their supplies and feeling fatigued.

Helmuth von Moltke the Younger led the Marne Campaign for the Germans.

FUN FACT

The First Battle of Marne was fought once the retreating French troops reached their destination and received reinforcements from the French and British armies.

World War I Germans medal Iron Cross.

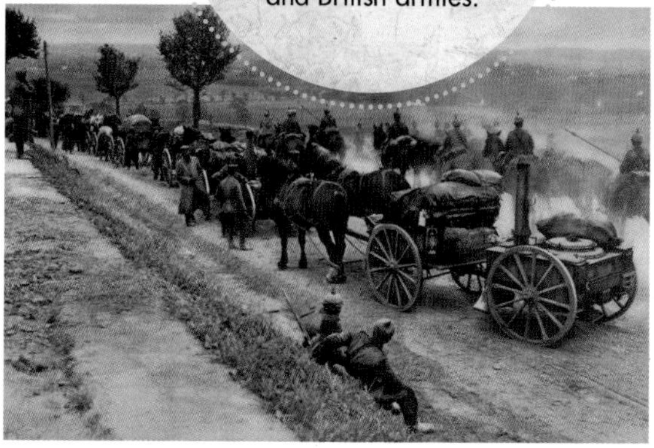

German invaders of Belgium came in long trains of supplies, such as these horse-drawn field kitchens.

The German Invasion

The Germans had to work towards reducing the effect of the Liege Fortress which protected Belgium. German troops crossed the frontier into Belgium and later Brussels with their 420 mm siege guns.

Battle of the Frontiers

The Frontier battles were fought on the French-German border in Alsace-Lorraine and the French-Belgian border in north-eastern France. Seven Imperial German Army contingents moved towards the west as per a carefully laid out plan, under Germany's tactical Schlieffen Plan. The Germans did not foresee such stiff resistance from the Belgian and French troops. The French plan was to have an offensive operation on Germany's eastern border and also on the north-eastern Franco-Belgian border of the Ardennes region. At the declaration of war between Germany and France, the French army moved towards both directions to battle the German troops. There were four major battles in the Battles of the Frontiers. They included, the Battle of Lorraine, the Battle of the Ardennes, the Battle of Charleroi and the Battle of Mons.

Charge of the "Ninth Lancers" during the "Great Retreat" from Mons to Cambrai attacking a German battery of 11 guns.

The largest battle

The Battle of the Frontiers was the largest battle of the war. At the time, it was declared the largest battle of human history as more than two million soldiers were involved in the battle. The German imperial princes commanded armies in Lorraine. Crown Prince Rupert of Bavaria sent his sixth army as a counter-attack before the French advance was successful. Crown Prince William of Germany also sent his army.

Heavily armed German soldiers advancing in Belgium.

The impact of the battle

The Battle of the Marne was the very large and visible wound caused by the offensive attacks and counter-attacks taken on by both nations. The Germans deployed about 50 per cent more troops than the French. Joffre's Plan XVII collapsed, but he quickly came up with a new plan and stationed a newly created sixth army to the north of Paris. Germans moved away from the original plan by Schlieffen due to Moltke's indecisiveness and also bad communication between his headquarters and field army commanders. It is said that Moltke can be blamed for Germany's losses.

German soldiers strain to move a huge siege gun into an attack position. The massive gun was designed shortly before World War I, to defeat the strongest fortifications such as those at Liege, Belgium.

Battle of Marne

The first Battle of Marne started in September 1914. It was started by the French army and the British Forces against the Germans, who had occupied Belgium and were very close to invading Paris. Within a few weeks, it seemed as if the German Schlieffen plan was falling apart and it had faced great resistance from Belgium.

FUN FACT

The Parisian taxis used to help move troops quickly around the battlefield came to be known as "taxis of the Marne". They were seen as an icon of France's determination to win the war.

French troops equipped for battle at a train station possibly during the Battle of the Marne.

How the battle was fought?

Belgium had managed to get more soldiers contrary to the German expectations. Germany needed to mobilise more men immediately, which they failed to do, while Russia managed to get together more men. This is why the battle of Marne was fought near the River Marne. It is believed that Moltke, distracted by the losses at the site of the German offensive in Lorrain had not issued orders to the first, second and third armies deployed for the Battle of Marine. Allegedly, after the German retreat, Moltke had announced that the Germans had lost the war.

A model of the taxi of Marne.

Exhausted troops

After the outbreak of the war, Germans had advanced into France and the French troops were fatigued after their retreat towards the Marne River which had lasted for more than 10 days. General Joseph Joffre took a risk with a counterattack and the allies exploited certain gaps within the German troops and sent the French troops in.

The surprise attack

Some 6,000 infantrymen were transported from Paris in 600 taxis. It was the first time that automotive transport of troops had happened in the history of war. This surprise night attack resulted in German retreat.

World War I, French dragoons with captured German prisoners, Doual, France.

The 33 m tall Memorial of Mondement commemorates the French victory of the Marne as well as the soldiers who protected France.

Austria Invades Serbia

After Archduke Ferdinand's assassination, a small period of diplomatic strategy was initiated between Austria-Hungary, Germany, Russia, France and Britain. It is now known as the "July Crisis". Austria-Hungary in its quest to finish the Serbian intrusion within Bosnia gave the state a series of 10 demands of which 8 were approved by Serbia.

Austro-Hungarian soldiers by the statue of Karađorđe in Belgrade in 1915. It was destroyed by the Austro-Hungarian government.

U-14, an Austro-Hungarian submarine was launched in 1912 as the French Brumaire-class submarine. During the war, she was captured and rebuilt for service by the Austro-Hungarian Navy.

First Austrian invasion

Austro-Hungary declared war on Siberia 28th July, 1914. The first Austrian invasion of Serbia began with a very small number of troops, but was quickly thwarted by the Serbian commander, Radomir Putnik. Austrians began a second attack against the Serbs on the Drina River.

Battle of the Kolubara

The Battle of Kolubara, also known as the "Battle of Suvobor", remained one of the most important battles that were fought between the Serbian and the Austro-Hungarian armies during World War I.

Both sides wanted to capture the Serbian capital of Belgrade. Between November and December 1914, there had been some fighting that had raged on in the 200 km long stretch from Belgrade to Guča and had brought the Serbian army to a situation of complete collapse. However, they managed to take over the First Army and took over against the well-equipped Austrian army. The Austro-Hungarians captured the city and entered the capital as conquerors. Nevertheless, the battle had led to great loss of soldiers on both sides. The Serbs launched a massive counter-attack on December 2 and the unprepared Austro-Hungarians were taken aback at the quick Serbian response. By 6th December, the Austro-Hungarian defences collapsed with many soldiers abandoning their weapons and becoming Serbian prisoners. The third Austrian attack was successful to a certain extent in the Battle of the Kolubara. Serbians were forced to withdraw from Belgrade, but a Serbian counterattack took back Belgrade which forced the Austrians to retreat.

Uniforms of the Austro-Hungarian Army.

Fort Sommo used from the Austro-Hungarian army during World War I.

World War I Taken to the Seas

German U-boat's torpedo passes the stern of a British vessel

At the start of the war, USA tried to get the British and German sides to agree to the Declaration of London. Even though Germany agreed, England did not. She did not want to give up her advantage. So, the German submarines trailed the waters near England and sank the ships carrying supplies.

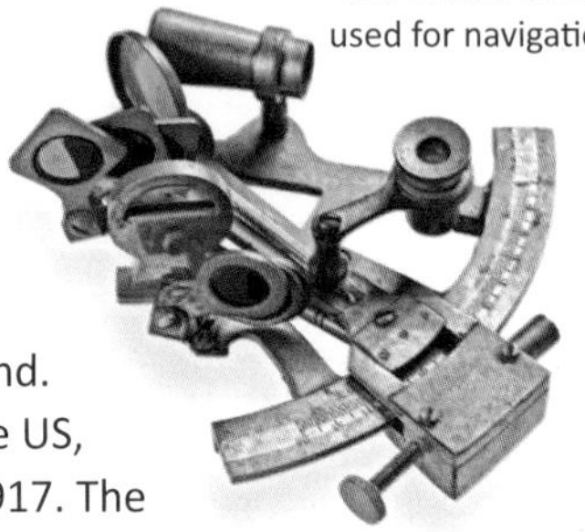
Old bronze sextant used for navigation.

Where was the war fought?

World War I was largely fought on land, but the sea was used to equip the Allies with both resources and manpower that helped them continue their armed assault. There were times when the Germans attacked British fleets. This led to great damage especially in the Battle of Jutland in 1916. This battle was also called the largest clash of battleships. Even then the Germans were unable to gain the upper hand on the seas although the successful attacks by German U-boats managed to leave some impact on the Allies. The United States joined the war owing to these attacks.

Stalking of seas

Soon the British navy began to stalk the seas to try and stop vessels from entering Germany. Both nations began to possess illegal goods from each others attacks. The USA and England then laid down stringent laws against the attacks and procedures followed by both nations.

Germany stalked areas around the North Sea. Here she could control the entry and exits of ships and submarines. At the time, USA had taken a neutral stand. Germany's high-handedness angered the US, who declared war against Germany in 1917. The reason for this was that USA aimed to safeguard the seas and uphold its rights as a neutral nation.

FUN FACT

The Declaration of London was a code of laws pertaining to maritime (sea) warfare made in 1909 at the London Naval Conference. It contained the declaration on illegal goods and nonstop voyage.

German U-boats on display.

The Submarine War of Germany

German submarines at Kiel, Schleswig-Holstein, on 17th February, 1914.

When World War I moved to the sea, Germany gained an upper hand with her use of submarines. At the beginning of World War I, 38 German U-boats attained prominent victories against British warships, but Germany wavered over using the U-boats on merchant ships because they anticipated a reaction from neutral countries like USA. However, in 1917, they went ahead with this plan and angered the US into joining the Allied forces and entering the war.

Use of U-boats during the war

The U-boats started sinking merchant ships that approached Britain or France. In 1917, the Germans sunk 430 allied and neutral ships. Towards the end of the war, Germany had built 334 U-boats and around 226 submarines were still under construction. The U-boats used by the German troops were fitted with 150 mm guns. The fortunes of the allied powers changed with the entry of the US in the war. At the time, the US was a major player in the shipping industry. Before the Great War, submarines were generally armed with self-propelled torpedoes that were used to attack enemy ships. During the Great War, the submarines were enhanced to have deck guns pre-fitted on the body of the submarines. The soldiers within the submarines would first approach the enemy merchant ships at a safe distance and signal them to stop. If the enemy ship pursued, they would be targeted and then sunk with the deck guns.

Germany lost its early advantage with this great response from the US. It is said that during the World War I, 60 U-boats were at sea at one time. World War I proved that despite their small size and robust build, the U-boats could be massive weapons of destruction as they destroyed tons of merchandise from hundreds of ships.

FUN FACT

German Chancellor Bethmann Hollweg was the one who announced Germany's decision to opt for unrestricted submarine warfare.

German sailors standing on the conning tower of a U-boat after torpedoing a British cargo ship.

Treaty of London

The Treaty of London is also referred to as the London Pact. It was a secret treaty whose main goal was to get Italy on the side of the Allied powers against Germany. The treaty was signed between the nations of the Triple Entente (Britain, France and Russia) and Italy. While Russia signed to protect Serbia, France and Italy signed to agree that they would not attack each other.

Treaty of London 1867.

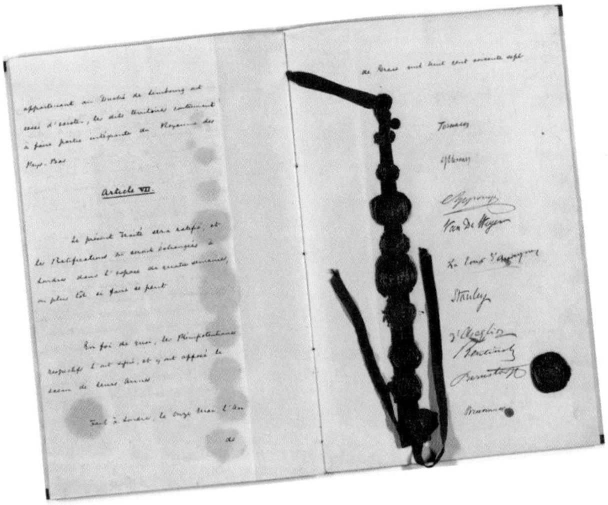

Italy's demands

The Allied forces were very eager for neutral Italy to join their side in the First World War. The main reason for this was that Italy bordered Austria. In return for their participation, Italy demanded certain territories which it was to gain if the Allied Forces won the First World War. Italy was promised the northern part of Dalmatia, Trieste and some eight more territories. So, even though most Italians wanted to remain neutral, the government of Italy decided to join the Allied forces in the war against Austria-Hungary.

Italy's additional share

In the treaty, it was also decided that Italy would gain a share in the Mediterranean region (which lies next to the Adalia province) in the event of a partition in Turkey. Italy also demanded that they be the official representatives of Albania in its relations with Foreign Powers. Italy was promised a share of war indemnity matching to its efforts and participation. Also, Great Britain was to give Italy a loan of 5,00,00,000 pounds.

Disavowal of the treaty

At the end of World War I, Britain and France refused to meet their promises which they had made in the pact. They split up the colonial territories amongst themselves which further upset Italy. In the Paris Peace Conference, USA had urged the nations against meeting the terms of the Treaty of London as it was a secret pact. It was decided here that all nations were to keep their pacts and promises public. The Treaty of London and all of its contents were revealed to the world when it was published in a Russian journal by the Bolshevik Russian State. Italy saw the refusal of Britain and France to meet the pact as a blatant betrayal.

1915: Treaty of London is signed

1918: Pact is nullified by the Treaty of Versailles

FUN FACT

In 1918, US President Woodrow Wilson announced his "Fourteen Points" which was to be a blueprint for peace. He had prepared these points after a careful and thorough inquiry with his team of 150 advisors.

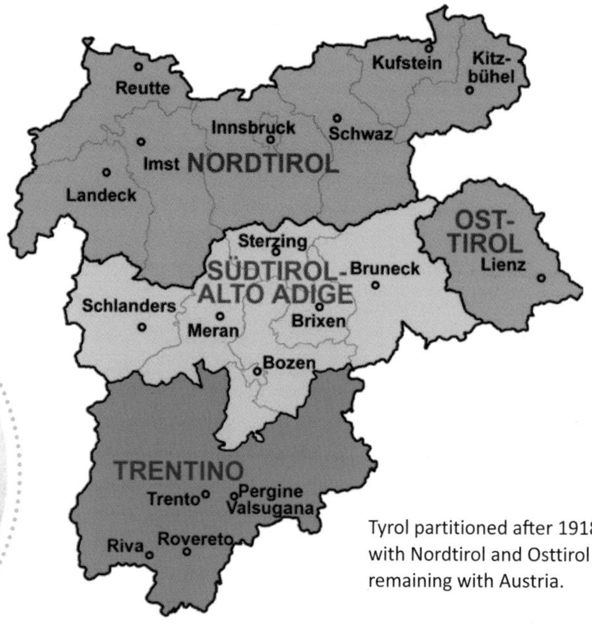

Tyrol partitioned after 1918, with Nordtirol and Osttirol remaining with Austria.

Germany Suffers Huge Losses

Togoland was a German colony in West Africa. On 5th August, 1914, Britain had declared war on Germany. Soon after, the allied parties had cut up the sea cables between Monrovia and Tenerife to weaken the radio connections between Germany and Togoland. Then, British and French troops captured and divided Togoland for themselves.

The graves of the Belgian soldiers who fought in World War I.

Operation Michael

At the start of World War I, in 1914, Amiens had been a base for the British Expeditionary Force. It was then captured by the German soldiers. The French re-captured this base. In 1918, the Germans launched a Spring Offensive called "Operation Michael". The Second Army of the Germans fought and drove away the Britain Fifth Army. On 4th April, 1918, the Germans managed to successfully capture Villers-Bretonneux, which overlooked Amiens. However, on the same night, Australian troops counter-attacked and re-captured it from the Germans. During their attempts to capture Amiens, the German troops had bombed repeatedly and created great loss to life and property. The Battle of Amiens was then launched in August, 1918 by the British Expeditionary Force. The end of this battle led to an Armistice with Germany and ended the First World War. Thus, the war ended with the German armistice and surrender to the Allies.

German prisoners in a French prison camp.

Toll of destruction

More than 40 crore soldiers from the Central and Allied forces were left injured or wounded by the war. Many of the soldiers even went missing and were never to be found again. Many civilians lost their lives as well. Many parts of the world had to be reconstructed and re-planned due to the heavy damage and destruction caused by repeated bombing and war tactics.

German economy collapses

The British navy blocked German ports, which meant that thousands of Germans were starving and the economy was collapsing. The German navy suffered a major mutiny. After Kaiser Wilhelm II abdicated on 9th November, 1918, the leaders from both sides met at Compiegne, France. The peace armistice was signed on 11th November. The Russian, Ottoman, German and Austro-Hungarian empires had collapsed because of the war.

Statue of a soldier, a World War I memorial in the town of Pleneuf, France was built to commemorate victims of World War I.

1914: German troops attack Amiens

1918: The Battle of Amiens ends World War I

US Enters World War I

The American flag.

The United States entered World War I in 1917, almost two and half years after it had started in 1914. This was because of President Wilson's policy of being neutral towards the war. However, the incident with Germany's submarines as well as the US's urge to gain world peace forced Woodrow Wilson, the Commander-in-Chief (a title earned as the President) to enter into the war and protect themselves against the attacks by the German submarines.

1917: The US joins the Great War

1918: Costa Rica and other countries support Allies

US as a moneylender

German U-boats had sunk three American merchant ships causing heavy loss of life. This was when the US declared war against Germany. The entry of the US in the war turned the tables against Germany. By 1917, the allies had exhausted their coffers by paying for essential supplies and armaments. As the US had joined the side of the Allied Forces, they made financial contributions in purchasing armaments and supplies. At this point, only the US could afford the supplies. The US made many loans to the allies from 1917 to the end of the war. These loans built up to more than seven billion dollars.

A postcard depicting Americans creeping on the Germans with hand grenades.

American Army troops parading in Scotland.

Germany as the enemy

The US also sent food to the nations and armies of the Allies. They entered the war with money and soldiers, both of which were needed desperately by all nations. The US dispatched more than 10,00,000 soldiers under the US commander General John J. Pershing. Its navy focussed on the construction of destroyers and submarine chasers to protect the allies from German U-boats. Owing to the US declaration of war against Germany, other nation states like Cuba, Panama, Haiti, Brazil, Guatemala, Nicaragua, Costa Rica and Honduras joined the war against Germany by July 1918.

Peace Move by the United States

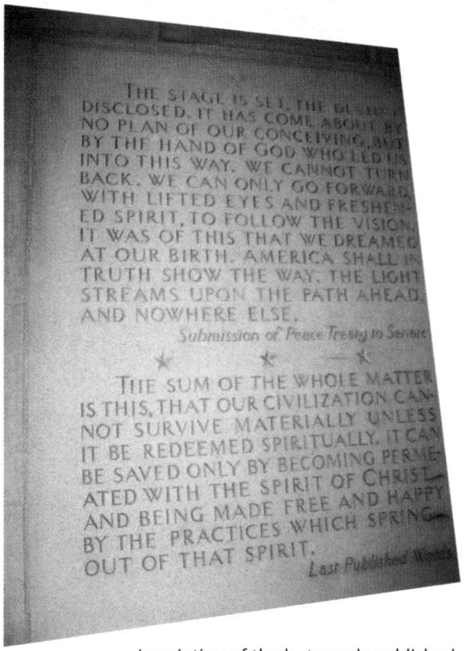

Inscription of the last words published by Woodrow Wilson on the west wall of the Wilson Bay in Washington National Cathedral.

Francis Joseph, Austria's emperor, died on 21st November, 1916. Charles I succeeded him as the new emperor. He wanted to initiate peace with the Allied and Central powers but this failed. Later, a German Reichstag member named Matthias Erzberger, tried to negotiate peace. His attempts were also met with failure. Another peace move was made in London by Lord Lansdowne, who suggested negotiations on the basis of the status quo antebellum, "the state existing before the war", but this was rejected. US President Woodrow Wilson became the spokesman of peace and came up with a plan called "Fourteen Points".

Wilson's Fourteen Points

Woodrow Wilson's Fourteen Points asked for an open declaration of peace and the abandonment of secret diplomacy. It also asked for the freedom to navigate on the high seas during the time of war and peace as well as the freedom to trade between nations. It also asked for a definite decrease of armaments, a neutral colonial resolution obliging not only the imperial powers but also the people of their colonies, the mass departure of nations from all Russian territories and respect for Russia's right to self-determination, the complete restoration of Belgium, a total German withdrawal from France, a readjustment of Italy's borders on the basis of ethnicity, an open vision of independence for the people of Austria-Hungary, restoration of Romania, Serbia and Montenegro, with access to the sea for Serbia, the prospect of autonomy for non-Turkish people of the Ottoman Empire, a sovereign Poland with access to the sea, "a general association of nations" and to guarantee the independence and integrity of all states both great and small. Wilson's peace campaign became one of the reasons that led to the fall of the German government in October 1918.

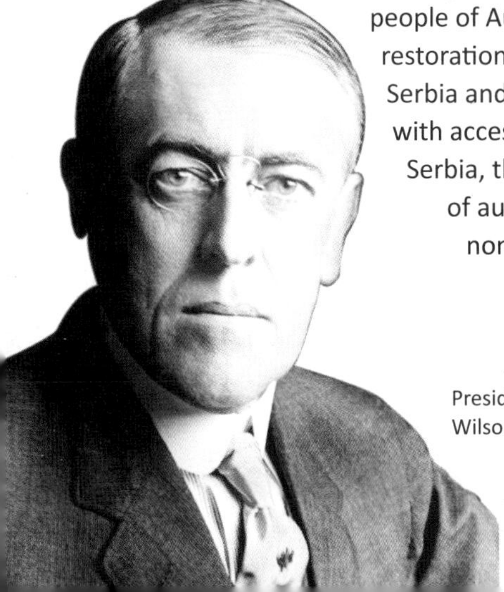

President Woodrow Wilson (1856-1924).

William Howard Taft with the newly inaugurated President Woodrow Wilson during the inauguration ceremony on 4th March, 1913.

FUN FACT

In the Fourteen Points laid down by Woodrow Wilson and his team, the first five points dealt with matters of international concern and the next eight were to do with specific border and territorial matters.

The 14-Point Declaration

President Woodrow Wilson believed in remaining peaceful and neutral. Until the incident with Germany, he was determined to maintain a neutral stand in the World War I. Once the US entered the war from the side of the Allied Forces, President Woodrow Wilson put in many resources and a lot of money to earn a victory. After the war, he returned to the peace strategy and laid down the fourteen-point plan for peace. Other members of the Allied Forces believed the plan to be too idealistic.

The 14-Point Declaration

1. Open agreement to peace, after which there shall be no private international understandings. Diplomacy must be carried out frankly and in the public view.
2. Complete freedom of navigation upon the seas during peace and war.
3. The elimination of all economic barriers and the creation of equal trade conditions among all the nations agreeable to peace.
4. Reduction of armaments in all the nations.
5. A free, unprejudiced and totally neutral adjustment of all colonial claims.
6. The evacuation of all Russian territories and the cooperation of nations towards Russia's quest to be an independent state.
7. Belgium must be evacuated and restored.
8. All French territory should be freed and the invaded portions restored.
9. Italy's borders must be readjusted as per familiar lines of nationality.
10. Austria-Hungary should be given the choice to be autonomous.
11. Romania, Serbia and Montenegro should be evacuated and Serbia should get free and secure access to the sea.
12. The Turkish portions of the present Ottoman Empire should be guaranteed safe sovereignty.
13. An independent Polish state must be put up.
14. A general union of nations must be formed under specific agreements to enable shared guarantees of political autonomy and territorial integrity for both large and small states.

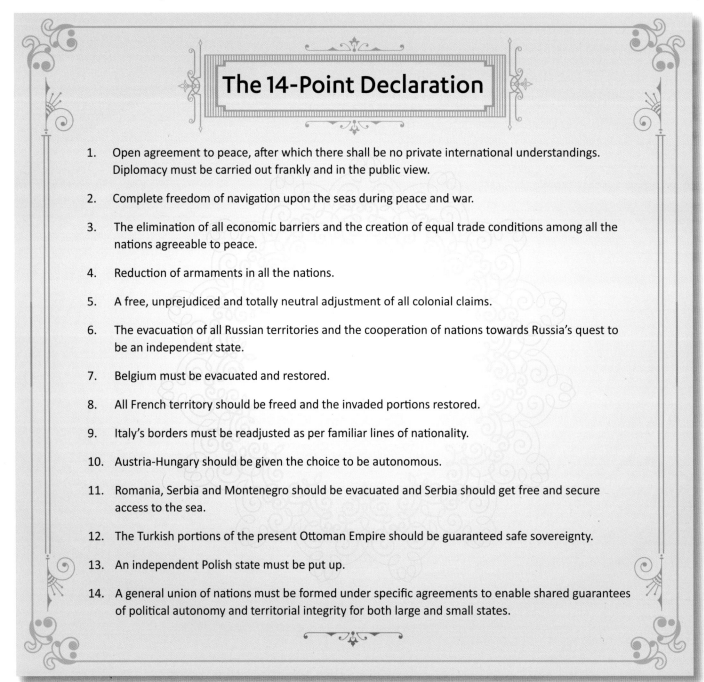

Woodrow Wilson (1856-1924) addressing the Congress in 1917.

FUN FACT

Johannes Bell, a German jurist, was one of the representatives from Germany who signed the Treaty of Versailles.

1918: Announcement of the 14-point plan

1918: Germany signs the Treaty of Versailles

Objectives of the plan

US President Woodrow Wilson had outlined the objectives of US involvement in the war in his Congress speech where he used these "Fourteen Points". His points were seen as extremely idealistic and they met with resistance in the Paris Peace Conference. But it did become the foundation for Germany's surrender in November 1918. However Wilson's administration via its diplomatic channels managed to get France and Italy's support for the Fourteen Points. This campaign was part of Woodrow Wilson's discourse that with German officials. The situation, for Germany, had gone from bad to worse and this deteriorating situation ensured that they approach the Allies for help. In 1918, when the German Chancellor Prince Maximilian of Baden, sent a note to President Wilson, requesting an immediate armistice and opening peace negotiations on the basis of the Fourteen Points.

This led to the meeting by Allied and Central Powers at Paris to discuss the Treaty of Versailles. Germany was blamed for all the destruction and devastation caused by the battles of the war. Germany felt thoroughly defeated. They were unable to defend themselves when so many powers were speaking against them. Thus, they had no other choice but to accept all the conditions put upon them by the Treaty of Versailles. They needed the help of the other powers to restore themselves as a nation.

President Woodrow Wilson (1856-1924), weakened by a severe stroke in 1919.

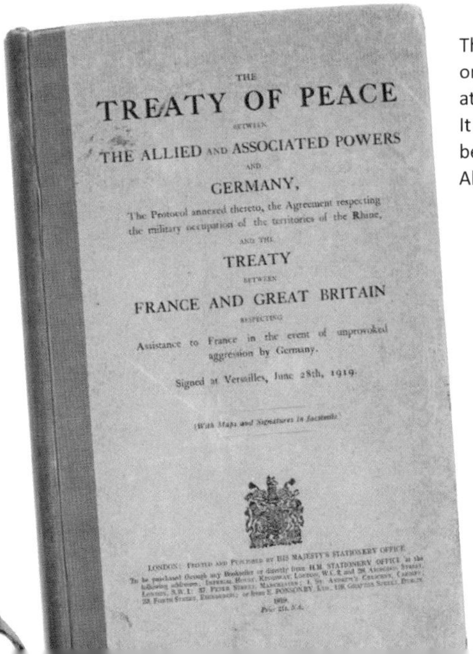

THE
TREATY OF PEACE
BETWEEN
THE ALLIED AND ASSOCIATED POWERS
AND
GERMANY,
The Protocol annexed thereto, the Agreement respecting the military occupation of the territories of the Rhine,
AND THE
TREATY
BETWEEN
FRANCE AND GREAT BRITAIN
RESPECTING
Assistance to France in the event of unprovoked aggression by Germany.
Signed at Versailles, June 28th, 1919.
(With Maps and Signatures in facsimile)
LONDON: PRINTED AND PUBLISHED BY HIS MAJESTY'S STATIONERY OFFICE.

The Treaty of Versailles was one of the peace treaties at the end of World War I. It ended the state of war between Germany and the Allied Powers.

Russian Revolution of 1917

The Russian Revolution was a movement started by the Bolshevik Party of Russia. This revolution aimed to end the Tsarist system followed in Russia and led to the formation of the Soviet Union. The Russian Empire came to an end with the abdication of Tsar Nicholas II. A temporary government was formed in February 1917 which had members of the Bolshevik Party.

Formation of a new republic

By 1916, Romania was fighting alongside Russia. By March 1917, the nationalist uproar in the Russian Empire quickly spread and there was widespread support for the efforts made by the moderate Socialist revolutionary, Aleksandr Kerensky. By April the National Moldavian Committee insisted on autonomy, land reforms and the use of the Romanian language. A move towards complete sovereignty was further pushed due to the events in Ukraine, where a council called as the "Sfat" was formed based on the model of the Kiev Rada, which proclaimed Bessarabia as an autonomous republic of the Federation of Russian Republics.

Bolshevik parade in St Petersberg during the Russian Revolution in the spring of 1917.

Military help

The Sfat appealed to the allies for military help. The Bolshevik Revolution of November 1917 put an end to the provisional government formed by the Bolshevik Party and got the Marxist Bolsheviks under the leadership of Vladimir I. Lenin came to power and put an end to Russia's contribution to the war. Acknowledging the possibility of isolation and taken aback by the affectation of the Ukrainian government, the Sfat voted for conditional union with Romania in April 1918. Reservations about the union were deserted with the defeat of the Central Powers and the creation of Greater Romania. An unconditional union was voted at the final session of the Sfat in December 1918.

A statue of Lenin.

FUN FACT

Did you know that a treaty under the Paris Peace Conference signed on 28th October, 1920 by Romania, Great Britain, France, Italy and Japan, documented the union of Bessarabia with Romania? All signatories (except Japan) finally ratified this.

Bolshevik revolution, 1917.

China Sides Up with the Allies in World War I

A bronze statue of Sun Yat-sen emplaced in the Memorial Hall in Guangzhou, China. Sun (1866-1925) was a revolutionary and political leader and the founding father of Republican China.

China soon sided up with the Allies when World War I entered its fourth year. World War I was at first limited to European nations but then began to include countries in Africa and Asia. The two competing nations, Japan and China, also had their role to play in the war. Japan was an old ally of England and had already declared war on Germany in 1914 and had captured Tsingtao, a German naval base at the Shantung Peninsula in China. After the capture of Shantung, Japan wanted direct control over Shantung, the southern parts of Manchuria and East Mongolia. It also wanted to capture the islands in the South Pacific which were under Germany's control.

Sun Yat-sen declares himself emperor

Sun Yat-sen, founder of the Kuomintang (KMT), used the anger of the Chinese people over Japan's demands and declared himself emperor. The opposition from China's military forced him to accept republican government. China declared war on Germany on 14th August 1917 to regain control over the Shantung Peninsula and to regain its power.

International delegates in the Palace des Glaces (Hall of Mirrors) during the signing of the Peace Terms ending World War I in Versailles, France.

Diplomatic meeting between the French and Chinese delegations.

The Paris Peace Conference

The Paris Peace Conference took place in January 1919 at Versailles and was called to put up the peace terms post the Great War. Although there were 30 different countries that participated, it was the United Kingdom, France, USA and Italy also known as the "Big Four" who became the dominant forces who were responsible for the formulation for the Treaty of Versailles, a treaty that ended World War I. During the Paris Peace Conference, the Allied Supreme Council backed Japan in its claim to control Shantung. This angered the Chinese leaders present in the peace conference.

World War I Takes to the Skies

While the war was fought primarily on land and sea, planes were often used to conduct survey missions. Fighting in the skies began with very minor exchanges of fire shots between these missions. It was only in 1915 that fighter aircrafts with machine guns and planned bombings of enemy air bases were initiated.

World War I aircraft in a dogfight. Britain vs Germany over the battlefields of Europe.

Planned bombing during World War I

The First World War witnessed the development of many lethal defence mechanisms and technologies including the machine gun, poison gas, flame-throwers, tanks and aircrafts. These weapons and defence technology had greater power and prowess to kill. The First World War also saw the introduction of weapons like the Big Bertha, which was a 48-tonne gun that had the capability to fire a shell over 9 km. However, it took around 200 men and many hours to assemble. Target bombing began with England's bombing of Cologne, Düsseldorf and Friedrichshafen in 1914. German aeroplanes strategically bombed Britain in the years of 1915 and 1916. England then targeted factories.

Wreckage of a World War I German Albatross fighter biplane.

London bombed by the Germans

The air raids conducted during World War I were largely destructive and took many lives. Air raids could easily help strike at the enemy's vital resources. Most of such air raids occurred from 1914 to 1918. The East End of London became one of the most popular targets for such air raids.

England used air strikes as per the attacks from German submarines, but Germany remained steadfast in attacking the towns of England. In June 1917, Germany bombed London with 118 high-explosive bombs. These raids were taken very seriously by England. They began to look at strategic bombing with more thought and planning. German raids on Britain, for example, caused 1,413 deaths and 3,409 injuries.

FUN FACT

The first separate air service in the world "the Royal Air Force" was initiated in 1917.

British two-seater monoplane fires on a World War I German Taube fighter. A rifle is used to shoot at the pilot of the German plane.

Collapse of Austria and Hungary

Cavalry Austria and Hungary.

After World War I, Austria began to fall apart. Its leaders approached the Allied Forces and requested for peace. They ordered the retreat of the Austrian army. Austria, Hungary and Czechoslovakia split from the Austria-Hungarian Empire. Also, Ireland became an independent state and split from the United Kingdom, remaining a part of the British Empire. Yugoslavia was formed from the Kingdom of Serbia.

The Black Hand

Austro-Hungary was the power whose territorial ambitions played a large part in the coming of war in 1914. Although head of an increasingly fossilised and outdated regime, the Habsburg emperor Franz Josef was an expansionist. In 1914, his latest addition to the Austro-Hungarian Empire was Bosnia-Herzegovina. Bosnian Serbs resented the Austrian rule and sought the protection of independent Serbia. It was a member of this Bosnian Serb group, the Black Hand, who had assassinated Archduke Franz Ferdinand in Sarajevo.

Austria declares war on Serbia

Austria quickly sent Serbia an ultimatum and declared war on the 28th July, 1914. A few days later, on 1st August, Germany declared war on Russia. Russians and Germans considered themselves to be the champions of the Slav people.

Austrian mountain troops in the Isonzo district, clinging to rocks and helping each other along by ropes. They were climbing over mountain pass to surprise an Italian detachment.

Law for a free state

The Czechoslovak committee in Prague passed a law for a "free state", while a parallel Polish committee in Krakow brought together Galicia and Austrian Silesia into unified Poland. Soon, the German members of the Reichsrat in Vienna announced the formation of an independent state of German Austria.

German Chancellor, von Bethmann Hollweg, addressing the Reichstag during the crisis of July 1914, when the Central Powers (Austria-Hungary) and the Triple Entente initiated the World War I.

Austria surrenders

An Austrian delegation arrived in Italy to surrender unconditionally. That same day, Hungary formally declared its independence. On 3rd November, all the terms of the Austrian armistice (peace treaty) were in place and on the following day, Austria-Hungary formally ceased to exist.

Austria became the successor state of Cisleithania and the Austria-Hungarian Empire. Also, Turkey became a successor state of the Ottoman Empire. Estonia and Finland gained independence from the Russian Empire. France, Italy, Britain and Japan regained many of their old territories which were captured by the Central Forces during World War I.

The Allies Emerge Victorious

World War I, The New York Tribune, caption of illustration reads: "A Yankee Terrier Gets Its Teeth in a German Sea Wolf".

Germany signed a peace treaty with the new Bolshevik government in Russia. Because of this, Germany could deploy all of its forces against the allies on its western border. But Germany was unable to succeed. The allied troops pushed back the Germans with the added strength of the American troops. The US deployed fighter planes and tanks in the Argonne Forest, which was the strongest part of the German line.

War spoils

In 1918, the Allied armies had advanced into the Western Front and soon the Germans had to abandon their naval bases on the Belgian coast. Many of its U-boats were surrendered to the Royal Navy as spoils of war. But there were many losses on both sides including human and property losses.

End of the war in sight

By September 1918, German army leaders met with German chancellor Kaiser Wilhelm and reported that they had lost the war. Wilhelm asked his foreign secretary to send a secret message to the US President Woodrow Wilson. President Wilson asked if Germany was willing to accept the peace proposals that he had offered months ago. Germany declined the proposition. At the time, German troops slowly began to run away from the army. Strikes broke out amongst the civilians. Industries refused to produce war-related goods. The Allied Forces launched the Hundred Days Offensive to crush the German opposition. Sailors of the Imperial German Navy began a mutiny and a German Revolution broke out. Which is why the German government decided to sign an armistice even though their troops were still stationed in Belgium and France. In the armistice, the Germans were asked to evacuate Luxembourg, France and Belgium with immediate effect within the next 15 days. Rhineland was to be occupied by the Allied troops.

FUN FACT

The Polish Government also faced an uprising in December of that year after the armistice which left Poland as a German concern.

Two German U-boats washed up on the rocks at Falmouth, England, in 1921. Both were sunk during World War I.

Peace terms

The peace terms stated that Germany must withdraw its forces from all of the territories it had occupied. It had to agree to evacuate from Alsace-Lorraine and give up its weapons including airplanes, submarines and battleships. Germany was to hand over trucks, railroad engines and other supplies. The German delegation refused to sign such an agreement. But with no stable German government at the helm as Kaiser Wilhelm had resigned and fled the country, a decision had to be made. After much argument, Germany agreed to the allied terms and signed the peace treaty. The prolonged World War I brought forth an end to the imperial dynasties especially for states like Germany, Austria-Hungary and Russia.

Yanks and Tommies (British soldiers) celebrate the armistice ending of World War I.

German delegation meets the allies

A German delegation attended a meeting at the Allied military headquarters to discuss peace terms. The delegation was met by the Supreme Allied Commander, Marshal Ferdinand Foch of France who wanted Germany to officially ask for a ceasefire. Only then would the peace terms be offered to Germany. After some resistance, Germany had no other choice but to accept the armistice.

A crowd at Times Square holding up headlines reading "Germany Surrenders," on 7th November, 1918.

Demands from Germany

A series of battles known as the "Hundred Days Offensive" were fought and this included the battle of Amiens, the Second Battle of Somme, and many more near the Hindenburg Line. Soon the Germans were forced to retreat back to Germany. The exhausted German forces wanted an armistice to negotiate and come to terms with a peace treaty. However, there was little time and lots of pressure from the Allied forces. The internal strikes in Germany also led to a quick surrender.

1914: Start of World War I

1918: Germany announces an armistice

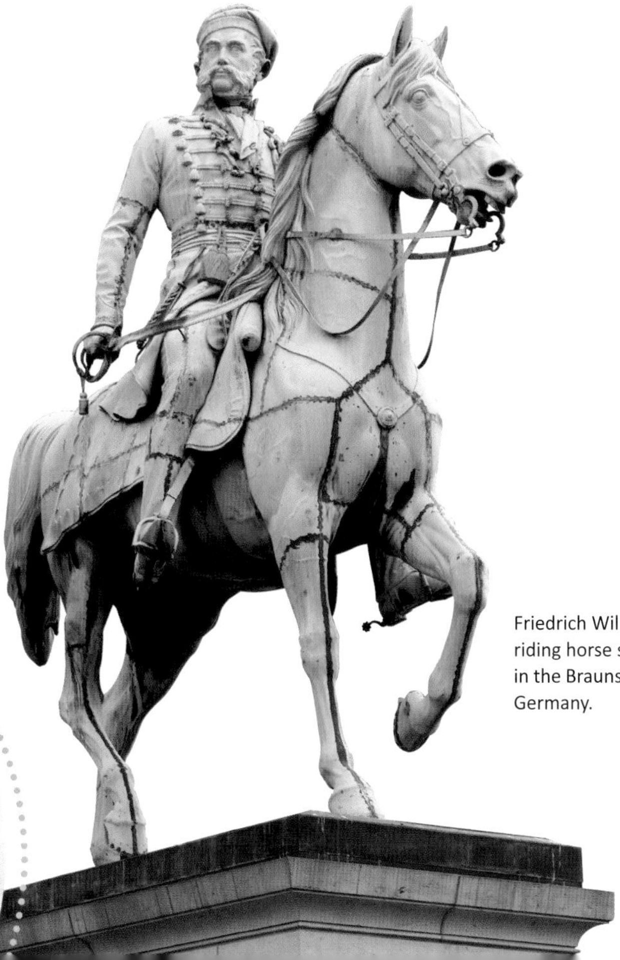

Friedrich Wilhelm riding horse statue in the Braunschweig, Germany.

FUN FACT

The fabric of Europe changed after the Treaty of Versailles, and also changed states from empires into autonomous states. The League of Nations was formed and it was expected that it could work towards negotiating peace and dealing with international disputes through negotiations.

End of the German War

Awaiting the appointment of a new chancellor, Ludendorff and Hindenburg gained the German Emperor's permission to urgently initiate peace. In his efforts, he met national political leaders and gave an update on Germany's weakening military strength. The new chancellor Prince Maximilian of Baden requested an armistice and negotiations based on Wilson's own pronouncements.

Trouble brews

The Social Democratic Party led by Friedrich Ebert was Germany's leading party. They urged Kaiser to abdicate so that Germany could be saved from its troubles. There was a fear that the extremists would take over the leadership of Germany which could lead to total anarchy. Kaiser went to Holland and on 11th November, 1918, an armistice was finally declared and the troops were asked to return.

Shortage of food

There was a severe food shortage in Germany. Farmers did not have enough young men during the harvest season because many of them had joined the army. Milk production also decreased and the supply of potatoes also reduced. It did not help that with such severe lack of food, people lacked the immunity to fight diseases like the flu. It is no wonder then that in Germany around 7,50,000 died in the war of which some lost their lives due to the flu.

Even after November, the Allies UK, France and USA maintained a food blockade to keep Germany submissive.

Disturbances in Hamburg and Bremen, the Social Democratic Party withdrawing their support from Prince Max's government and the abdication of Kaisher Wilhem's title made matters worse.

Germany becomes a republic

The Hohenzollern monarchy came to an end, just like those of the Habsburgs and Romanovs. The power was handed over to Friedrich Ebert, a Majority Social Democrat. Ebert formed a provisional government and Philipp Scheidemann, a member of the government announced that Germany was a republic.

Friedrich Ebert (1871-1925), socialist leader of the Social Democratic movement in Germany was president of the Weimar Republic from 1919 to 1925.

FUN FACT

The Blockade of Germany also extended to the Central Powers of Europe. This was started in order to delay the supplies of food, raw materials and weapons to the nations of the Central Powers.

A bronze statue of King Maximilian Joseph of Bavaria in front of the opera in Munich, Germany.

The Terms of the Armistice

The Armistice was an accord signed by representatives of France, Great Britain and Germany to agree to end fighting and work towards peace negotiations. It would be called the "Treaty of Versailles". The term "the Armistice" was used to refer to the agreement to end World War I.

Telegram read to the 5th Australian Field Ambulance by Crowther to announce the Armistice on 11th November, 1918.

Meaning of armistice

The Armistice between the Allies and Germany became an agreement that ended the fighting going on in the Western Front of Europe. Armistice comprises the Latin word "arma" meaning "arms" and "stitium", meaning "stoppage". The armistice ended the fighting, but negotiations at the 1919 Paris Peace Conference where the terms of the Treaty of Versailles were completed and signed on 28th June, 1919.

Surrender of the German Army on the Western Front, Nov 1918.

Signing of the armistice

The Armistice was signed in Ferdinand Foch's railway carriage in the Forest of Compiegne, near Paris. The World War I Armistice with Germany was signed on 11th November, 1918 by representatives from Britain, France and Germany and managed to bring more than 52 months of fighting to an end. The terms had to ensure that Germany could not restart the war. They had to give up 2,500 heavy guns, 2,500 field guns, 25,000 machine guns, 1,700 aeroplanes and all their submarines. With the signing of the Armistice and Treaty of Versailles, Germany accepted the blame for the First World War and was asked to pay reparations (compensation) for the damage caused, estimated to a total of about 22 billion pounds. While Germany thought the terms of the treaty were very harsh, the French thought they were very lenient.

FUN FACT

Did you know that Germany paid off its war debt in 2010, with a final payment of 59 million pounds?

Admiral Beatty reading the terms of the surrender of the German Navy.

World War I and the Destruction Left in its Wake

The four years' of World War I remained the worst assault on Europe. More than 85,00,000 people died, and 2,10,00,000 were wounded. The war proved to be extremely expensive. Many parts of France, Belgium and Poland lay devastated and many valuables remained destroyed at sea. It is estimated that eight million soldiers died and many more were physically or mentally affected, while nine million civilians died. The war had destroyed 3,00,000 houses, 6000 factories, 1000 km of railway lines and 112 coal mines.

Luxemburg women wave allied flags from their windows to greet the Occupation of the American Army at the end of World War I.

Loss of life

The USA was part of World War I only for around seven and a half months. In those seven months of actual combat, close to 1,16,000 were killed and around 2,04,000 were injured. In fact, the Battle of Verdun in 1916 witnessed over a million casualties within 10 months.

Post World War I scenario

Empires had fallen and new ideologies had come forward. Woodrow Wilson had asked for new democratic diplomacy. Revolutions began in Berlin and Russia. Anti-imperialist ideas were shared and became popular among revolutionaries. The war weakened the economic status that European powers had thus far enjoyed. World War I cost $186 billion in direct expenses and another $151 billion in indirect expenses. It was the first war to have employed aeroplanes, tanks, long-range artillery, submarines and poison gas, which had left at least seven million men permanently disabled. World War I brought Germany towards the brink of an economic collapse and thousands of Germans were starving. It resulted in the mutiny in the German navy. Economically, the war severely upset the European economies; thereby, making USA the chief creditor and industrial power.

FUN FACT

A few historians believe that there was no second war. It was just one war with a long ceasefire in between!

16 soldiers leaving Camp Dix, New Jersey, in a car after 11th November, 1918.

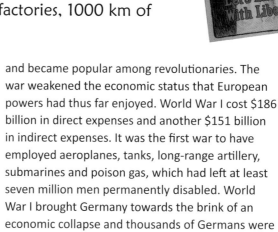

WORLD WAR II

1939–1945

The twentieth century witnessed two world wars. The First World War (World War I) was fought from 1914 to 1918. The Second World War (World War II) was fought from 1939 to 1945 and was fought in different parts of Europe, Russia, North Africa and Asia.

World War II had disastrous consequences and was called the deadliest war in human history, as 40 to 50 million people died.

World War II started in Europe, but spread throughout the world. It was fought between the Axis Powers comprising Germany, Italy, Japan and the Allied Powers comprising Britain, the USA, Soviet Union and France. Many other countries were also involved.

Much of the fighting occurred in Europe and in Southeast Asia (Pacific). The war ended with Germany's surrender on 7th May, 1945 while the war in the Pacific ended when Japan surrendered in September, 1945.

The Axis and the Allies

The Axis alliance emerged as a result of several agreements between Germany and Italy. These were followed by the declaration of an "axis" combining Rome and Berlin, which stated that henceforth, the world would move around the Rome-Berlin axis. After this, the German-Japanese Anti-Comintern Pact against the Soviet Union was signed in 1936. Later, a complete military and political alliance was formed between Germany and Italy. Finally, all the three powers signed the Tripartite Pact on 27th September, 1940.

World War II German and American soldiers with weapons.

Old postcard showing Polish attack of Soviet tanks.

The US joins the Allies

At the beginning of World War II, Russia and Germany were on the same side, but Russia joined the Allies when Hitler ordered a surprise attack on Russia in 1941. The US wanted to be neutral during World War II, but they joined the Allies after the surprise attack at Pearl Harbor by the Japanese.

The Anti-Comintern Pact

In 1936, Germany and Italy signed a friendship treaty and established the Rome-German Axis.

The Italian dictator Benito Mussolini used the term axis to describe their alliance. Soon, Japan and Germany signed the Anti-Comintern Pact—a treaty against communism; thus, forming the Axis Powers.

In November 1936, the Foreign Minister of Germany Joachim von Ribbentrop negotiated an agreement between Germany and Japan wherein the countries openly declared opposition to international communism.

In the event of a Soviet Union attack on Germany or Japan, the two nations would discuss with each other the measures to be taken to protect their interests. They also agreed that they would not make any political treaties with Russia.

FUN FACT

Around 100 million people of the armed forces were engaged in World War II. It is considered as the most devastating war in history, in which close to 2.5 per cent of the world's population died.

World War II photo of soldier hiding and covering behind a burning jeep wreck.

US Navy F4Us, Corsairs, in flight over South Pacific in 1943, during World War II.

Outbreak of World War II

World War II began owing to the rise of authoritarian, military regimes in the states of Germany, Italy and Japan, which resulted from the Great Depression that swept across the world during 1929 and 1930. Post World War I, an overpowered Germany, disenchanted Italy, and a determined Japan were eager to regain power. These countries were against Communism. The other states were unprepared and not ready to engage in war again after World War I. It did not help that the League of Nations was weakened as the US had defected from it and the supposed union of nation states at a global level was unable to promote disarmament.

Soviet Foreign Minister Molotov signs the German-Soviet Nonaggression Pact with German Foreign Minister Joachim von Ribbentrop.

Events leading to World War II

The second Sino-Japanese War in 1931 also did not help matters as treaties were violated and states became even more aggressive. Adolf Hitler again prepared the German army. Benito Mussolini invaded and conquered Ethiopia. The Spanish civil war from 1936 to 1939 also added to the distress in Europe and both Germany and Italy helped fascist Francisco Franco win. In 1938, Germany conquered Austria and soon a British and French appeasement policy with the Axis powers ended with the handing over of Czechoslovakia to Germany as per the Munich Pact.

The Nonaggression Pact

German dictator Adolf Hitler wanted to invade and occupy Poland, which had the support of France and Britain. Soon, negotiations between Germany and Poland led to the signing of the German-Soviet Nonaggression Pact, as per which both Germany and Russia agreed that Poland will be divided between them. On 31st August, 1939 Hitler ordered his forces to invade Poland; Britain and France responded by declaring war on Germany on 3rd September and thus, the Second World War began.

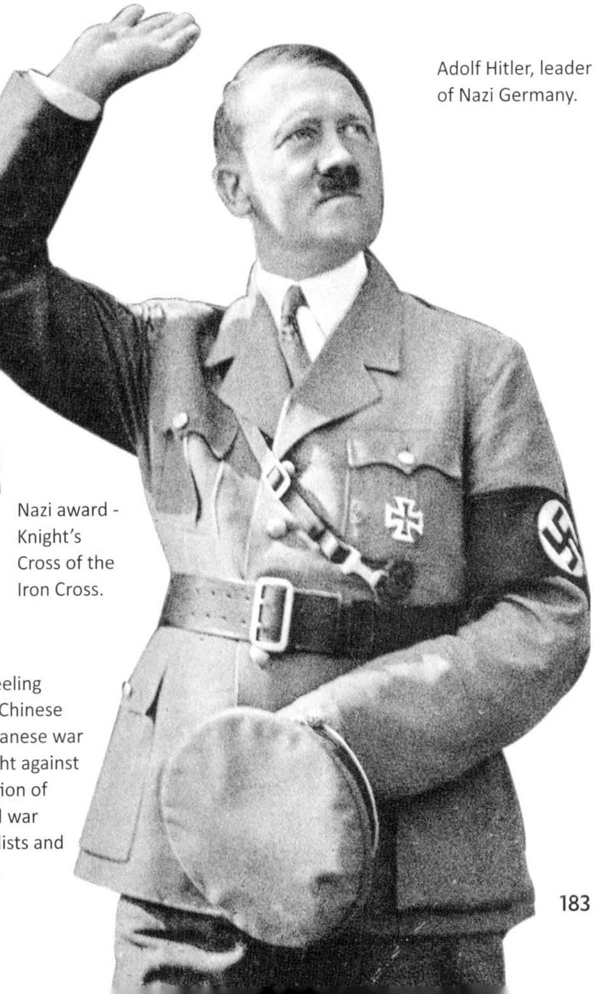

Adolf Hitler, leader of Nazi Germany.

Nazi award - Knight's Cross of the Iron Cross.

Two Chinese men kneeling prior to execution by Chinese soldiers. The Sino-Japanese war (1937-1945) was a fight against the Japanese occupation of China as well as a civil war between the Nationalists and Communists in China.

World War II Douglas Dauntless Dive-Bomber.

An old hand grenade and bullet.

World War II Weaponry

A larger number of countries were involved in World War II than in World War I. By the end of World War I, tanks and military aircraft had become a pre-requisite for a better defence and offence, due to the huge and quick destruction they caused. However, World War II was the largest armed war in human history. This period witnessed dramatic and significant scientific developments that resulted in the use of nuclear weapons in warfare for the first time.

FUN FACT

Between 1939 and 1945, the Allies dropped around 27,700 tons of bombs per month.

Use of arms

By the end of World War I, the victorious Allied forces had begun to believe in their supremacy and so their pace of introducing newer weapons and artillery in their armies seemed to slow down. However, the defeated nation of Germany had started developing tanks and begun to aggressively build a better and stronger army by 1935. In stark comparison, England by 1939 had not even started work towards building an armoured division.

Three US Navy Dauntless dive bombers on a fighting mission in the Pacific in 1943.

Aerial combat

By the end of World War I and the beginning of World War II, the use of the sky in defence tactics had also altered to a great extent. During the interim period between 1918 and 1939, the range and size of aeroplanes had developed to a considerable degree. With better speed, engine power and performance, aircrafts were slowly becoming more sophisticated. Better aircraft technology in terms of instrumentation, power-assisted flight controls and radar tracking began to emerge. These developments made use of aircrafts integral to defence and offense tactics during World War II. Dive-bombers, monoplane fighter planes, machine guns, light and medium bombers were some of the weapons employed in air warfare during World War II. Radar stations were built on the coasts of England to warn of impending attacks from hostile planes.

Vintage American M24 Tank.

Russo-Finnish War

The Russo-Finnish war, also known as Winter War, was fought between Russia and Finland. It started on 30th November, 1939 and ended on 10th March, 1940. Due to Finland's rejection of Russia's request for a naval base in 1939, Russia with a heavy force of around a million soldiers attacked Finland and the Finnish army with its smaller force put on a brave front.

1939: Start of Russo-Finnish

1940: End of Russo-Finnish War

Birth of the Republic of Finland

From the twelfth century to the early 1800s, Finland was a part of Sweden. Napoleon persuaded Alexander I of Russia to declare war on Sweden, and Finland became the prize of victory during that war. Finland remained a part of Russia from 1808 to 1918 under the Tsar. However, during Russia's Revolution of 1905, Finland managed to create for itself a modern, unicameral parliament with elected representatives and it also became the first European country to offer women political suffrage at the national level. By 1917, Finland declared its independence. A civil war erupted between the Red faction backed by the Soviet Bolsheviks and the Germany-backed White faction. In 1918, General Mannerheim with Germany's assistance defeated Russia. General Mannerheim established the Republic of Finland.

Carl Gustaf Emil Mannerheim (1867-1951).

Russia's foreign policy of 1939

Russia signed treaties of mutual assistance with Lithuania, Estonia and Latvia, which allowed Russia to establish military bases in all these Baltic states. In October 1939, Russia invited Finnish representatives to Moscow to discuss land issues around the Finnish/Russian border. Russia wanted certain Finnish islands in the Gulf of Finland, including Suursaari Island, in order to establish a military base. In return, Finland would get Soviet Karelia. Finland viewed Stalin's demands as an attempt by Russia to re-establish its authority over Finland, so Stalin's proposal was rejected. By the end of November 1939, a war between Finland and Russia seemed inevitable.

Frozen bodies of dead Soviet (Russian) soldiers killed in the Russo-Finnish War.

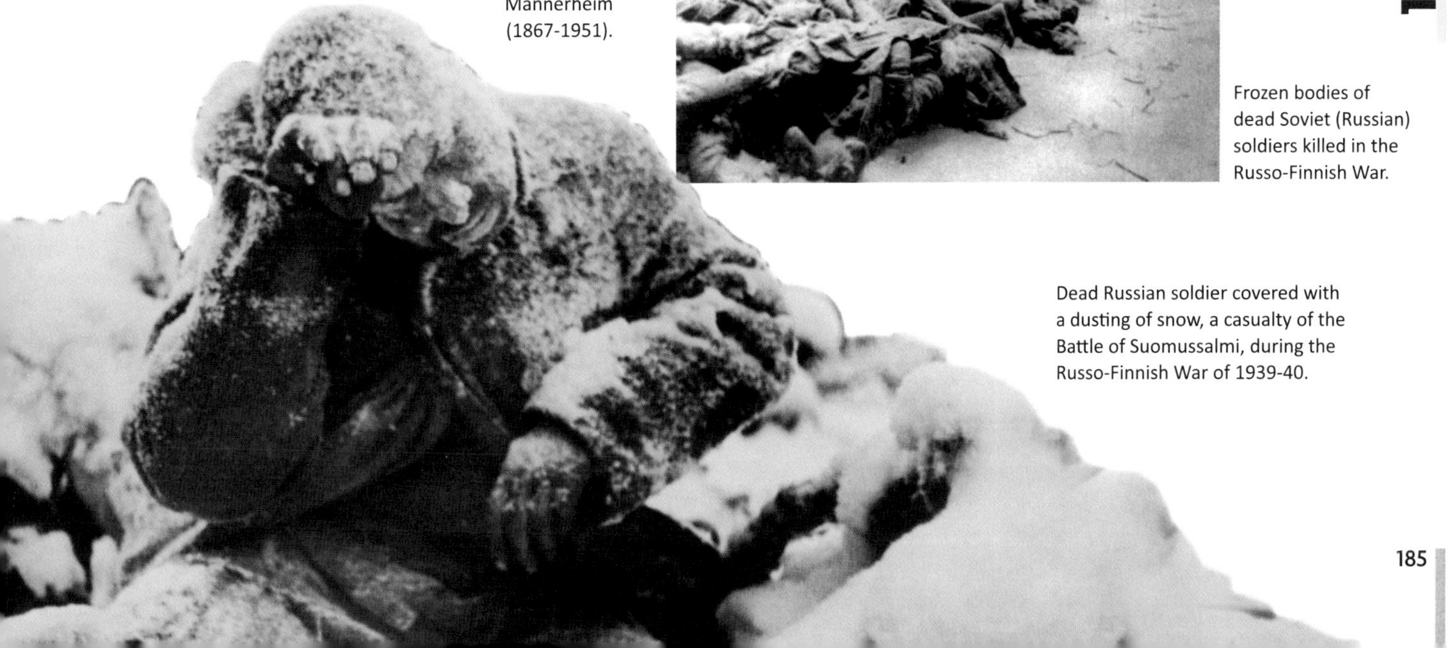

Dead Russian soldier covered with a dusting of snow, a casualty of the Battle of Suomussalmi, during the Russo-Finnish War of 1939-40.

Hitler's Role in World War II

Adolf Hitler became one of the most powerful and notorious dictators in history. He joined the National Socialist German Workers' Party and soon took over the reins of Germany by 1933. Hitler joined the German army and rose to the rank of corporal and despite not being popular amongst his comrades he was awarded Germany's highest award for bravery—the Iron Cross. His main job in the army was also to meet political organisations and understand their learnings—left or right.

1933: Hitler heads Germany

1939: Germany attacks Poland

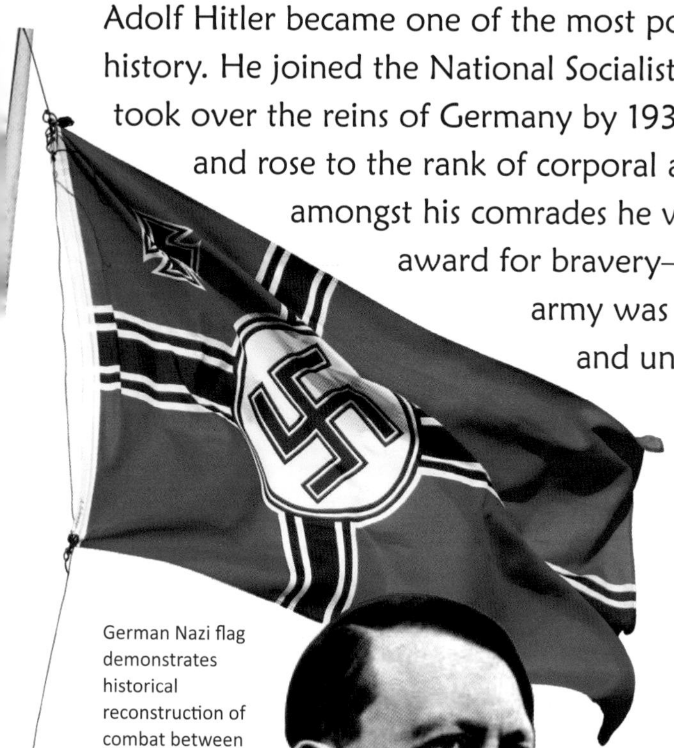

German Nazi flag demonstrates historical reconstruction of combat between Soviet and German armies during World War II.

Adolf Hitler

Hitler's role in World War II

Hitler established several concentration camps to imprison Jews. He believed that they were a danger to Aryan superiority and this view led to the death of more than six million people in the Holocaust. Germany attacked Poland in 1939 and this sparked off World War II. By 1941, Hitler's troops had occupied much of Europe and north Africa.

Hitler's entry into the politics of Germany

Hitler evaded military service in Austria-Hungary and went to Vienna. He volunteered for the Bavarian army and served during World War I and soon became a member of the Nationalist Socialist German Workers' Party. He soon controlled the National Socialist German Workers Party and after a coup attempt and a jail sentence later, he called for the restructuring of Germany on the basis of race.

FUN FACT

Eva Braun, a shop assistant from Munich, became Adolf's mistress. He married her much later towards the end of his life.

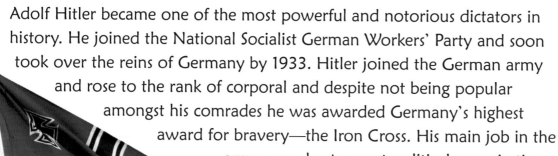

Adolf Hitler in Nuremberg to attend a Nazi Party Convention in September 1934.

Hitler's Views on Race

German Chancellor, Adolf Hitler, shaking hands with a Brownshirt during the Nazi Party Day in Nuremberg, 1937.

As Germany's ruler for 12 years, Adolf Hitler became the reason for the deaths of many. After being recognised as a veteran for his work in World War I, he became a part of the German Workers' Party and renamed it as the National Socialist German Workers Party (in short Nazi Party). He unsuccessfully tried to overthrow the German Weimar Republic and was jailed for this. In prison, he wrote his manifesto, Mein Kampf (My Struggle), and became popular because of his strong oratory skills. By 1933, he became the Chancellor and brought in new rules.

Germany declares war on Poland

Hitler believed that Germany must wage wars to acquire land in order to enable more Germans to prosper and raise big families. By the time he came to power, Germany had started military preparations to wage such wars. He was determined to wage a war against Poland and to do so aligned with Russia. Before the full attack on Poland, German troops seized Norway in April 1940 to facilitate the navy's access to the North Atlantic. After reaching France, Hitler decided to wage wars against the US and Russia.

Liberated prisoners of Wobbelin concentration camp taken to a hospital for medical attention on 4th May, 1945.

Hitler's War

The term Hitler's War is often used in reference to World War II because it was due to his will and push that led to the start of World War II. Hitler became infamous for his dictatorial ways and his hatred towards the Jews, which led to the construction of concentration camps where millions of people were tortured and killed.

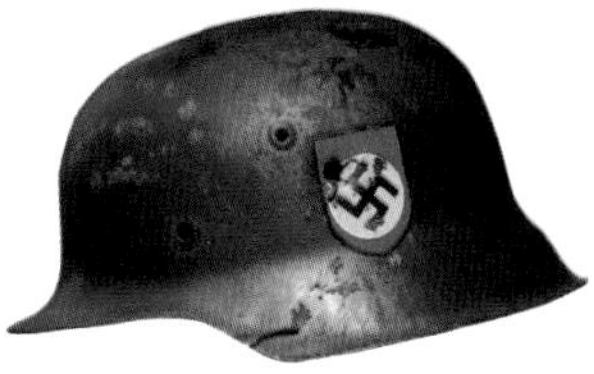

Nazi helmet

FUN FACT

Despite being the person responsible for building concentration camps that imprisoned Jews, Hitler never visited a concentration camp in his lifetime.

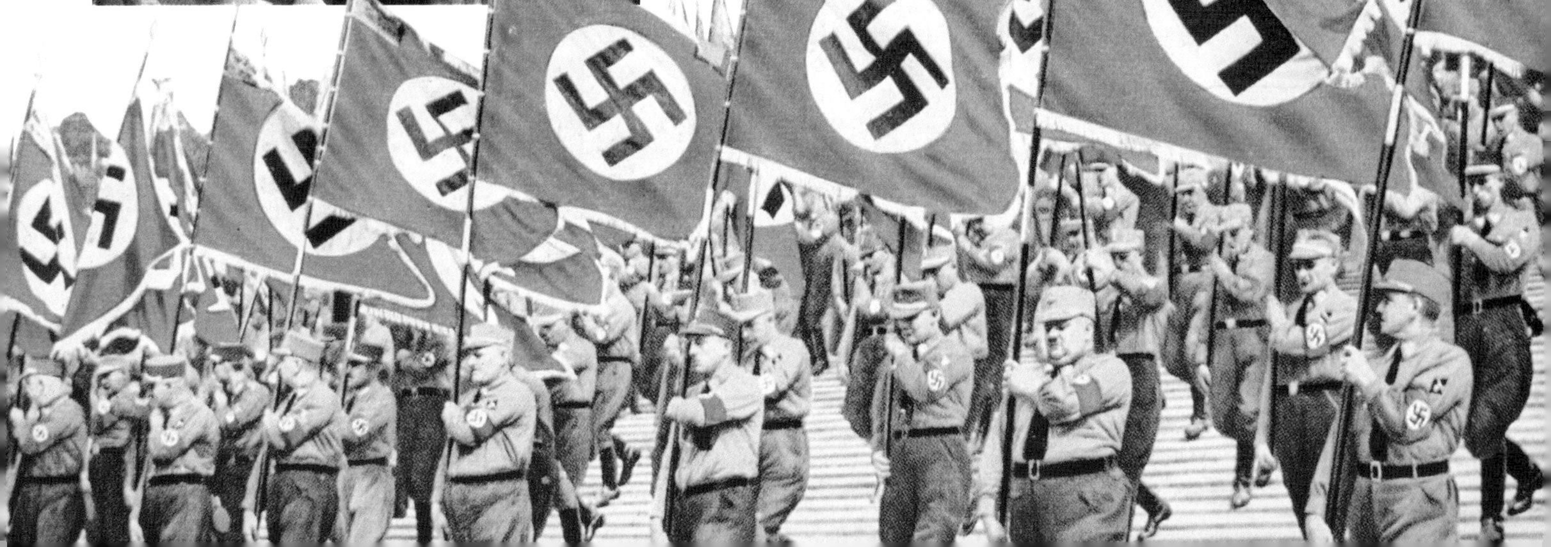

Entrance of Nazi flagbearers at the Party Day rally in Nuremberg, 1933.

Invasion of Norway

A few months after the start of World War II, Adolf Hitler realised that controlling the Norwegian coastal waters would be important from many perspectives, as that was how the Swedish iron ore was transported to German blast furnaces. The German occupation of Norway would prevent the entry of the Allies into Germany. Consequently, Hitler issued the order to invade Norway under the code word Weserübung, which also included the invasion of Denmark. So, Germany invaded Norway on 9th April, 1940.

German 1943 poster depicts men carrying Nazi banner going off to fight.

Germany's interest in Norway

The control of Norway's extensive coastline became important since it would mean the control of the North Sea and could provide German warships and submarines easy access to the Atlantic Ocean. Furthermore, through Norway, Germany could get easy access to importing iron ore from Sweden.

Germany occupies Denmark

By April 1940, Nazi troops were able to occupy Denmark without much of a fight. No sooner than they occupied Denmark, they made way to attack Norway. On the first day, they brought in the infantry into Norway and gained control over quite a large area of Norway.

By 15th April, English troops reached to assist the Norwegian forces, but a strong attack by the German forces forced the English troops to flee Norway.

Further, the German troops were able to slip through the mines that the English forces had laid near Norwegian ports. This was possible as local garrisons had been commanded to permit Germans to enter, under the orders of a Norwegian commander loyal to Norway's pro-fascist former foreign minister Vidkun Quisling.

Heavy fire from German troops led to a hasty evacuation of 360,000 Allied troops from Dunkirk to England.

Monument for Soviet soldiers in Kirkenes city, Norway who liberated northern Norway from Nazi occupation in 1944.

German soldiers invade Poland in armoured and motorised divisions in September 1939. It was the beginning of World War II.

The German Attack

The German armoured cruiser SMS Blücher, launched on 11th April, 1908 and sunk at the battle of Dogger Bank on 24th January, 1915.

German forces, led by Erwin Rommel, struck at the weak extension at Maginot Line in the Ardennes Forest and succeeded. Both attacks met quick success. Norway with a population of three million and a small population meant a smaller army. While the German occupation attempt was relatively successful, it was not without its glitches, because the Norwegian forces managed to sink Germany's new cruiser called SMS Blucher at Oslo. This act gave the forces some time to delay the German possession of the capital Helsinki and also gave an opportunity to the members of the Norwegian royal family and government to escape.

Germany invades Norway

Just after Germany invaded Norway, there was a demand for Norway's surrender, but the Norwegian government rejected this demand. So, the German troops established another regime under Quisling. Soon after the invasion, a German minister in Oslo demanded that Norway surrender. The Norwegian government did not accept and the Germans responded with a parachute invasion, and the establishment of a puppet regime under Quisling. The Norwegian forces rejected Germany's rule in the guise of a Quisling government and continued fighting along with British troops.

General Rommel standing in a jeep in the North African desert. Rommel's German-Italian forces were supplied tanks and fuel in January 1942. He soon captured Benghazi, Libya.

Effects of the German invasion of Norway

The economic impact of the German invasion resulted in Norway losing all its major trading partners, resulting in Germany becoming its main trading partner. Germany confiscated a major portion of Norway's output and left Norway with around 43 per cent of it. Norway faced scarcity of basic commodities, including food. There was an increased risk of famine so the Norwegians grew crops to feed themselves.

German soldiers in Frederikshavn, Denmark, before being sent to Norway.

Swastika armband from World War II.

FUN FACT

Quisling soon became a word synonymous with traitor, owing to Quisling's siding with Germany in World War II.

Invasion of France

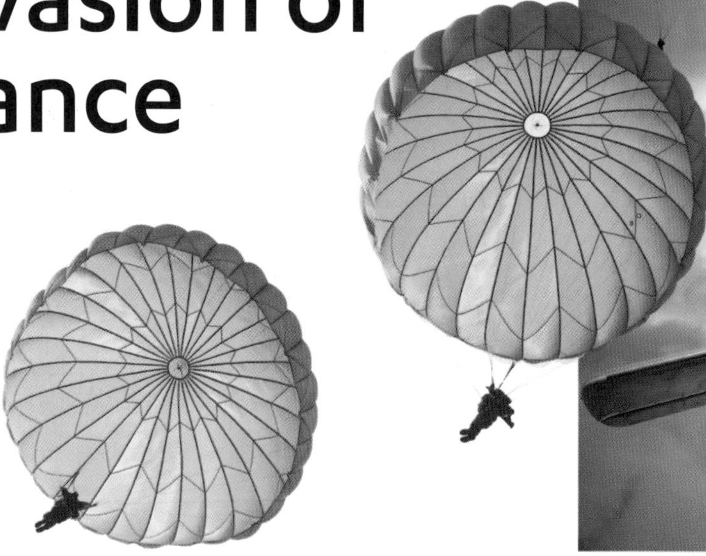

Biplanes with airborne infantry.

Germany set its sights also on France. By 1940, German bombers had targeted air bases in France, Luxembourg, Belgium and the Netherlands and had destroyed many Allied planes. German paratroopers had also dented France's defence plans.

The Netherlands is invaded

German troops moved through Netherlands, northern Belgium, Luxembourg and into the Ardennes forest towards France. Oblivious to Germany's move to the south, the British and French army were stationed in large numbers in Belgium. However, Dutch resistance slowed down the advance of the German troops into Brussels and The Hague, but the German air force (Luftwaffe) bombed Rotterdam, just as surrender negotiations with the Netherlands were going on. The Rotterdam attack killed over 800 civilians, leading to the surrender of Netherlands.

German bunker in Normandy from World War II.

Belgium is invaded

Attack on a German radar. Troops of the covering force and paratroopers practise withdrawal to the landing craft.

Britain and France's plan to defend Belgium went awry because the German paratrooper units captured the forts between the cities of Antwerp and Liege on the first night of the invasion. Soon, the German forces attacked the Allied forces from the Ardennes forest in the south. Trapped between two determined German forces, the Allied forces could not stop the German advance towards Paris and the English Channel.

The Allied forces tried to battle it out with the 136 German divisions that entered Holland and Belgium. Simultaneously, around 2500 German aircrafts proceeded to bomb airfields in places across Belgium, Holland, France and Luxembourg. This was followed with 16,000 German airborne troops parachuting into Rotterdam, Leiden and The Hague. The Belgian bridges were soon captured by 100 German troops that came via air gliders. The Dutch army were outnumbered and defeated in five days. The day after, Belgium was invaded when the soldiers at Fort Eben-Emael surrendered.

Evacuation from Dunkirk

Even as the French forces remained trapped between the two German troops, the British Expeditionary Force (BEF) was pushed back towards the French port of Dunkirk. With no hope of reaching the French forces, the English government ordered the BEF to retreat. Known as Operation Dynamo, the evacuation started on 27th May, 1940. Over seven days more than 800 civilian and military sea vessels were used to bring back close to 338,000 men to England. This evacuation meant that France was left to fight its own battle with Germany.

Ship leaving Dunkirk carrying defeated British and French soldiers to England. In the background the French port of Dunkirk burns under German advance.

France invaded

German tanks broke through the main fronts along the Somme River and the fortified Maginot Line, and entered Paris. To provide support, British Prime Minister Winston Churchill flew to Paris to offer his personal encouragement, but he could not spare any British military assistance because he needed them for England's defence. Italy opportunistically supported Germany and within four days the French capital fell and the French officials fled to Bordeaux. The French surrendered on 25th June, merely seven weeks after the invasion of France. Britain's forces at the Maginot Line surrendered at St Valéry as Prime Minister Churchill was reluctant to take any risk. On 22nd June, 1940, France signed an armistice with Germany. Hitler insisted that the armistice be signed in the same railway car that Germany had surrendered to France in 1918, at the end of World War I.

Leader of the National Socialists; and later Imperial Chancellor – Adolf Hitler.

Statue of Winston Churchill outside the Petit Palais near the Seine river.

FUN FACT

Winston Churchill had served as Britain's Prime Minister for only 16 days when the evacuation started.

Military evacuation of Dunkirk during World War II. Thousands of British and French troops wait on the dunes of Dunkirk beach for transport to England.

Italy Enters World War II

The Italian Government introduced military conscription in 1907. However, only about 25 per cent of those eligible for conscription received training and by 1912 there were only 300,000 men in the Italian Army. Over 5.2 million men served in the Italian Army during the First World War. Italy's total wartime casualties was 420,000 killed and almost 955,000 wounded.

Mussolini's statue on display at Militalia.

Signing of the Pact of Steel on 22nd May, 1939 in Berlin.

Benito Mussolini comes to power

Post World War I, Vittorio Orlando, the Italian representative at the Paris Peace Conference (1919) was criticised for changing Italy's stand. Benito Mussolini engineered the entry of Italian right-wing groups into the Fascist Party.

In 1920, the next Prime Minister Francesco Saverio Nitti was forced to resign and a series of riots beset Italy. Orlando also came under attack and was forced to resign in 1920. In 1922, King Victor Emmanuel III appointed Benito Mussolini in order to stop a communist revolution and consequently Mussolini became the head of a coalition comprising fascists and nationalists.

The Italian parliament continued to function for a while, but the murder of socialist leader Giacomo Matteotti in 1924 by the Fascists changed the face of Italy. Soon, communist or left-wing parties were censored. By 1929, Italy had become a one-party state.

Liberty Ship SS Rowan explodes after being hit by a German bomb, near Sicily on 11th July, 1943.

Hitler and Mussolini in Munich, Germany on 18th June, 1940. Hitler was at a high point, as his army had accomplished a string of victories and was completing its conquest of continental Western Europe.

Pact of Steel

Hitler had for long been inspired by Mussolini's achievements. When Hitler came to power he wanted to develop a close relationship with the Italian dictator and secure for Germany another partner to fight against the Allies.

In 1936, Hitler secured Mussolini's partnership, after which the two leaders of Germany and Italy signed a military alliance thus, forming the Berlin-Rome Axis. By 1939, post the Italian invasion of Albania, Benito Mussolini signed a complete defence alliance with Germany, known as the Pact of Steel.

FUN FACT

Benito Mussolini, the supreme dictator of Italy, believed in the concept of a fascist government, which has only one leader and one party that has complete power. The fascist government controls all the aspects of the lives of citizens..

Mussolini Plans to Invade Ethiopia

The African countries of Eritrea and Somalia were under Italy, but Ethiopia had managed to evade Italy's influence. Benito Mussolini was keen to occupy Ethiopia. In October 1935, Mussolini sent the Italian army under General Badoglio to Ethiopia. The League of Nations condemned Italy's move and imposed sanctions on Italy. Around 400,000 Italian troops fought with the poorly armed Ethiopian army and soon captured the capital Addis Ababa. In May 1936, Emperor Haile Selassie fled to England.

Mussolini and Hitler in Berlin.

Italian invasion of Ethiopia

Italy had previously tried to capture Ethiopia in 1896. But the Ethiopian forces had defeated Italy in the Battle of Adowa. A border skirmish between Ethiopia and Italian Somaliland in December 1934, gave Mussolini an excuse to invade Ethiopia. After Ethiopia's capture, Mussolini declared Italy's king Victor Emmanuel III emperor of Ethiopia and appointed Badoglio as viceroy.

Hitler and Mussolini join hands

Mussolini had always been an inspiration for Adolf Hitler. Hitler wanted a close relationship with Italy. Hitler extended an invitation to Mussolini to visit Germany. Post his visit, they signed a secret pact that promised Germany of Italian collaboration on certain diplomatic issues. When Mussolini visited Germany he saw many mass parades, military exercises and did a tour of the Krupp munitions factory. He left Germany as an altered individual who had new-found respect for the German dictator.

Hitler visits Mussolini

Similarly, when Hitler visited Mussolini's banquet, the German dictator promised that he would never break his Italian counterpart's trust and would never invade the Italian border.

In 1936, the two dictators joined hands in a military alliance. Italy entered World War II on Germany's side in 1940; thereby, declaring war on the Allies.

Statue of Haile Selassie.

FUN FACT

In 1919, Mussolini started the Fascist Party. He wanted to bring back the days of the Roman Empire. The members of the Fascist party wore black clothes known as "Black Shirts".

Stamp showing Benito Mussolini and Adolf Hitler 1941.

Adolf Hitler and Benito Mussolini being given a military salute during Hitler's visit to Venice, Italy.

Hitler Plans to Invade Britain

V1 flying bomb used by the Germans to attack London, England.

In 1940 Hitler issued Directive 16, that authorised the preparations to invade Britain. Hitler called the planned invasion as Operation Sea Lion. However, in reality, the operation was never carried out because Germany's plans went awry and they were ousted in the Battle of Britain.

Directive 16

Six weeks after Germany's invasion of France, the French signed an armistice with Germany. Britain remained the only country that continued to resist Germany's dominance. Hitler assumed that after France's surrender, the British would follow suit and also surrender. Nonetheless, when Britain remained steadfast in their resistance against the Germans, then Hitler issued Directive Number 16, which authorised a detailed plan to invade Britain, under Operation Sea Lion. The directive stated that the objective of the operation was "to eliminate the English motherland as a base from which war against Germany can be continued, and, if this should become unavoidable, to occupy it to the full extent".

Firemen at work in a bomb-damaged street in London during the Battle of Britain.

Germany's plan

The German Directive 16 included a plan to land along the southern coast of England, that extends from Dorset to Kent. The plan was that the German navy would defeat the Royal Navy in the Mediterranean and North Sea. The Royal Air Force had to be defeated and only then the actual invasion could happen.

London's Big Ben surrounded with barbed wire and soldiers on guard during World War II.

Germany plans an air attack

Germany had control over the North Sea and France, which meant that the entire coastline near France was under its control and they could use the *Luftwaffe* (German air force) to attack Britain.

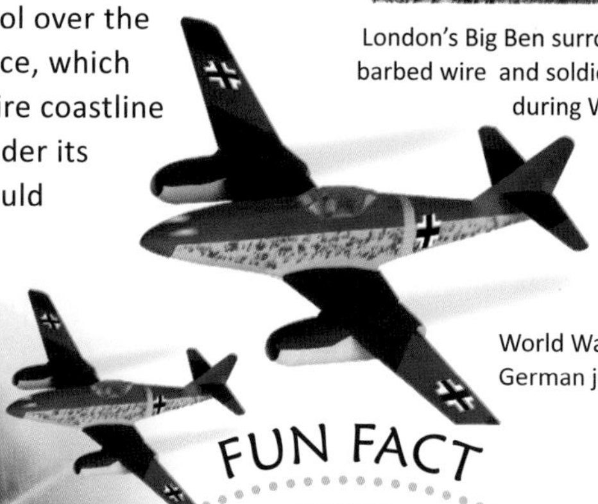

World War II German jet fighters.

FUN FACT

Luftwaffe is a German term for air force and it became the official name for the Nazi air force. Founded in 1930 and commanded by Hermann Goering, the *Luftwaffe* became one of the largest commanding air forces in Europe during World War II.

Finnish and Russian Face Off

The Finnish Army was trained to use their terrain to the utmost advantage and were well adapted to the forests and snow-covered regions of their land. Finnish ski troops despite being mobile and well trained were not trained in large-scale exercises.

Soldiers of Finnish Guard sharpshooter battalion during Battle of Gorni Dubnik (Russo-Turkish War 1877-78).

A Finnish ski patrol, lying in the snow on the outskirts of Northern Finland, waiting for Russian troops on 12th January, 1940.

Winter war

Russia used 45 divisions with each division having 18,000 men (which in effect meant close to 25 per cent of Finland's population) and deployed 1500 tanks and 3000 planes. Finland did not have enough ammunition to fight the war. Russia was unequipped to handle a winter war and the winter of 1939-1940 was particularly severe.

Signing of the Moscow Peace Treaty

The Russians fought near the Russian–Finnish border and some parts of the 965 km border were utterly impassable. The Russian air force was also used only for a short while owing to the winter. The Russians saw heavy casualties and lost 800 planes. However, after renewed and reorganised military tactics, Russia managed to overcome the Finnish troops at the border. Finland agreed to give more territory to Russia and the Moscow Peace Treaty was signed.

Details about the treaty

As per the treaty, Finland ceded most of Finnish Karelia to Russia. The army and Finnish civilians were evacuated to the other side of the new border. The treaty also allowed free passage to Soviet civilians to Petsamo to move towards Norway. Under the treaty, Finland also ceded part of the Salla municipality and the islands near the Gulf of Finland. Further, as per the treaty Finland had to rent out the Hanko Peninsula for 30 years to the Soviets, who would proceed to use it as a naval base.

FUN FACT

Finland gave around 11 per cent of land and Russia got Lake Ladoga, giving Russia the safeguard that was required to protect Leningrad.

Old Russian tank used during World War II.

Italy Declares War Against Britain

A rusted helmet and machine-gun tape.

Dictator Benito Mussolini declared war on Great Britain and France and entered World War II. Mussolini's desire to expand Italy's empire to the Mediterranean and North Africa, made the dictator take this step, even if it meant going against the Italian monarch, King Vittorio Emmanuel III's wishes. The King mistrusted Germany, but his wishes went largely unnoticed and unheeded by Mussolini.

Mussolini's reasons for declaring war

Mussolini was upset with the sanctions placed by the League of Nations after its war with Ethiopia. Particularly since, the two countries that imposed sanctions, France and Britain, were themselves ruling over the rest of Africa. This pushed Mussolini towards agreeing to a pact with Hitler.

Allies push Italy to a war

The Allies ignored Italy's offer to declare a ceasefire when Germany invaded Poland. Soon, the Allies realised that Italy would get involved in the war and they started seizing German coal shipments that were making way to Italy. Italy was further humiliated and Mussolini condemned the Allies for this act and called it as piracy, since it was done to a state that was not at war with France and Britain.

The League of Nations condemned Italy's aggression and imposed sanctions, which included a ban on countries to sell arms, rubber and metals to Italy. There was opposition to the sanctions by some political leaders from France and Britain who thought that it would push Mussolini to form an alliance with Germany. In 1939, Italy invaded Albania and Mussolini signed a treaty to form an alliance with Hitler.

The town of Cassino was completely destroyed in one of World War II's worst air bombings. The Monte Cassino Abbey was bombed in the same operation on 15th February, 1944.

German soldiers during World War II.

Turmoil within Italy

Mussolini had comprehended that while peace would be more beneficial for Italy and a long drawn war could prove problematic for the country, he feared that if he did not join the war then he may not reap any benefits from it if the war was won by Germany—who would receive all the fruits of war.

Italy had begun to think that war was inevitable and the defeat of France and Britain seemed like a foregone conclusion, and Mussolini had a desire to dissolve the Italian monarchy. In fact, Italian Royalist members like Balbo, De Bono and De Vecchi asked King Emmanuel to revoke Mussolini's powers, but they did not make a strong push.

A British heavy gun in action, British soldiers preparing artillery shells and manning a large artillery piece.

Italy declares war on Britain

When Germany invaded Poland in 1939, Italy was not ready for a war, but Mussolini urgently wanted to join the war to be part of a historical event that could potentially change the map of Europe.

Italy had no great industrial prowess to brag about. In fact, it was not at all equipped like the countries of Britain, France or Germany as far as production of guns, ammunition, artillery, tanks, etc., was concerned.

Mussolini was perturbed at the shipping incident with the Allies. The Allies had not been overtly friendly towards Italy since World War I and the fact that now Italy's trade would also depend on the Allies was too much for Mussolini to handle. In 1940, he declared war on Britain.

Italy took part in the Battle of Britain along with Germany in 1940. Mussolini sent around 200 aircrafts to bomb Britain. However, the Italians achieved limited success due to the inferior quality of the Italian aircrafts.

They carried only 1,500 pounds of bombs per aircraft and conducted raids only during the nights or occasionally during the day.

1939: Italy invades Poland

1940: Battle of Britain begins

Early 1900s World War II postcard depicting soldiers receiving machine gun instructions.

Kaiser Wilhelm II and King Victor Emmanuel III.

FUN FACT

Poison gas was first used during World War I to dismantle the trench warfare stalemate. During World War II, Japan (in China) and Italy (in Ethiopia) used chemical weapons.

Battle of Britain

World War II German bomber.

The Battle of Britain began on 10th July, 1940 and lasted for three months with Germany bombing England. The name Battle of Britain comes from UK Prime Minister Winston Churchill's speech where he had reportedly said, "The Battle of France is over. The Battle of Britain is about to begin".

German Heinkel 111 bomber over London. Below is the river Thames and Tower Bridge.

Beginning of the battle

By the summer of 1940, German and British air forces had started battling it out in the sky over Britain and that was when the deadliest bombing campaign began. The Battle of Britain was fought essentially in the skies, but it ended when Germany's *Luftwaffe* couldn't supersede the efforts of the Royal Air Force despite Germany's continued targetting of Britain's air bases and posts.

Defeating the Royal Air Force

German troops soon realised that the British Royal Air Force (RAF) was a difficult adversary and hence if Britain had to be conquered, the RAF had to be destroyed. So, the German troops concentrated on destroying airport runways and targetted radar systems and infrastructure. The RAF and British forces continued to battle it out with Germany; whereby, Hitler decided to change strategy and started bombing large cities, starting with London.

Britain puts up a good defence

German troops began to feel that they were very close to conquering England, but the RAF shot down many German planes. Although the German troops continued bombing London and other targets in Britain, the raids had to slow down because the RAF were fighting on their homeland, and they also had the advantage of radar facilities. They could, therefore, defend their aircrafts well.

FUN FACT

The Battle of Britain was the first battle to be fought almost entirely in the air. Germany lost around double the aeroplanes of Britain.

The first mass German air raid on London on 7th September, 1940. Tower Bridge stands out against a background of smoke of fire.

Detail of the Battle of Britain Monument on the Victoria Embankment, London.

The USA Supports Britain

Although USA and England had similar ideologies, many in the US questioned its involvement during World War I. So, as far as possible USA did not want to get involved in World War II.

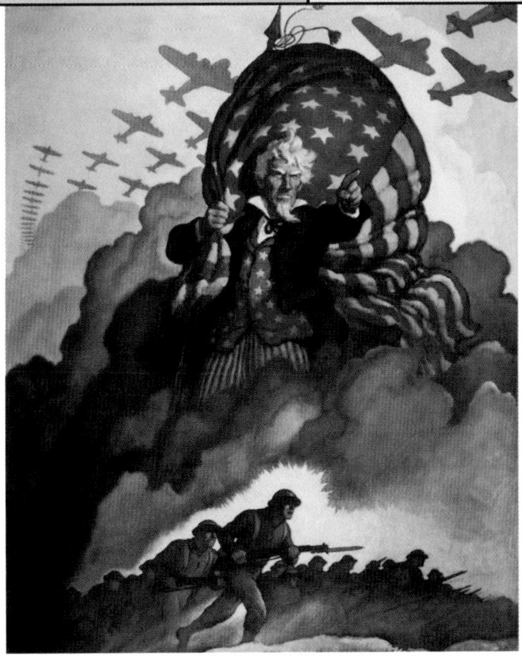

A 1942 World War II poster of Uncle Sam. He holds a US flag and points his finger as fighting troops, with airplan es flying overhead, advance from a cloud of smoke.

The Neutrality Act and the USA

At the advent of World War II in Europe, US President Franklin Roosevelt understood that the war could prove to be a menace for US security, so he sought ways to help European states without getting directly involved. The Neutrality Act came into existence when the law was passed by the US Congress and signed by President Franklin Delano Roosevelt in August, 1935. It was meant to keep America out of any European conflict by banning shipment of any war material to the belligerents and it forbade US citizens from travelling on these ships and if they did it would be at their own risk. During the 1940s, when France had been invaded and Britain seemed to be the only democracy left, the USA began to trade arms under the fourth Neutrality Act that allowed USA to trade arms with the Allies.

Chinese soldier guards a line of American P-40 fighter planes, 1942.

Lend-Lease Act

In March 1941, Theodore Roosevelt allowed the lending, leasing, selling or bartering of arms under the Lend-Lease Act, which permitted ammunition and food to be given or leased to any state that the President deemed vital to the defence of USA. The Lend-Lease Act of 1941 began a programme under which the USA could provide goods and services to the Allies in their war against Germany, Italy and later Japan during World War II. As per the terms under the Lend-Lease Act, the Allies could repay America by way of returning the goods or using them in support of the cause or by a similar transfer of goods.

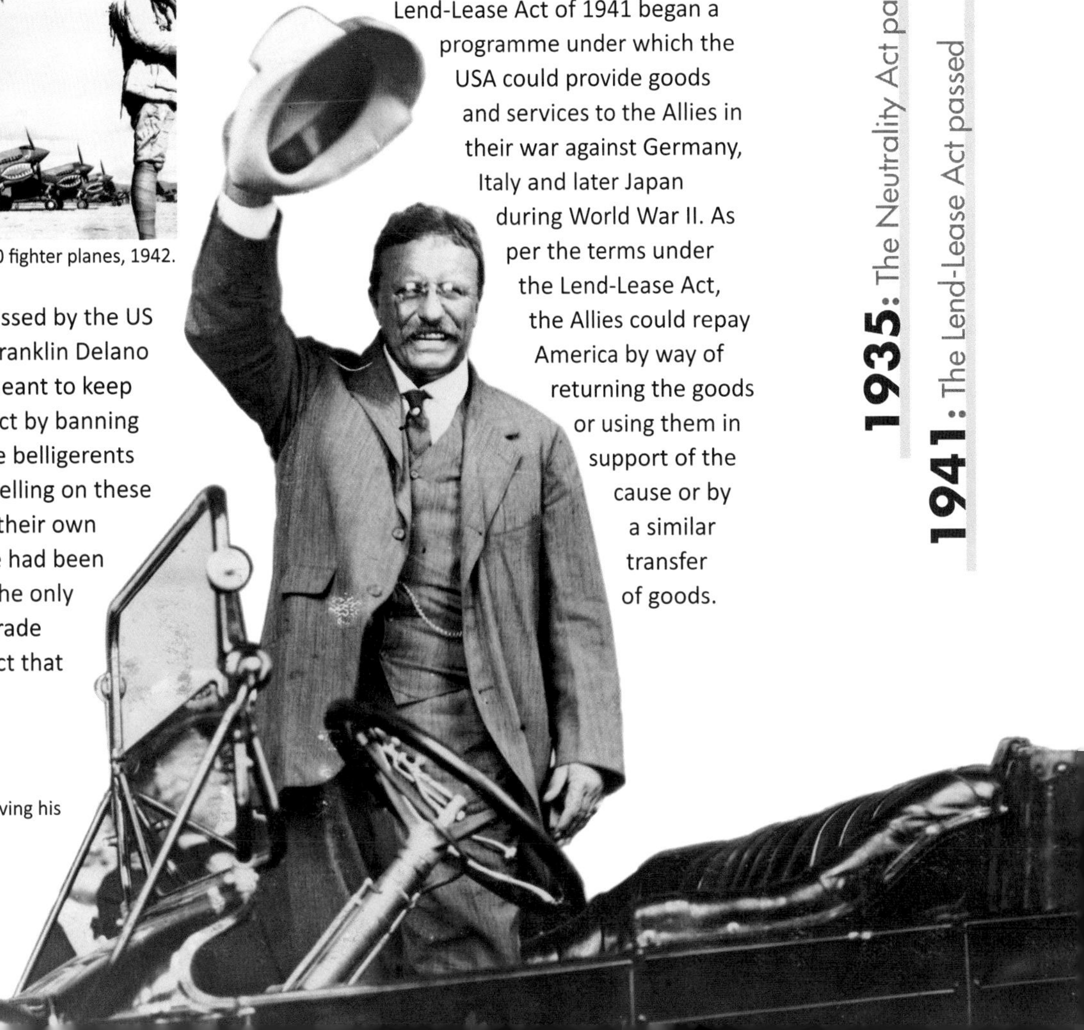

Theodore Roosevelt, waving his hat, as he stands in car.

1935: The Neutrality Act passed

1941: The Lend-Lease Act passed

USA and Britain's Association

USA was pulled into World War II when its naval and air force began accompanying British convoys that were transporting the Lend-Lease material across the seas, in a bid to defend them from the German U-boats. Winston Churchill kept urging US President Theodore Roosevelt to enter the war. They met at the 1941 Atlantic Conference, where Roosevelt had said that people should have the right to choose their own government.

The USS Shaw on fire after being hit by a Japanese bomber in Pearl Harbor.

The final trigger

The 1941 Japanese bombing of the US Pacific fleet at Pearl Harbor became the final trigger that ensured the entry of USA into World War II. After the bombing, the US Senate unanimously voted in favour of entering the war, except for one congressman. Four days later, Germany declared war on USA.

USA enters World War II with Operation Torch

In November 1942, the combined armed forces of USA and Britain began an ambitious operation against the French-held territories in Algeria and Morocco. The campaign was called Torch.
It was born out of several rounds of discussions and disagreements.

In 1942, Operation Torch or the invasion of North Africa became USA's first offensive during World War II. Allied troops steadily cornered German forces in North Africa and Germany surrendered in Tunisia in May, 1943. The Allied forces realised that Russia needed help. Churchill's plan of an attack through Italy at the Casablanca conference was approved and Operation Husky or the invasion of Sicily began in July 1943. By June 1944, the Allied forces had captured Rome.

Operation Torch plaque.

Eight US Navy Douglas SBD-3 Dauntless dive bombers and six Gruman F4F-4 Wildcat fighters on the flight deck of the escort carrier USS Santee (ACV-29) during Operation Torch, the November 1942 invasion of North Africa.

Operation Barbarossa

Operation Barbarossa: Germans inspecting Russian planes.

The operation by Germany to invade Russia on 22nd June, 1941 was code-named Operation Barbarossa. It became the largest military attack during World War II and had lasting effects on the people of Russia. Around three million Axis troops and 3500 tanks were part of this operation. Germany's win against the Allies in France a year earlier was a trigger for the operation.

The Soviet surviving

Germany in its triumph was happy to note that the Soviet army had previously faced defeats at the hands of Finland in 1939. This operation became one of the crucial moments of World War II. Unlike what Germany had in mind, the Soviet forces fought and survived, and ensured that the German offensive was thwarted.

Blitzkrieg and Operation Barbarossa

Operation Barbarossa was based on the idea of a huge attack that follows the blitzkrieg method—blitzkrieg is the German word for lightning war—it was a military tactic that was designed to create a huge disruption within enemy lines through the use of mobile forces and fire arms. Three German army groups attacked Russia on 22nd June, 1941.

Marcks plans attack on Russia

Erick Marcks, the German General, came up with an initial plan that involved a huge attack on Moscow followed by a second attack on Kiev with two

Destroyed Soviet tanks at Junourcia, during the German invasion of the USSR (Russia) in 1941.

subsequent attacks in the Baltic near Leningrad and in Moldavia in the south. After Moscow's decline, Marcks planned another attack on Kiev. Marcks' plan was reworked by Halder, but the final change was made by Hitler who code-named it Barbarossa.

German soldiers at Lubnica, where Soviet (Russian) forces attacked their left flank in 1941.

FUN FACT

Hitler had outlined his desire to invade the Soviet Union in his 1925 book *Mein Kampf.* Operation Barbarossa was a culmination of this desire.

Hitler's Plan

As per Hitler's plan, the main military action would happen in the north, which meant that Leningrad would become an equally important target along with Moscow. The attack involved the combined military strength of the Axis powers – three million soldiers, 3580 tanks, 7184 artillery guns, 1830 planes and 750,000 horses. On the seventeenth day of Operation Barbarossa, 300,000 Russians were captured. More than 2500 Russian tanks, 1400 Russian artillery guns and 250 Russian aircrafts were captured.

Nazi anti-Semitic poster of the early 1940s.

Russia is devastated

The German troops advanced very quickly and took over the Russian army's supply and communication lines. Hitler ordered his troops to move southeast towards Kiev. Another set of troops was asked to move to the north. This diversion meant that his central troops were left exposed without two of its most powerful groups.

Major success in Russia

The German troops saw many successes in the north and south. Many Russian soldiers were captured and held as prisoners. The German troops also amassed huge quantities of Russian arms and ammunition. The unprepared Soviet forces were taken aback with the sudden blitzkrieg attacks from Germany along the long border that stretched for close to 2900 km. The Soviet forces had to face terrible losses and in a week's time the German army had advanced 322 km into Soviet territory. The Germans had destroyed close to 4000 aircrafts and had either killed, captured or injured close to 600,000 Red Army troops. However, the diversion also impacted the time that the German troops took to advance further. Further, the German Army was caught in the midst of terrible cold and the freezing temperatures, which also affected their advance.

German infantry advancing on a burning village in Russia.

German anti-tank gun team on road with a flaming tank in background in Russia.

A Soviet military SSh-40 helmet emblazoned with the red star.

FUN FACT

Blitzkrieg is a German word, which means lightning war. It refers to a military tactic involving a quick, sudden and overwhelming attack on the enemy.

1939: German-Soviet Pact signed

1941: Operation Barbarossa begins

Invasion of USSR

Germany along with the Axis powers invaded the Soviet Union under Operation Barbarossa on 22nd June, 1941. It was one of Germany's biggest military operations during World War II. Around 4.5 million troops attacked from Polish territory that was under Germany's control. Despite the non-aggression pact signed in 1939, both the countries had been expecting aggression from the other side, but both were only waiting for the right time to strike.

First day of the German Invasion of the Soviet Union in June 1941.

Reenactment of breaking the siege of Leningrad.

Beginning of the Russian invasion

Hitler had always wanted to remove the communist threat from Russia and had, therefore, seen the 1939 German-Soviet nonaggression pact with Russia as just a temporary arrangement. After the German invasion of France and the other Low countries (Belgium, the Netherlands and Luxembourg), Hitler signed Directive 21, which gave the first operational order for the invasion of the Soviet Union under Operation Barbarossa.

Two years after signing the German–Soviet Pact, Germany made a move to invade Russia. The German troops saw success in Minsk and Smolensk and soon reached Kiev.

Russian soldiers burned to death during the German invasion of the Soviet Union in 1941.

During the winter and autumn of 1941, special units of German Security Police and Service were deployed at the front lines.

Severity of winter

The winter of December 1941 proved to be very harsh for the German armed forces as they marched their way to Moscow.

The winter gave Russia that much needed break from a continuous battle with Germany, but there were huge losses from both sides.

Order of German Cross in gold.

Failure of Barbarossa

Red Army section in Olšanské cemetery.

Hitler's strategy relied heavily on the internal collapse of the Red Army. But that was not how things panned out. The Germans had not anticipated the harsh winter and difficult terrain of Russia, which would make managing its army difficult. The Russian army was initially debilitated. However, soon it reorganised and its counterattacks soon forced the weary and resource-deficit German army to accept defeat.

Difficulty in coordination

Hitler deployed his armed forces to different places – Leningrad, Moscow and present day Ukraine. During the first six weeks Russia fought back, but soon German forces reached Leningrad and invaded Smolensk and Dnepropetrovsk in Ukraine.

However, coordinating with various army groups spread over a million kilometres proved to be very cumbersome and it was something that Hitler had not counted upon.

Unforeseen obstacles

The German troops trudged towards Moscow during the severe winter and were slowed down by Russia's counterattacks, forcing the Germans to retreat. The German soldiers were tired; they had ill-planned their warfare and could not provide for food and medicines. The distances were too large and the end goal was huge. The German armed forces also had to deal with poor Russian roads and harsh weather. Further, the Germans underestimated the resistance that they would face from the Red Army.

The German Falke Division crossing the Bug River, while advancing towards Kiev in September 1941.

German troops reach Stalingrad

Russia managed to drive the Germans back from Moscow. However, after a short while the German troops regrouped and continued their offensive in the city of Stalingrad, moving towards the Caucasus oil fields.

Operation Barbarossa became one of the most crucial events during World War II. Despite suffering huge losses, Russia bravely fought and continued to fight the Germans until 1942.

Russian soldiers preparing to cross a river in Stalingrad during the Battle of Stalingrad.

War in China

In 1941, Japan attacked Pearl Harbor thus, forcing the US to join World War II. The attack and the simultaneously occurring second Sino-Japanese war led to Japan making many enemies. In 1933, Japan left the League of Nations and became a threat for the European powers and USA. At the start of the second Sino-Japanese war, USA imposed economic sanctions on Japan.

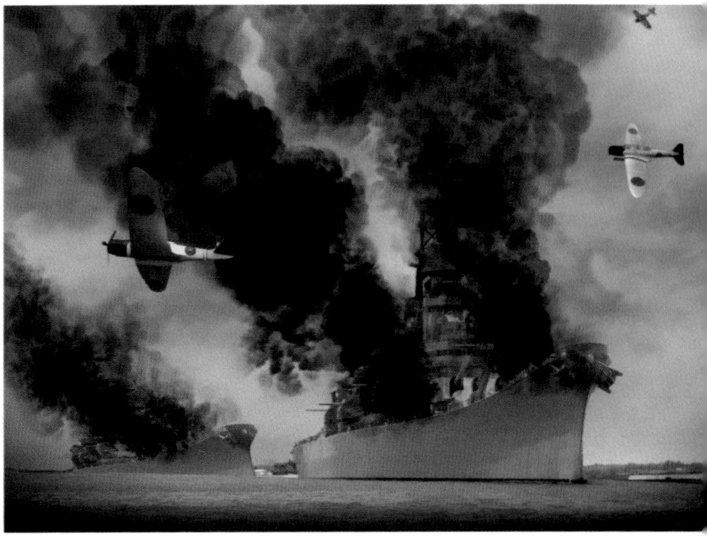

Digital oil painting of an attack during World War II.

Japan vs China

The second Sino-Japanese war began in July 1937 when the Japanese fired at Chinese troops at the Marco Polo Bridge near Beijing as an excuse to launch an invasion on China, using Manchuria as their base.

Soon, China's most important port, Shanghai was conquered and later the capital Nanjing (Nanking) was captured in December 1937. Following this, in 1940, Japan joined the Axis powers and signed the Tripartite Pact along with Germany.

In 1941, the Chinese Nationalists fought with the Japanese forces under the leadership of Chiang Kai-Shek. Chiang's forces were not well trained and were unequipped. World War II had reduced the foreign aid that China used to receive.

In 1942, the US Congress approved a US$ 500 million loan for China as USA saw China as its main ally against Japan.

End of the Sino-Japanese war

There were delays in supplies reaching China and it did not help that Chiang and his allies could not reach a consensus on how to use the foreign aid. However, China kept resisting the Japanese attacks.

FUN FACT

The second Sino-Japanese War (1937-1945), fought between China and Japan, was the largest war in Asia of the twentieth century.

Chinese soldiers marching on the Burma Road toward the fighting line on the Salween river front in 1943.

By 1944, Japan had invaded Kiangsi and Kwangsi and later controlled Peking-Hankow railway.

However, the second Sino-Japanese war came to an end when the US dropped the world's first atomic bombs on the cities of Hiroshima and Nagasaki, Japan on 6th and 9th August, 1945. The bombings led to Japan's surrender.

Hiroshima bomb explosion on 6th August, 1945.

Fall of Mussolini

Benito Mussolini, the founder of fascism, was Italy's supreme leader and dictator from 1922 till 1943. He became an important ally of Germany and Japan during World War II. In May 1938, Mussolini decided to partner with Hitler during the war. However, his armed forces were not prepared for war and could, therefore, offer no resistance to the Allied forces. Even internally Mussolini faced resistance to his dictatorship, which resulted in him becoming unpopular in his own country. He was overthrown in 1943. The Italian insurgents who opposed him captured and murdered the former Italian dictator. Thus, Mussolini's reign ended.

Meeting of Adolf Hitler and Benito Mussolini in Stepina, 1941.

(From left) Emilio De Bono, Benito Mussolini, Italo Balbo and Cesare Maria De Vecchi during the march to Rome.

Benito becomes Italy's supreme leader

Mussolini was involved in socialist politics and was a journalist in the socialist press. He joined the Italian army in September 1915.

By 1919, he formed the Fascist Party and got support from unemployed war veterans. He armed these party members and they began to be called Black Shirts. Mussolini's Black Shirts terrorised political leaders and were finally asked by the Italian king to join the coalition government in 1921.

Mussolini forms a government

In 1922, Mussolini was asked by King Victor Emmanuel to form the government. He became the Prime Minister of Italy. Slowly and steadily, he dissolved the various democratic institutions in the government and silenced all his political opponents. By 1925, he declared himself as a dictator and took the title of "Il Duce".

He wanted to re-establish Italy as a great European power and with that intent he invaded Ethiopia in 1935. Mussolini helped the Spanish dictator Franco in the Spanish Civil war. He signed the Pact of Steel with Germany and introduced an anti-Jewish legislation in Italy.

Mussolini with Italian troops in the Adriatic front.

1919: Mussolini forms Fascist Party

1925: Mussolini takes title of 'Il Duce'

Mussolini Declares War on Allies

In 1940, Mussolini declared war on Britain and France, and met with a series of defeats in north and east Africa and the Balkans. By 1943, Italy was severely defeated and the Allied forces had captured Sicily.

Anzio War Cemetery for allied military personnel who were killed in World War II.

Mussolini signs an armistice with the Allies

Mussolini was removed from office and jailed by his ex-colleagues in the Fascist government. Italy signed an armistice with the Allies. The German troops came and rescued Mussolini. He was reinstated as the leader of the government, but in reality he did not have any influence.

Fall of Mussolini

Mussolini had dreamt of establishing a Fascist Italy and bringing it back to its former glory as an empire, but Italy suffered many military defeats during World War II. By 1943, opposition groups in Italy had come together to overthrow Mussolini and make peace with the Allies, but the Germany's army stopped such an act. However, after Italy lost its ground, Mussolini was soon deposed in a coup.

Announcement of surrender

After Italy signed an armistice with the Allies, General Eisenhower—the commander-in-chief of the Allied forces—announced the surrender by the Italian government, which had agreed to put an end to all hostilities with the Allies.

In a personal message to his people, Prime Minister Badoglio confirmed the surrender. It was suggested to sign an armistice in August in a neutral territory. Finally, the armistice was signed on 3rd September, 1943 in Sicily. They decided to keep the armistice a secret until the Allies had completed its invasion of Italy.

Benito Mussolini met with a series of defeats between 1940-43.

Bomb-struck area in Germany.

Russia Declares War on Japan

A World War II US fighter plane shooting down Japanese torpedo bomber over Saipan.

In the east, the Japanese army had been eyeing the Siberian part of Russia for a very long time and tried several times to challenge the Russian forces in the region. The two countries eventually signed a ceasefire and the two countries remained friendly right up to World War II. As per his agreement with the Allies, Stalin led Russia to declare war on Japan just three days after the Hiroshima atomic bomb attack, after which Russia invaded Manchuria.

Ruins of Nagasaki, Japan, after the atomic bombing of 9th August, 1945. Battered religious figures are seen amid the rubble.

Operation August Storm

In a surprise move for the Japanese, Russia declared war on Japan on 8th August, 1945 and launched Operation August Storm. After the destruction of Hiroshima, Japan still had ammunition and fought the Russians. Once the Russians invaded Manchuria, they defeated the Japanese army. Soon, the Soviet forces launched an attack on the south of Sakhalin Island, after which they planned to invade the island of Hokkaido. Japan understood that it would not be possible for its army to fight both the Allies and Soviet armed forces, both of which would be attacking its territory from different directions. The Soviet invasion decimated the Japanese armed forces. On 9th August, 1945 USA dropped another atomic bomb on Nagasaki and by 15th August, 1945 Emperor Hirohito of Japan officially surrendered to the Allies.

The Atomic Dome, ex Hiroshima Industrial Promotion Hall, destroyed by the first atomic bomb in Hiroshima, Japan.

Russia continues fighting with Japan

Russian forces continued fighting with the Japanese Kwantung Army. After two weeks, the Japanese forces lay defeated and Japan's official surrender to the Allies was quickly signed on 2nd September, 1945 on the US Battleship Missouri.

Mushroom cloud of the atom bomb that exploded over Nagasaki, Japan, on 9th August, 1945.

FUN FACT

An American B-29 bomber dropped the first atomic bomb over the Japanese city of Hiroshima. It destroyed around 90 per cent of the city and killed 80,000 people. Soon, many more perished due to radiation. The second bomb dropped on Nagasaki killed around 40,000 people.

Allies Invade Italy

The Allied invasion of Sicily became the reason for the fall of Mussolini's government. He was forced to resign by the Fascist Grand Council and was soon arrested. After the Italian dictator was deposed, Pietro Badoglio became the leader of the Italian government. He held secret negotiations with the Allies notwithstanding the presence of German troops in Italy.

US B-17 Bomber falling after its wing was shot off during invasion of Sicily in July 1943.

The Eighth Army

The Allied invasion of Italy was led by Field Marshal Bernard L. Montgomery, who along with the Allied troops crossed the Straits of Messina from Sicily and headed towards Calabria, also known as the "toe" of Italy. Montgomery's British Eighth Army began advancing through the Italian mainland. As per Italy's surrender terms, the Allies would be lenient with the Italians if they would help the Allies in defeating the German armed forces in Italy.

Italy's invasion begins

By 1943, the Allied forces had begun their invasion of European countries under the control of the Axis powers. It started with the island of Sicily as they faced very little struggle from the dispirited Italian troops. In just three days, around 150,000 Allied troops arrived on Italy's shore and soon the Allied invasion of Sicily was complete.

Secret negotiations with Allies

The collapse of Mussolini seemed imminent with the Allied conquest of Sicily. The Fascist Grand Council forced Mussolini to resign and he was soon arrested. Pietro Badoglio took over the reigns of the Italian government after secret negotiations with the Allies. Mussolini who was imprisoned in the Abruzzo mountains was rescued by German commandos and reinstated as a leader with very little power.

FUN FACT

Mussolini tried to escape from Italy, but was caught by Italian partisans and shot dead on 28th April, 1945.

World War II era bombing run on airport.

Operation Husky

World War II German bunker in Marina di Ragusa, Sicily, Italy.

The Allies wanted to challenge Germany by overthrowing the Italian regime. Further, invading Italy seemed like a good option because it would divert Germany's attention from the Allied plan of Germany's invasion. The Allies started the Italian campaign with Sicily's invasion. The Allies named the invasion of Sicily as Operation Husky.

Capture of Palermo

After defeating the German forces in the mountains of Sicily, the Allies successfully managed to send back the German forces. The capture of Palermo inevitably led to the collapse of Mussolini's government. In this attack, the Allies suffered casualties of over 23,000. The Allies decided on Operation Husky after they realised that the best way to tackle Germany would be by invading Sicily. General Dwight D. Eisenhower became the overall commander of the attack, while British General Harold Alexander became the overall ground commander. The invasion was done using gliders, parachutes and boats. Despite disruptions caused by the high winds, after a while the Sicilian capital of Palermo was conquered by the Allies and Sicily was secured.

A bronze statue of Dwight D. Eisenhower in his World War II jacket. The statue is on the grounds of the Presidential Library and Museum, USA.

German forces resist Allies in Italy

Despite the surrender of the Italian government, the German troops fought and resisted the fall of Rome. The German-fortified Winter Line across southern Italy kept pushing back the Allied forces for more than six months. Finally, in 1944, Rome was conquered and the German troops retreated towards a new line called the Gothic Line towards northern Italy, which they managed to control till 1945.

Allied ships in a southern Italian port being loaded with vehicles and supplies. They assaulted the southern coast of France, in Operation Dragoon on 15th August, 1944.

Mussolini is executed

The Badoglio government declared war on Germany and by April 1945 the Allied forces had started a new offensive. Mussolini was captured again and executed by Italian partisans.

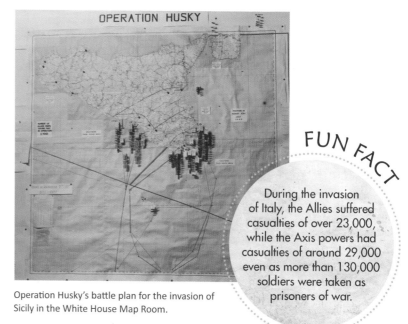

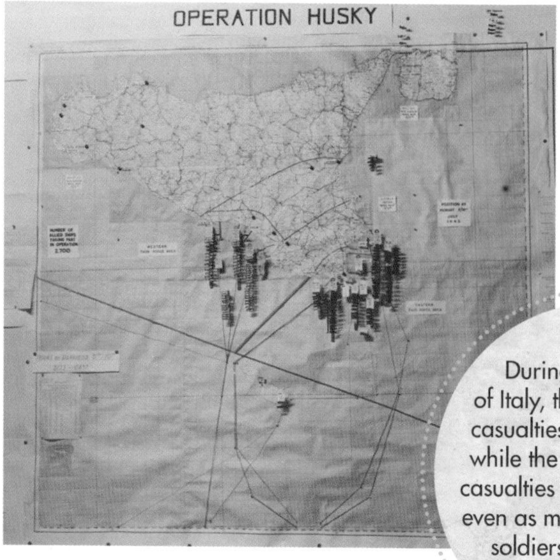

Operation Husky's battle plan for the invasion of Sicily in the White House Map Room.

FUN FACT

During the invasion of Italy, the Allies suffered casualties of over 23,000, while the Axis powers had casualties of around 29,000 even as more than 130,000 soldiers were taken as prisoners of war.

Allies Invade Western Europe

A-20 G Havoc light bomber with D-Day "invasion stripes" painted on wings. Plumes of smoke rise from the Forest Cerisy, where a German machine gun position blocked the US advance, 8th June, 1944.

The battle of Normandy lasted from June to August 1944. It led to the freedom of western Europe from Germany's control. Called as Operation Overlord and also known as D-Day, the Battle of Normandy involved around 156,000 Allied forces comprising British, Canadian and American soldiers who landed along the coastline of Normandy in France. The Battle of Normandy ended with the Allies freeing various countries in western Europe from Germany's control.

FUN FACT

The Normandy American Cemetery near the Omaha beach and the English Channel was the first US cemetery in Europe. More than 9300 of the US armed forces who died during the D-Day Normandy missions were buried in the cemetery.

The coast of Normandy is covered with deep craters from the bombardments on D-day.

Normandy landing

The Normandy invasion saw US, British, and Canadian forces land on five beaches in Normandy. Later, other countries also joined them. The invasion led by 12 countries involved three million troops.

D-day

Launched on 6th June, 1944, the first day of the Normandy landing is also called D-day. The Allied troops crossed the English Channel to reach Normandy in France. It ended in the defeat of the Germans and the liberation of northern France.

1943 American poster showing cannons, each with the flag of an Allied nation.

Beginning of end of World War II

Owing to the fact that the Battle of Normandy was fought on land and in water, a lot of planning was required to conduct detailed overtures that would mislead the Germans. By August 1944, the operation had succeeded in liberating northern France and by the next spring the Allies had defeated the Germans. It is no wonder that the Battle of Normandy is also called the Beginning of the end of World War II, at least in Europe.

D-Day landing crafts head for Omaha beach during the Normandy invasion on 6th June, 1944. In the right is the cruiser USS Augusta, flagship of the Western Naval Task Force.

Operation Overlord

Formation of Douglas A-20s over France during the D-Day invasion in June 1944.

On 5th June, 1944, more than 5,000 ships carrying troops and supplies left England for France, even as over 11,000 aircrafts were being readied for air warfare to support the invasion of France. The invasion began on the morning of 6th June, 1944. Around 156,000 allied troops effectively invaded the beaches of Normandy. Within a week the beaches were fully secured.

Choltitz refuses Hitler

Paris finally became free after four years of Nazi occupation when the French 2nd Armoured Division and the US 4th Infantry Division were able to overcome the weakened German resistance. Hitler ordered the German army to bomb Paris's major landmarks and burn the city before the Allies reached and liberated the city. However, General Dietrich von Choltitz, the commander of the German garrison, did not pay heed to Hitler's orders and signed a formal surrender.

Germany deterred

Due to the absence of Commander Rommel (who was on leave), Hitler did not send divisions close to Normandy to counterattack the Allies. The German troops came from other places and were delayed as many bridges had been destroyed by the Allied forces. Soon, the port of Cherbourg was conquered and more Allied forces entered Normandy.

France liberated

By the end of August 1944, the Allied forces had liberated Paris and soon the German forces were pushed back. The Allied forces entered Germany. On the other side, Russian forces too had begun to advance into Germany. When Germany was unable to defeat the Allies in Normandy, it had to concede its failure in defending what it had wanted to create—"the European fortress". The loss of Normandy led to the end of World War II.

German bunker at Point du Hoc in Normandy, France.

1944: Operation Overlord begins

1945: Second World War ends

Mulberry harbour developed for the D-Day invasion of Normandy. Installed on Omaha beach after D-Day, the steel roadway was supported by prefabricated concrete caissons.

German Offensive in the West

American soldiers, stripped of equipment, lie dead, face down in Belgium during the Battle of the Bulge. The soldier in the foreground has bare feet.

The Battle of the Bulge started in December 1944 and earned its name owing to the bulging shape in the map. It became the last big offensive on the Western Front and was the biggest battle that the US fought. The battle was fought during the winter from 1944–1945 and was the final major German attack against the Allies in World War II.

Divide and rule

The Battle of the Bulge was Hitler's final attempt to split the Allied forces. It started on 16th December, 1944 and was carried out because Hitler believed that the Allied forces were weaker in western Europe. He believed that a major attack would completely destroy the Allies.

Battle of the Bulge

In a desperate attempt at regaining lost ground, the German army launched the attack against the Allies in the thickly forested Ardennes region in Belgium, which proved to be costly for the Allies.

The Battle of the Bulge got its name because the attack created a 113 km wide and 80 km deep bulge in the American defensive line thus, separating the British and American forces.

Russian old gun in Prokhorovka on 30th January, 2013. The largest tank battle of World War II happened here.

Germany faces shortage of fuel

Despite heavy casualties, the US army did not give up. Soon, the German forces faced a shortage of fuel, while the Allied troops led by General Patton regrouped and fought hard to retrieve the town of Bastogne in Belgium.

The main reason for the shortage of fuel was that the American troops had bombed and destroyed the German fuel depots, which led to the German tanks running out of fuel. The Germans lost the battle.

German soldier waving his unit members forward in the first few days of the Battle of the Bulge.

Valiant US Troops Don't Give Up

During the Battle of the Bulge, the American troops near Bastogne, Belgium were surrounded by the Germans army and they were ordered to surrender or die. But the US troops led by US General McAuliffe did not give up and held out till more reinforcement troops arrived. The courage of these valiant soldiers ensured the victory of the Allies in the battle.

Gestapo officials recording data on incoming prisoners at a German concentration camp.

Bodies of dead inmates in the yard of Nordhausen, a Gestapo concentration camp. The photo was taken shortly after the camp's liberation by the US Army on 12th April, 1945.

Germany surrenders

In April 1945, the commander of the German home guards (Gestapo), Heinrich Himmler, entered into negotiation talks for peace with the Allies, that is, Britain and USA. Meanwhile, rather than face arrest by the Allies, Adolf Hitler committed suicide in Berlin on 30th April, 1945. Soon, the Allies demanded that the German troops immediately surrender at all their fronts.

End of the European phase of war

In 1945, Colonel General Alfred Jodl became the German High Command. He was Hitler's successor. In the beginning, General Jodl did not want the Germans to surrender at all the fronts, but wanted only the forces that were fighting in western Europe to surrender. However, the Allied commander General Dwight Eisenhower wanted a complete German surrender. Eisenhower gave the indication that if Germany failed to completely surrender, then the Allies would seal off the western front and not allow the Germans to escape to the west, which meant that they would ultimately fall in front of the approaching Soviet forces. On 7th May, 1945, early in the morning, Colonel General Alfred Jodl signed the terms of unconditional surrender and after five years, eight months and seven days, the European phase of World War II came to an end.

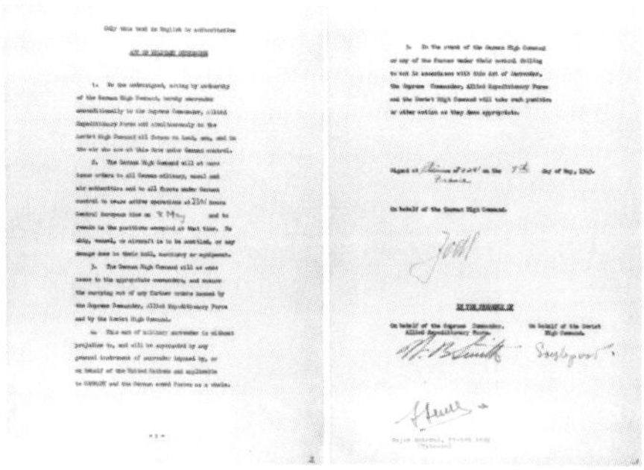

Germany surrender document signed by Gen. Alfred Jodl, Chief of Staff of the German Army. It was signed at the Allied Headquarters at Reims, on 7th May, 1945.

FUN FACT

The Gestapo was the political police of Nazi Germany, that ruthlessly eliminated opposition to the Nazis within Germany and its occupied territories. Working in partnership with the Sicherheitsdienst or the Security Service, it was primarily responsible for the roundup of Jews throughout Europe for deportation to extermination camps.

Allied POWs in a variety of uniforms at a prison camp in Zossen, Germany.

The German Collapse

The Allied forces extensively used air warfare in their final attack on Germany. The air offensive included 800 RAF aircrafts and 400 US aircrafts and resulted in the death of around 25,000 people and destruction of various cities across Europe.

Bodies of prisoners who died of starvation lie on the floor of a concentration camp in Nordhausen, Germany after liberation by First US Army on 11th April, 1945.

Germans and the self-destruct mode

The German troops were asked to follow Hitler's idea of self-destruction. Hitler had declared that "the battle must carry on without consideration for our own population" and that all "all industrial plants, all the main electricity works, waterworks and gas works" must be destroyed to create a desert-like environment for the Allies. Hitler's self-destruct idea met with opposition from his Minister of War Production Albert Speer, who secretly met army and industrial heads and asked them not to heed Hitler's idea.

Allied forces enter Berlin

The Allied forces comprising mainly Americans and British soldiers crossed the Rhine river and easily reached Berlin. Simultaneously, Russia took the offensive towards Vienna and soon the Russians too reached Berlin.

Germany was bound to lose the war from the beginning

Germany's strategic position even at the start of the war had never been optimum, for it was at war with countries like France and UK that together had a population of around 90 million.

They were industrialised nations that received help from neutral countries like Belgium and the Netherlands—countries who were in essence enemies of Germany. Germany had a population of just 79 million.

Further, the French and British navies prevented Germany from accessing its natural resources. Thus, due to these factors Germany was bound to run out of the raw materials required to fight this prolonged battle.

Consequently, Germany was forced to surrender in the end.

FUN FACT

The German air force had 22 infantry divisions, two armour divisions and 11 para-troop divisions. Further, 84 German army generals were executed by Hitler.

In May 1941, Nazi Germany bombed British cities.

Hitler with Baldur von Schirach, who was the leader of the "Hitler Youth".

Hitler Stays in Berlin

During the last 10 days of his life, Hitler met his top men and fellow Nazis. He met Josef Goebbels and Himmler, Ribbentrop and Alfred Jodl among others on his 56th birthday in Berlin. They asked him to leave the now doomed Berlin and go towards the mountainous terrain of the German–Austrian border, where he had his villa. They urged him to go there and could continue to hold the fort in the mountains of western Austria and southern Bavaria.

The fall of Hitler

Hitler knew that if he moved out of his bunker in Berlin he would risk being captured. He did not want to be alive and end up being caught and displayed by his enemies, especially the Russians. Therefore, he did not leave, but gave permission to his personal bunker staff to leave. A few of his personal staff stayed with him, including his top aide Martin Bormann, some soldiers, some of his private secretaries and his long-time companion, Eva Braun. Hitler chose to stay in Berlin and married his mistress Eva Braun two days before he committed suicide with her in the chancellery ruins. Around this time the Russian troops were just a few kilometres away from Hitler's complex.

As infantrymen march through a German town, a shocked old woman stares at the ruins in Germany in 1945.

Germany surrenders

Hitler's successor, Dönitz, wanted to save Germany's civilians and he worked towards this aim. The Allied forces finally broke through the German defences. The surrender document was signed on 29th April, 1945 and the attacks soon stopped by 2nd May, 1945.

The European World War ends

The German forces surrendered and signed a surrender document at Montgomery's headquarters and another one at Reims in front of the American, British and French delegations. By midnight of 8th May, 1945 the war in Europe was formally over.

Helmet and rifle monument to dead soldiers on a shell-blasted beach.

FUN FACT

The United Nations was formed at the end of World War II with an aim to prevent such wars in the future.

US Troops Continue Attacks on Japan

Aerial view of Hitachi Aircraft Co., in Tachikawa, Japan. It was bombed by US B-29 Superfortresses in 1945.

Towards the end of 1942, the Japanese soldiers had begun to occupy or attack different places across the South Pacific. Hoping to stop Japan in its tracks, the US Navy Admiral Chester Nimitz followed a strategy of island hopping, that is, to capture strategic islands near Japan one by one, so that eventually the US bombers would reach within closing distance of Japan.

USA uses firebombs

After securing the Japanese island of Iwo Jima, USA tried a new strategy of night strikes using napalm firebombs. The Tokyo bombing on 9th and 10th March, 1945 devastated the city and killed more than 80,000 people and rendered over a lakh Japanese homeless.

Aerial warfare against Japan

The American troops continued to bomb cities like Kobe, Yokohama, Toyama, Osaka and Nagoya. It seemed as if Japan did not require any invasion on land and that simple air warfare would suffice. The USA with its Manhattan Project under its US Office of Scientific Research and Development soon developed an atomic bomb that was tested in the desert area near Alamogordo, New Mexico, in July 1945. The atomic bomb had the same potency as 15,000 tons of dynamite. President Truman saw the possibility of using the atomic bomb in Japan, particularly because Japan did not respond well to the Potsdam declaration. The Hiroshima bombing had a devastating effect. It killed more than 70,000 people and many more died due to radiation exposure. The second bombing on Nagasaki killed around 40,000 people. Finally, Japan's Emperor Hirohito surrendered to the Allies.

An Army B-25 bomber takes off from the USS HORNET in the first US air raid on Japan led by General James Doolittle on 18th April, 1942.

The Japanese Surrender 1945

By the summer of 1945, the Japanese navy and air force had been decimated. Further, the Allies had blocked access to the seas and were conducting bomb raids over Japan, leaving the country in shambles. With the US capture of Okinawa, it was inevitable that the Allies would invade the main Japanese islands. US General Douglas MacArthur was to launch Operation Downfall in November 1945, but it was abandoned as Japan agreed to surrender.

Charred bodies lie amidst the destruction caused by the atomic bombing of Nagasaki.

Potsdam Declaration

The Allies issued the Potsdam Declaration that demanded unconditional surrender of the Japanese armed forces and if they did not accept the declaration then they would be responsible for the devastation that was to follow the country.

Japanese Prime Minister Kantaro Suzuki told the press that his government would not heed the ultimatum of the Allied powers.

After this, US President Harry Truman gave the order for the devastation to begin, which started with the dropping of the atomic bomb on Hiroshima by the US B-29 bomber Enola Gay.

Effects of the bombing

The atomic bombing of Hiroshima killed around 80,000 people and fatally wounded many more. Even after the Hiroshima attack, members from Japan's Supreme War Council were in favour of surrender, but the majority remained steadfast in their resistance to unconditional surrender.

On 8th August, 1945 USSR declared war against Japan, and a few days later the Soviet forces attacked Manchuria. This was quickly followed by the dropping of a second atomic bomb on the Japanese coastal city of Nagasaki, killing 39,000-80,000 people. Over the following months, many more died due to exposure to radiation.

Douglas MacArthur

FUN FACT

The Japanese were guilty of many war crimes during World War II and were responsible for the death of more than 20 million Chinese under a terrible policy called "Kill All, Burn All and Loot All".

Battleship Missouri Memorial at Pearl Harbor in Honolulu on the island of O'ahu. Japan surrendered aboard the deck to end World War II.

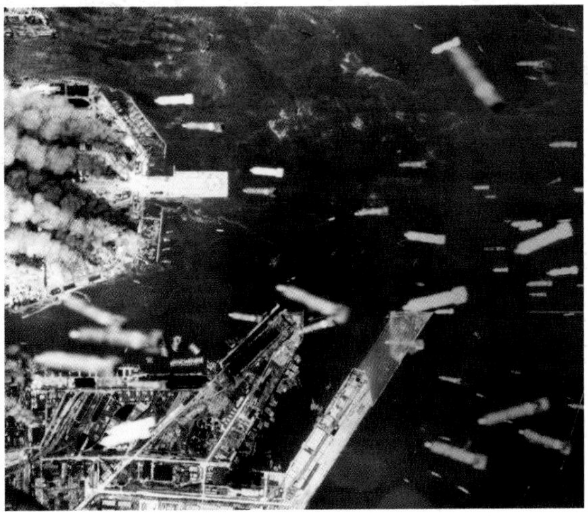

A costly battle

After the atomic attacks, the US planned to invade Japan under Operation Downfall in November 1945. However, the August atomic bombing of Hiroshima and Nagasaki and the Soviet invasion of Manchuria brought Japan to its knees. Faced with further destruction, Emperor Hirohito decided to surrender.

In response, the USA sent a message on 12th August, 1945 that "the authority of the Japanese emperor and government would be subject to the Supreme Commander of the Allied Powers". After a debate, Emperor Hirohito got work started on the wording of Japan's official surrender.

US 21st Bomber Command dropped incendiary bombs on Osaka, Japan on 1st June, 1945.

Military coup crushed

On 15th August, 1945, Major Kenji Hatanaka took over control of the imperial palace and the military coup managed to burn down Prime Minister Suzuki's residence.

However, the coup was soon squashed. By noon, Emperor Hirohito made a national address on the radio telling people that the country was about to surrender to the Allies.

Japan surrenders

USA accepted Japan's surrender. MacArthur led the Allied occupation of Japan as the Supreme Commander of the Allied Powers.

On 2nd September, 1945, Japan surrendered on the battleship, the USS *Missouri* in Tokyo Bay, Japan. The final surrender ceremony was stalled till the rest of the Allied delegates arrived.

In front of the Allied representatives, Japanese Foreign Minister Mamoru Shigemitsu and General Yoshijiro Umezu signed the Japanese Instrument of Surrender.

End of World War II

MacArthur signed on behalf of Allied forces, who made a declaration that "a better world shall emerge out of the blood and carnage of the past".

USS *Missouri* Battleship at Pearl Harbor in Hawaii.

Soon, the other allies including China, Britain, the USSR, Australia, Canada, France, the Netherlands and New Zealand signed the agreement and finally World War II came to an end. However, the war formally came to an end when the Treaty of San Francisco was enforced on 28th April, 1952.

1945: Atomic bombing of Japan

1945: Japan surrenders and World War II ends

Huge crowd packed in Times Square, in a premature celebration of Japan's surrender.

End of Japanese War

The US forces were making strides towards Japan and were increasingly relying on air warfare. Aerial bombing was the focal point of the US strategy for Japan. This strategy began with the dropping of 2000 tons of incendiary bombs over the city of Tokyo. Conducted over two days, the bombing completely burned more than 16 sq km of land in and around Tokyo—the Japanese capital.

Tokyo burns under B-29 firebomb assault. In this raid, 464 B-29s fire bombed the area immediately south of the Imperial Palace on 26th May, 1945.

Bombing of Tokyo

The Tokyo bombings were crucial for USA in terms of the devastation that it caused in the Japanese capital. It killed around 80,000-130,000 Japanese in a single fire-storm, making it the worst of its kind in history. From 1944 to 1945, the US forces carried on with the continuous long-range bombing of Japan using B-29 bombers. But the US forces had other plans for the island of Iwo Jima, because they realised that if Iwo Jima was captured, then it would become an important base for USA.

Raising the flag on Mount Suribachi

Joe Rosenthal took the historic photograph of *Raising the Flag on Iwo Jima* on 23rd February, 1945. It shows five Marines and a US Navy corpsman hoisting a replacement American flag on top of Mount Suribachi. Later, Felix de Weldon used the picture to sculpt the 1954 Marine Corps War Memorial, next to Arlington National Cemetery.

1944-45: Aerial bombing of Tokyo

1945: Battle of Iwo Jima

Tokyo's shanty town, where post-World War II homeless Japanese set up housekeeping in small huts during wartime bombing.

Marine Corps War Memorial. The memorial features the statues of servicemen who raised the second US flag on Iwo Jima during World War II.

Iwo Jima attack

Iwo Jima was severely bombarded by the US troops using naval guns, rockets and napalm bombs, but the Japanese troops had protected the island very well and it seemed unaffected. The US marines and Japanese troops began fighting on 19th February. After fierce fighting, the US flag was planted on Mount Suribachi and the island was secured on 16th March, 1945. The attack saw Japanese casualties of over 21,000 and US casualties of over 6000.

Costs of World War II

World War II became the most terrifying and significant event of the twentieth century. It was responsible for many social changes that ended European colonialism and brought forth the US civil rights movement. In addition, it may have paved way for the start of the women's rights movement.

Emergence of two superpowers

After World War II, two major powers emerged —USA and Soviet Russia. Soon, the two countries would delve into a war of another kind — the Cold War that would last for the remainder of the twentieth century.

Cost of World War II

World War II was the worst war in history and although the exact figure of human lives that were lost across the world is not known, it is estimated that more than 50 million defence personnel and civilians might have died during World War II. The countries that suffered the most in terms of losses, both human and material, included Japan, China, Germany and Russia.

Soldiers on a farmhouse after World War II.

Loss of life

American military truck in Pilsen City Czech Republic Europe - Anniversary at the end of World War II.

Estimates suggest that around 70 million people died owing to the constant battles that were fought between 1939 and 1945. Around two-thirds of this figure actually comprised civilians who had not engaged in war, which made it the deadliest war in history. Close to one in 10 Germans perished during the war. Germany lost around 30 per cent of its total armed personnel. More than 15 million Chinese died during World War II, while the Soviet Union saw casualties of around 27 million. Poland lost 16 per cent of its population, mainly Jews who were exterminated as per Hitler's final solution plan. In a nutshell, World War II witnessed killings of around 30,000 people every day.

World War II Memorial in Washington DC.

End of European Colonialism

Soviet communistic background.

After 100 years of the Emancipation Proclamation, the African Americans in USA, especially in the southern states, were still living a segregated life with no right to vote and discrimination. Segregation remained a daily reality they had to face along with instances of violence owing to their skin colour. They had no access to public schools and bathrooms.

End of colonialism

World War II brought an end to European colonialism. Colonies were waking up to the concept of people power and many colonies both in Africa and Asia were revolting against their imperial rulers. Uprisings to seek independence and communism were also the effects of World War II. Countries in eastern Europe and China seemed influenced by Soviet Russia and soon became communist states.

Civil rights movement in USA

In USA, African Americans joined the civil rights movement under Dr Martin Luther King Jr, which aimed at ending racial discrimination and segregation of African Americans. Mahatma Gandhi's non-violence message was propagated during the civil rights movements in USA.

In South Africa, however, racial discrimination continued even under the new government and apartheid or separateness in South Africa existed until 1994. Soon, a women's rights movement would also begin in USA.

Advances in technology

A space race began between the USA and USSR as each country tried to develop space programmes. Quickly, technology developed during the war became better and sophisticated, ranging from sonar, radar to the use of chemicals, plastics, etc.

FUN FACT

USA sent the first men on the moon on 20th July, 1969.

Bronze statue of Nelson Mandela in Johannesburg. Nelson Mandela is credited with peacefully ending apartheid in South Africa.

The Martin Luther King Jr Memorial located on National Mall on the Tidal Basin in Washington DC.

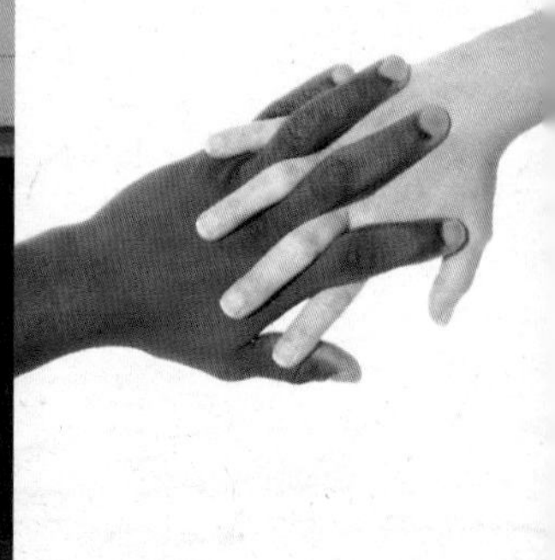

Europe after World War II

World War II had destroyed Europe, right from roads and bridges to communication. In all practical terms, Europe had to be rebuilt from scratch, but it was difficult since many governments did not have the resources to do so, since lot of money had been used during the war.

Europe overcomes the economic crisis

Countries like the USA were worried about the spread of communism and this meant that western Europe needed to be rebuilt quickly. The US economy and territory had not been greatly impacted because the war had not been fought on US soil. This made it the richest country in the world at the end of the war. Hence, the onus of helping Europe get over the economic crisis fell on the shoulders of USA.

The Marshall Plan

To help Europe pull through the after effects of the war, the US came up with the Marshall Plan, named after US Secretary of State George Marshall. It envisaged providing assistance and financial help to European countries to help them recover from the impact of World War II. Also known as the European Recovery Program, the Plan managed to channel over $13 billion to support the European economic recovery in the years after the World War II, especially between 1948 and 1951. The Plan managed to revive the economy and restore confidence of the people of Europe.

Assistance by the USA

By 1948, the USA had given $13 billion as assistance to west European countries and also to Soviet Russia, which did not accept the financial help. Although Japan was not part of the Marshall Plan, USA also offered financial assistance to the Asian country. At the end of the funding, the economies of most of the European countries were able to make a recovery.

George Marshall, US Secretary of Sate.

FUN FACT

George Marshall was awarded the 1953 Nobel Peace Prize for his Marshall Plan.

Far East after World War II

The destruction left in the wake of World War II in China made a country that was already suffering from overpopulation, underdevelopment and over 50 years of war and political unrest, even more wretched. Japanese forces had taken over quite a bit of the Chinese territory and it did not help that the Chinese economy was in depression. After indiscriminate bombing fighting, famines and epidemics, cities and villages were left in shambles.

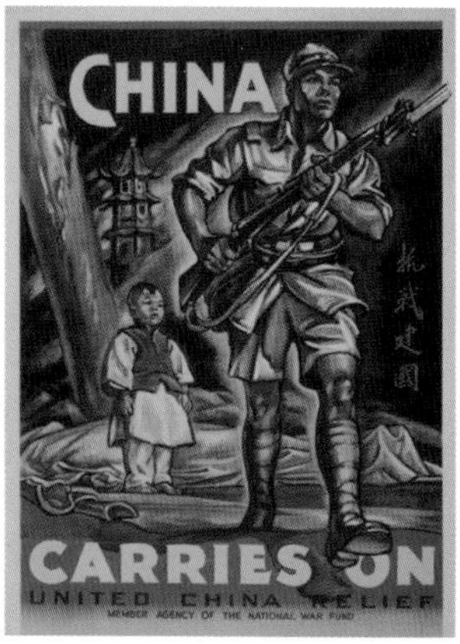

China Carries On poster by United China Relief, member agency of the National War Fund.

State of Japan

Japan saw 14 million civilian deaths during World War II. The Japanese had a forced labour system where many civilians and prisoners of war who eventually died in these camps. It is also said that the Japanese also massacred many civilians eerily similar to that of the Nazis.

Indian fate

India suffered a similar fate. Famines were a part of life and the Indians could not pay the heavy taxes levied by the colonial rulers. Philippines had also suffered under its three years of occupation by Japan. Owing to World War II, the British altered its stand towards India because Britain required India's labour and manpower to help them fight the war. It was agreed upon that in exchange for India's support during World War II, it would offer Indians more political power.

Mother of a starving child begging in India in 1943.

Japan in ruins

Japan was in a bad shape due to the arbitrary aerial bombing and dropping of the atomic bomb. Almost 40 per cent of Japanese cities were destroyed and thousands rendered homeless.

The aftereffects of the atomic bombings included the debilitating effect of radiation, which continued to have repercussions several years after the atomic bombings.

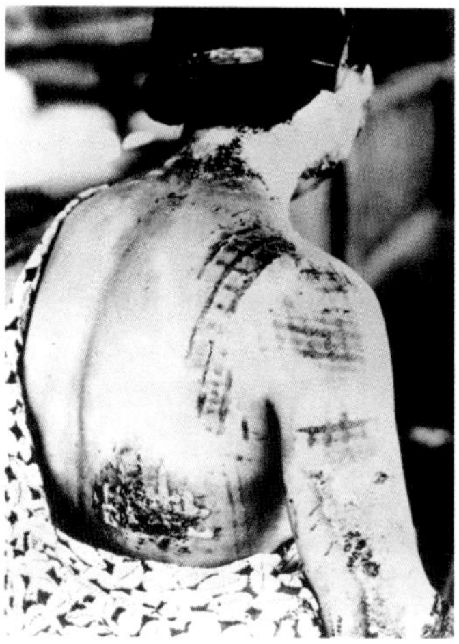

Injured female survivor of the Nagasaki atomic bombing. Her skin is burned in a pattern corresponding to the dark portions of a kimono worn at the time of the explosion.

FUN FACT

Japan and the Soviet Union made peace when they signed the Soviet–Japanese Joint Declaration of 1956.

Three Chinese civilians in Chungking witness a Japanese air-raid.

Independence Struggle of the World's Largest Democracy

1900–1942

The history behind Indian independence is about India's struggle by millions of faceless Indians, who fought for the freedom of their country. The year 1857 is often referred to as a benchmark in the history of Indian independence, which later turned into a Sepoy Mutiny by Indian soldier Mangal Pandey. Pandey was hanged and this fanned the revolution further, but soon the revolt was eventually stopped by the British army.

The beginning of the 1900s saw several revolutionary groups emerge in different parts of the country including Bengal, Punjab, Gujarat, Assam and the southern states. Political groups like the Congress came together to voice out the suffering of million natives to the British Empire in a peaceful manner. The prominent leaders of this period were Mahatma Gandhi, Subhash Chandra Bose, Jawaharlal Nehru and Lala Lajpat Rai. The revolutionaries who took extreme measures to gain freedom included Surya Sen, Chandrasekhar Azad and Bhagat Singh.

Mahatma Gandhi's "Salt March" and the 1942's "Quit India Movement" saw public support swell for the freedom movement. The British Government imprisoned many leaders including Gandhi. Subhash Chandra Bose moved away from Congress and formed a new party named the All India Forward Block Party and started his own army called Indian National Army (INA) and tried to win freedom, but with the sudden death of Netaji the INA attempts became unsuccessful.

The British Rule

FUN FACT

E. M. Forster's, "A Passage to India" has good insights into the racial and social isolation towards native Indians, practiced by the British that continued right till the end of British Raj.

In 1858, British Crown rule was established in India; thus, ending more than 100 years of control under the East India Company, after the Indian Mutiny or the "First War of Indian Independence". This changed the structure of the political, social and economic rule that the British had established.

After effects of the Mutiny of 1857

The Indian Mutiny had an impact on the country despite its failure. First, it made the British sit up and take note of the activities of the East India Company and therefore abolished it. They successfully ended the Mughal Empire and soon Queen Victoria was announced as the ruler of India. This announcement automatically meant that Britain now had control over the previously controlled Indian territories by the East India Company.

Negotiating with the British

Even as the country was under the East India Company prior to the mutiny, it should be noted that nearly two-fifths of the sub-continent was independently governed by over 560 large and small principalities. A few had turned against the British in the mutiny, but soon entered into negotiations with the British Raj. Then, these princely states would become allies of the British who would help England with both financial and military support during the two world wars. The Nizam of Hyderabad is a good example of this.

Old illustration of British soldiers battling insurgents near Delhi.

Rise of nationalism

The rise of nationalism had made Britain understand that they would now have to work towards some amount of development of the country. They focussed a little on education under which the Ilbert bill was made, which stated that Indians could be as qualified and experienced as any Briton. However, in its true implementation, very few British people accepted Indians as equals; the majority felt that they were superior and more civilised than Indians.

Queen Victoria was proclaimed the first ruler of India after the fall of the Mughal Empire.

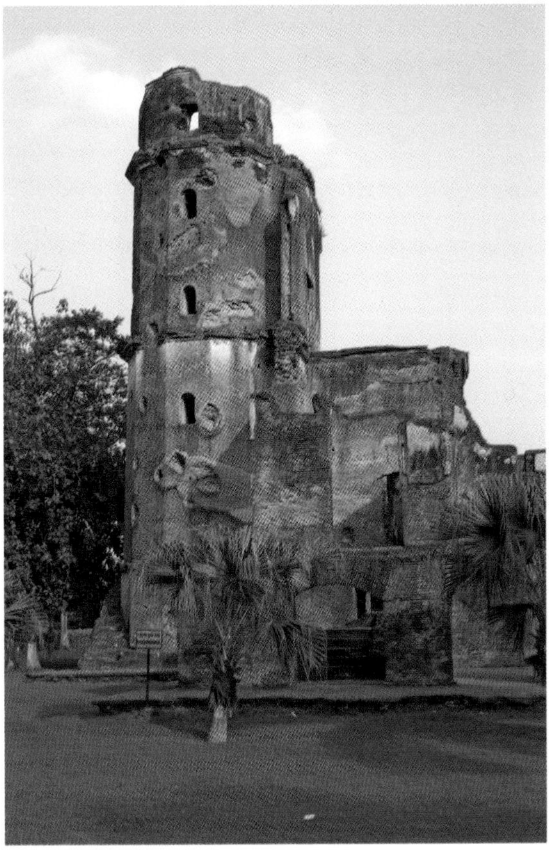

Old British Residency in Lucknow, India. Old derelict building which subject of a siege in the Indian Mutiny of 1857.

1857: Indian mutiny

1917: Edwin Montagu visits India

Growing racial gulf between Indians and British rulers

The Mutiny of 1857 created a racial gap between the Indians and British. This continued up until the end of the British Raj. E M Forster and Rudyard Kipling reflected this amply in their works. The British Empire appointed viceroys who had little experience about India and its people. It was only in 1917 that Edwin Montagu actually visited India on a fact-finding mission. It was understood then that just about a few thousand civil servants could not rule over 350 million Indians without having some Indians in the system.

Rudyard Kipling

British's economic benefits from India

Britain's main objective of being in India was because it made for a great economic investment. India was a good market for goods and services. Moreover, it required an army that the local natives had to pay for.

An ancient palace of the Nizams in Hyderabad, India.

FUN FACT

Edwin Montagu became secretary of state for India in 1917 and worked on the British policy towards "progressive realisation of responsible government" in India and recommended control of some aspects of provincial government passed to Indian ministers.

Investment in India under British Rule

In terms of investments, the British during their raj invested in infrastructure and built the railways network. They also built canals and other irrigation works and established the English education system.

The British built a strong railway network that is operational even today.

Rise of industrialisation

The latter half of the nineteenth century witnessed some amount of industrialisation with the first cotton textile mill that was set up in 1853 in Bombay by Cowasjee Nanabhoy. Soon, the first jute mill was established in 1855 in Bengal. A majority of the modern Indian industries were controlled by the British. However, overall the raj only made a formerly prosperous country into shambles, where people were made poorer owing to heavy taxations that were levied under the British Rule and resulted in famines. A drained Indian economy had to bear the burden of an expensive British bureaucracy and army.

Mutiny of 1857

William Hodson presented the heads of the two princes Mirza Mughal and Mirza Khizr Sultan. A scene in The Indian Mutiny, 1857.

In May 1857, Bengal army soldiers shot British officers and marched towards Delhi, and this mutiny added fuel to the rebellion that had started in northern and central India. The Revolt of 1857 was preceded by a series of instability in different parts of the country from the late eighteenth century onwards.

Start of the mutiny

Often referred to as the "First War of Indian Independence", it started with a series of rebellions in northern and central India against the British power and soon became the first united rebellion against the British in 1857-1858. Mangal Pandey, a Sepoy in the colonial British army, spearheaded the revolt, when he questioned British officers over violation of their religious beliefs. The introduction of the new cartridge for the Enfield rifle provoked the soldiers because the cartridges were wrapped in paper, coated with animal grease, making them offensive to both Muslims and Hindus.

Growing support for the mutiny

The uprising grew into a bigger rebellion when Mughal Emperor, Bahadur Shah, supported it.

Soon, the mutiny of soldiers transformed into a revolutionary war, with many Indian chiefs hastened to support it at the behest of Bahadur Shah, who wrote letters to all the heads and Indian rulers requesting them to come together to create a sort of a union of Indian states to counterattack the British regime. Soon, the Bengal army joined it followed by different parts of the country from Awadh, Rohilkhand, to Bundelkhand, then further towards central India and Bihar and East Punjab. Later, other princely support was received when other leaders like Rani Laxmibai of Jhansi and Tatya Tope joined in.

Statue of Rani Laxmibai of Jhansi.

A painting depicting the Mutiny of 1857.

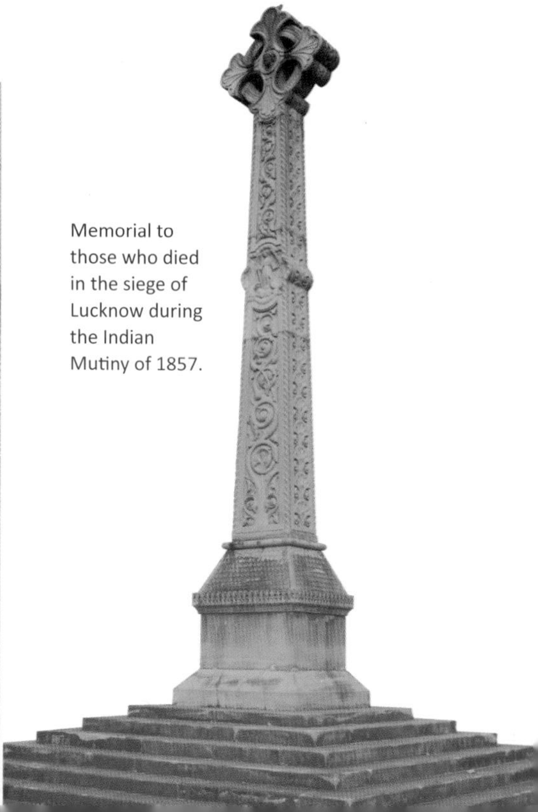

Memorial to those who died in the siege of Lucknow during the Indian Mutiny of 1857.

End of the East India Company

Sir William James Erasmus Wilson

From 1600 onwards, the East India Company, also known as the English East India Company, comprised the merchants of London, who traded into the East Indies, Southeast Asia and India. On 31st December, 1600 a group of merchants who called themselves as the East India Company were given monopoly privileges for trade with East India.

Move to China

In 1608, Sir Thomas Roe sought support from Mughal Emperor Jahangir after becoming an emissary of King James I in 1615. Soon, the Company established a factory at Surat. From the early eighteenth century, the trading entity soon embroiled itself into the local politics and became a British representative of the Queen in India. During the nineteenth century, the East India Company in China expanded and intensified British influence there.

The spice trade

The East India Company primarily wanted to have a pie in the spice trade share, which was originally monopolised by countries like Spain and Portugal. England defeated the Spanish Aramada in 1588, and soon England gained the control over the spice trade.

East India Company's trade expansion

The East India Company's rivalry with the Dutch East Indies from the East Indies led to struggles between the two. The East India Company traded with cotton, silk goods, indigo, salt and other spices from India. It soon expanded its activities from Persia to India.

Spices, silk goods, indigo, etc., were traded.

Its gradual decline

The monopoly of East India led to the joining of hands of the United Company of Merchants of England trading to the East Indies. The Regulating Act of 1773 and Pitt's India Act of 1784 established government control and steadily the company lost commercial and political control. Later, it just became a representative of the British government in India and after the Indian uprising of 1857 it was brought to an abrupt end.

FUN FACT

E. M. Foster's, "A passage to India" has good insights into the racial and social isolation towards native Indians, practiced by the British that continued right till the end of British Raj.

The old silk route, which was used for trading silk between China and Sikkim, India.

Formation of Indian National Congress

Indian National Congress, by name Congress Party, was formed in 1885 and fought for India's independence from Britain. Lord Dufferin, the Viceroy of India, had implied that Indian intellectuals needed to have a forum to forward the grievances of Indians so that they could be better represented to the government.

Indian National Union

Mr Alan Octavian Hume, a retired member of Indian Civil Service, helped establish the organisation and named it Indian National union. The first session of the Indian National Union was held on 28th, 29th and 30th December, 1885, and was presided over by W C Banarjee, A O Hume, K T Telang, Subramanya Aiyar and Dadabhai Naroji. Dadabhai, known as the grand old man of India, suggested that the Indian National Union be re-named as Indian National Congress. It also envisioned on gathering opinions from educated Indians and attempting to make changes for the welfare of India.

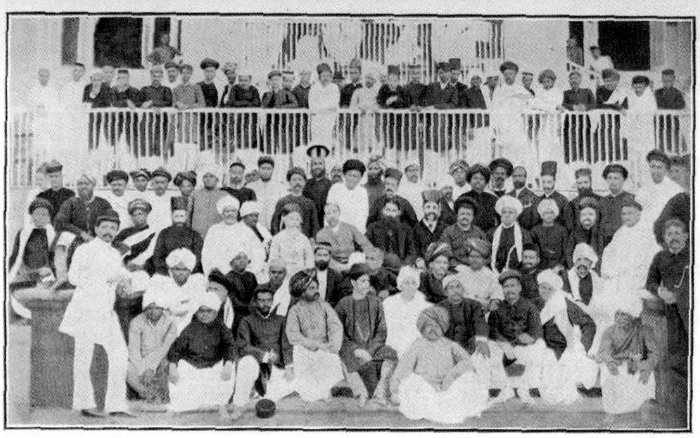

THE FIRST INDIAN NATIONAL CONGRESS, 1885.

Image of the delegates to the first meeting of the Indian National Congress in Bombay, 1885.

Resolutions passed after the formation of Indian National Congress

The resolutions of the Congress included the abolition of the India Council to hold the Indian Civil Service Examination in India as well to increase the age limit for appearing in the Indian Civil Service Examination, to have elected members in legislative assemblies and to establish legislative assemblies in the North-West Frontier Province, Oudh and Punjab.

Aim of the Indian National Congress

The primary aim of the nascent national congress was to simply put in place a base towards the creation of a secular and democratic national movement, to make people politically aware, to put in place a headquarters for this and to ensure that it becomes an all-India leadership entity that could organically help create an anti-British strategy and anti-colonial mentality. Therefore, at the beginning the Congress started its functioning with very humble objectives.

The grand man of India, Dadabhai Naroji.

A O Hume, Dadabhai Naroji and Wedderburn meeting at the Indian National Congress.

FUN FACT

During the post Independence period, the last important episodes in the Congress involved the final step to independence and the division of the country on religious lines.

Mahatma Gandhi became a global symbol of peace due to his peaceful method of solving disputes of which one was the Boycott of British Goods.

FUN FACT

On 12th March, 1930, Mahatma Gandhi led the Dandi March to produce salt from seawater, which was considered illegal at the time due to the British monopoly over the salt market in India. This march led to various other non-violence movements.

Boycott of British goods

By the early twentieth century, the Congress began the "swadeshi" movement. This movement urged people to boycott all British goods and encouraged them to use goods that were produced indigenously.

British social reformer Annie Besant and Indian nationalist Bal Gangadhar Tilak started the Home Rule wing in 1917. This was known as the extremist wing of the Indian National Congress. It addressed the diverse social classes of the country and encouraged them to boycott British goods and practice passive resistance.

Between the 1920s and 1930s, the Congress endorsed nonviolent non-cooperation against the British rule under the leadership of Gandhi. The Indian National Congress led the nationwide civil disobedience movement and advocated for the revocation of the tax levied by the British.

Move towards self rule

Gandhi's Civil Disobedience Movement of 1930-31 was kickstarted by the Salt March and became a unique symbol of the civil resistance movement. It helped undermine British authority and in a way brought together different sections of India together towards a common cause under the Indian National Congress and also facilitated the next stage towards India's struggle towards self-rule.

Quit India Movement

At the start of World War II in 1939, Britain entered the war and unwittingly dragged India into it as well. This upset many in the Indian National Congress, who declared that they would not support the war effort until India attained total freedom from the British rule.

In order to bring the British rulers to the negotiating table, Gandhi initiated his "Quit India" movement in August 1942 with a call to "do or die". Intense non-violent resistance resulted in the imprisonment of most of the Congress leaders.

It was only after the war that the British government of Clement Attlee passed an independence bill (1947) and in January 1950, India's constitution as an independent state emerged.

Discussing the "Quit India" movement with Nehru, 1942.

1930: Civil Disobedience Movement

1950: India has a constitution

Massacre at Jallianwala Bagh

On 13th April, 1919 around 10,000 or more unarmed men, women and children gathered at the Amritsar's Jallianwala Bagh to attend a protest meeting, despite a ban on public meetings. General Dyer ordered his soldiers to fire into the gathering, and for 15 minutes 1,650 rounds of ammunition were unloaded into the screaming, terrified crowd, killing 400 civilians and wounding another 1200.

Before the massacre

In protest to the Rowlatt Act, Amritsar had observed a peace hartal on the 30th March and 6th April, 1919 and the British government wanted to repress the protest. On 10th April, 1919, Dr Satyapala and Dr Kitchlew, two popular leaders of the province, were deported from Amritsar.

Effect of the massacre

The massacre instigated and fuelled nationalist feelings across Indians and had a deep impact on the leaders of the freedom struggle particularly on Gandhi. Gandhi had promised Britain that India would support the colonial ruler in World War I. This was to help create a base toward granting partial autonomy for India, but post the Jallianwala Bagh massacre, Gandhi was of the opinion that India should stop this request for partial autonomy and seek, and fight for complete freedom and total independence. The Jallianwala Bagh massacre became the trigger for the next level of India's struggle towards freedom and propelled Gandhi to start off India's first civil resistance movement called as the civil disobedience movement against Britain's tyrannical rule.

Close-up of a bullet mark from the massacre at Jallianwala Bagh.

The Jallianwala Bagh

Jallianwala Bagh was closed on all sides by houses and buildings and just a few narrow entrances, which were generally locked. The main entrance was a bit wide, but was secured by British troops. They had the backing of the armoured vehicles. There was no warning issued to disperse the crowds.

The main entrance was a bit wide, but was secured by British troops. They had the backing of the armoured vehicles. There was no warning issued.

Bullet-marked wall at Jallianwala Bagh, Amritsar, India.

FUN FACT

Although Queen Elizabeth II had not made any comments on the incident, during her state visits in 1961 and 1983, she spoke about the events at a state banquet in India on 13th October, 1997.

Jallianwala Bagh massacre

On Baisakhi day, Sunday 13th April, 1919, 50 British Indian Army soldiers, under orders from Brigadier-General Reginald Dyer were asked to reload their rifles many times and were ordered to shoot to kill.

Jallianwala Bagh memorial in Amritsar, Punjab, India.

Events of the massacre

"The Martyr's" well.

After the shooting, a number of people died in stampedes in their attempt to get away from the Bagh, but got caught at the narrow gates. A few jumped into the solitary well to escape the shooting. The wounded could not be shifted when the curfew was declared adding to the casualties.

Impact of the massacre

The Jallianwala tragedy had a deep impact. In fact, Rabindranath Tagore renounced his knighthood as a form of protest against the massacre. Gandhi returned the Kaisar-i-Hind medal given to him for his work during the Boer War. General Dyer's act was universally seen with contempt. Britain's prime minister too declared in the British parliament that the massacre was "one of the worst outrages in the whole of our history". However, Dyer found some support among senior British officers who appreciated his act and said that he was only trying to suppress another Indian Mutiny. The House of Commons debate censured his act and Winston Churchill stated, "The incident in Jallianwala Bagh was an extraordinary event, a monstrous event, an event which stands in singular and sinister isolation".

Hunter committee

The Jallianwala Bagh massacre brought forth strong public reaction in India and even in England. An enquiry committee was appointed to enquire about the massacre and Punjab disturbances. Indian National Congress boycotted the Hunter Committee and appointed another unofficial committee of popular lawyers, including Motilal Nehru, CR Das, Abbas Tyabji, MR Jayakar and Gandhi. Prior to the Hunter Committee beginning its proceeding, the government passed an Indemnity Act, which was criticised. General Dyer was found guilty of a "mistaken notion of duty" and was relieved of command.

1919: Jallianwala Bagh Massacre
1920: Dyer's commands are condemned

Monument of Rabindranath Tagore in Kolkata, India.

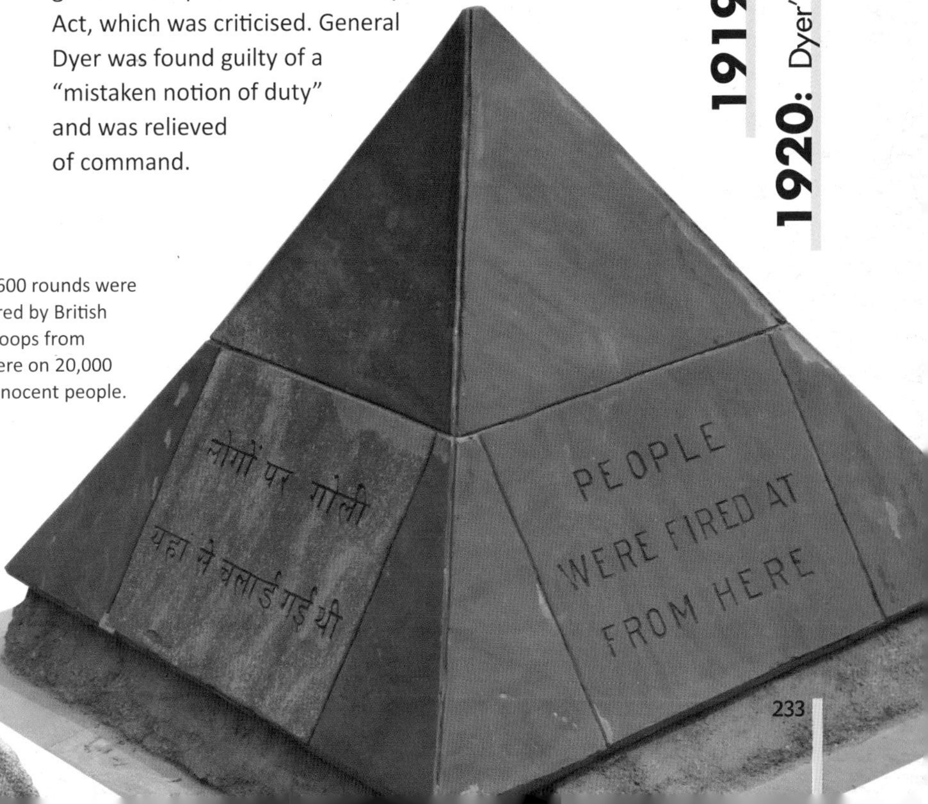
लोगों पर गोली
यहा से चलाई गई थी
PEOPLE
WERE FIRED AT
FROM HERE

1600 rounds were fired by British troops from here on 20,000 innocent people.

Non-cooperation Movement

The non-cooperation movement was spearheaded under Gandhi from September 1920 to persuade the British government to give India its right to self-govern. The movement was fuelled by Amritsar's Jallianwala Bagh massacre, where the British had indiscriminately killed innocent and unarmed Indians. The movement also gathered more steam because Indians were unhappy at the government's inability at taking an action against General Dyer, the man responsible for the massacre.

What triggered this movement

Impoverished farmers in Champaran in Bihar and Kheda in Gujarat were pushed towards growing cash crops in place of food crops, such as tobacco, indigo and cotton instead of food crops. Famine also meant no respite from paying taxes. Indian revolutionaries like Sardar Vallabhbhai Patel, Jawaharlal Nehru and Rajendra Prasad came together with Mahatma Gandhi to work towards India's independence. Muslim leaders came together to form the Khilafat committee to fight the British. The Jallianwala Bagh massacre had angered everyone and soon Gandhi came up with the idea of nationwide Satyagraha against the Rowlatt Acts.

Proposing non-violence

Gandhi presented the proposal of non-cooperation in the Calcutta session of the Indian Nation Congress and stated that, "The English Government is Saitan. Cooperation is not possible with it". He added that the government was not sad at its actions so, "we have to adopt a progressive nonviolent non-cooperation policy for the fulfilment of our demands".

Gandhi's idea faces opposition

The non-cooperation movement was launched on 1st August, 1920 and after the Indian National Congress met for a special session at Calcutta on 4th September, 1920. Gandhiji's idea faced opposition from veteran leaders particularly C R Das who did not approve of the boycott of legislative council elections, because it was believed that boycotting the new Councils would alienate Indians further from the fountainhead of political power.

Statue of historic leader, Mahatma Gandhi, in Parliament Square, London.

Monument of Sardar Vallabhbhai Patel (1875-1950).

Statue of Jawaharlal Nehru.

Aim of the movement

The aim was simple: to non-violently look towards mobilising masses towards the creation of a nationalist feeling. India's first mass-based political movement under Gandhi boycotted the use of foreign cloth; the forthcoming visit of the Prince of Wales in November 1921 had popularised the use of the charkha and khadi, which lead to the Jail Bharo (fill the jail by arresting everyone) by Congress volunteers.

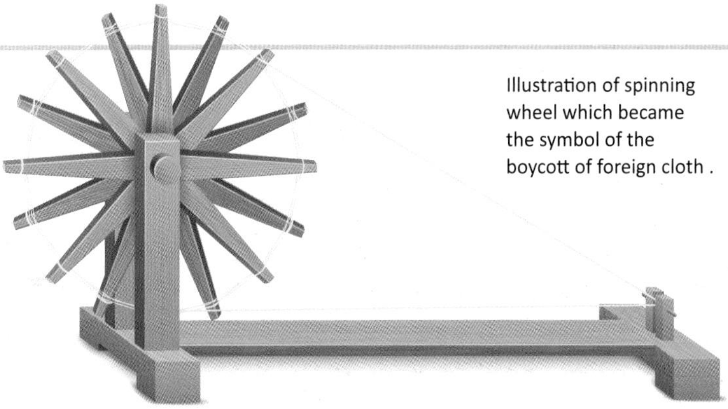

Illustration of spinning wheel which became the symbol of the boycott of foreign cloth .

Features of the movement

The non-cooperation movement or the "Asahayog Andolan" transformed the freedom struggle to another level since India's First War of Independence in 1857. It commenced in 1920 and its momentum lasted through 1922 with great support from the leaders and members of the Indian National Congress. The movement with its objective of resisting British rule via non-violence led to supporters of the movement refusing to purchase British goods and go back to using local handicrafts.

Elements of the movement

The largely non-violent movement urged people to resign titles, boycott government educational institutions, courts, government services, foreign goods, elections and also refuse to pay taxes.

Gandhi and Sardar Patel, Bardoli Satyagraha, 1928.

Violence erupts during the non-cooperation movement

In August 1921, the Muslim Moplah movement had violent altercations; this incident was followed by more violence in Chauri Chaura. Members of a Congress and Khilafat procession picketed the local bazaar in their bid to oppose liquor sales and high food prices. After being provoked by some policemen the crowd attacked them, in retaliation the police opened fire. And an enraged crowd killed 22 policemen and set the police station on fire. Gandhi called off the movement after this incident.

1920: INC meets for a special session

1921: Charkha and Khadi become popular

Gandhi during the Salt March, March 1930.

FUN FACT

Gandhi's commitment to non-violence was redeemed when (1930-1934) tens of millions again revolted in the Salt Satyagraha.

Civil Disobedience Movement

Gandhi during the freedom struggle in 1930.

Under Mahatma Gandhi's leadership, the Civil Disobedience Movement grew to become an important event in the history of India's freedom struggle. It started in 1930 and the main objective behind this movement was to challenge and confront the laws made by the British.

Gandhi's demands

Gandhi presented before Viceroy Lord Irwin a request that said that certain elements of the British Raj needs to be removed at an immediate basis and the list of demands given by him would need to be implemented else the civil resistance movement would be launched with the Dandi Satyagraha. The demands included the prohibition of intoxicants, change the ratio between the rupee and sterling, reduction of the land revenue rate, abolition of salt tax, reduction in military and civil administration expenditure among others.

Reasons behind the movement

The Simon Commission planned to appoint only British Parliament members to create a new constitution for India. The national political parties and social organisations across the nation rejected the commission. At Bombay's All-Party Conference of May 1928, formed to make more boycotts, gave Dr M A Ansari and Motilal Nehru the responsibility of the drafting committee to prepare the constitution for India. However, the British Government refused to pay heed to it. Soon, they were warned after the Calcutta Session of the INC in 1928 that it would start a Civil Disobedience Movement if India was not granted its own government.

Gandhi's demands

Mahatma Gandhi presented a request before Viceroy Lord Irwin, which said that certain elements of the British Raj needed to be removed at an immediate basis. He also stated that the list of demands given by him would need to be implemented, else the civil resistance movement would be launched with the Dandi Satyagraha. The demands included the prohibition of intoxicants, a change in the ratio between the rupee and sterling, reduction of the land revenue rate, abolition of salt tax, reduction in military and civil administration expenditure among others.

FUN FACT

Gandhi began the Salt March with a mere 78 followers, but this number grew to tens of thousands by the time he reached Dandi.

Mahatma Gandhi leading a movement.

India adopts civil disobedience

Mahatma Gandhi

The Civil Disobedience Movement began with the Dandi March, where Gandhi marched with his followers to protest against the taxes levied on salt. Millions joined his march and illegally picked up salt from the coastal areas.

This movement further gained momentum when people all over the country began boycotting British goods and services. Peasants began to risk their lands and livelihoods when they started refusing to pay taxes. Several forest laws imposed by the British government in Maharashtra, Karnataka and other central provinces were blatantly defied by the masses.

Calling-off the movement

The British were anxious on the increasing popularity of the movement and therefore arrested all major Congress leaders. In April 1930, Abdul Gaffar Khan, a political and spiritual leader and follower of Gandhi was arrested. His arrest led to protests, which were suppressed by the British who arrested around 10,000 protestors including women and children, and thrashed them. This made Gandhi call off the civil disobedience movement.

Lord Irwin

Gandhi–Irwin Pact

In March 1930, Gandhi signed the Gandhi-Irwin Pact with the Viceroy Lord Irwin that outlined two important elements; first, the participation of Congress in the round table conference and the calling off the civil disobedience movement. It was attended by Sarojini Naidu and Gandhi. The conference was held in London, but Lord Willingdon in Gandhi's absence adopted the repression policy violating the Gandhi-Irwin Pact. Soon, the civil disobedience movement started again.

Ordinances from the British Government

The Congress Working Committee came up with the decision to restart the civil disobedience movement by January 1932. To retaliate, the British Government came up with four ordinances to deal with the prevailing situation, wherein police could arrest anyone based on mere suspicion. Sardar Patel and Gandhi were arrested along with the supporters of Congress. The movement continued for six months. Gandhi fasted for 21 days from 8th May, 1933 and the movement finally came to an end on 7th April, 1934.

Salt march statue.

Dandi March

The Dandi March or Salt Satyagraha spearheaded by Gandhi started in March–April 1930 and became the first act of civil disobedience or satyagraha, where Gandhi garnered widespread support from Indians and soon became very popular for his staunch support to a non-violent movement.

Protests against the salt tax

The production and distribution of salt within India had been under the control of the British, who had banned Indians from producing or selling it independently, which meant that Indians had to buy salt that was very expensive, because this commodity was heavily taxed. A great majority of poor Indians could not afford it and soon there was a public outcry over this, and protests against the salt tax began.

The Dandi March

At the start of 1930, Gandhi started a demonstration against the salt tax and marched into Gujarat from his Sabarmati Ashram to the town of Dandi near the Arabian Sea coast, accompanied by many followers. The march halted at different villages along the route, where more crowds would gather to listen to Gandhi who spoke against the unjust practice of taxing the poor. On 5th April, the group reached Dandi after a journey of 385 km and on 6th April, Gandhi and his followers picked up a handful of salt from the shore and proclaimed that they had broken the law.

Consequences of the march

Later, many were arrested and imprisoned, including Jawaharlal Nehru and Gandhi. The marches to other salt works continued with 2500 people under poetess Sarojini who were attacked and beaten by the police. At the end of these marches, around 60,000 freedom fighters were in jail. Gandhi after his release from jail started negotiations with Lord Irwin and a truce was declared. Soon, Gandhi, representing the Indian National Congress, was invited to attend the second session of the Round Table Conference in London.

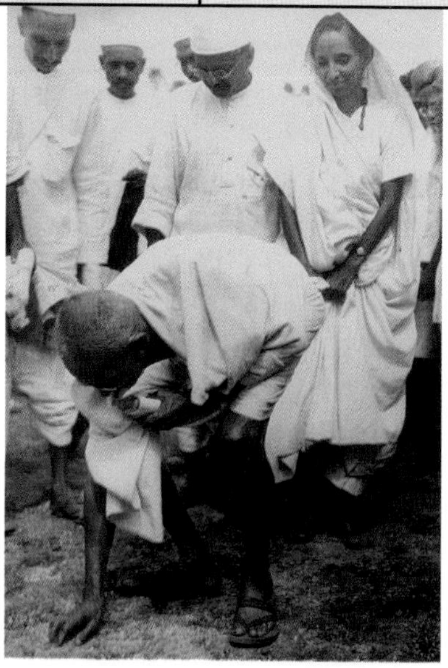

Gandhi at Dandi, South Gujarat, picking salt on the beach at the end of the Salt March, 5th April, 1930. Behind him is his second son Manilal Gandhi and Mithuben Petit.

A picture of Gandhi and Sarojini Naidu during the Dandi March.

Rise of Gandhi

Mohandas Karamchand Gandhi was born in Porbandar, to a wealthy family. He was the fourth child of Karamchand Gandhi and was an average student. At the age of 13, he was married to a girl named Kasturba. He studied law under his father's insistence, although he wanted to study medicine and went to England to pursue his education in 1888. After attaining bar in 1891, he tried to practice law in Rajkot and Bombay, with very little success.

"The weak can never forgive. Forgiveness is the attribute of the strong."

-Mahatma Gandhi

Quote by Mahatma Gandhi

Encounter with racism

Gandhi accepted an offer to represent a firm in Pretoria, the capital of Transvaal in the Union of South Africa. While travelling in a first-class train compartment in Natal, he was asked by a white man to leave the compartment. Gandhi got off the train and decided to work towards eliminating racism. He called for a meeting of Indians in Pretoria and spoke against the whites who practiced racial discrimination. This launched his campaign of improved legal status for Indians in South Africa, who suffered discrimination at that time. He was lynched by an angry mob when he aired his views against racism.

Gandhi returns to India

Gandhi returned to India in January 1915 and by then, he had attained the title of "Mahatma" for his simple life and the development of the concept of Satyagraha that he had started in South Africa. Gandhi spoke of a new, free India and convinced people to stand against the British rule. After the Jallianwala Bagh Massacre, he called for a non-cooperation movement against British institutions including British courts, stores and schools. He soon became an icon for the masses. He began the Khadi movement with the intention of making people spin their own clothing rather than buy British goods. His belief was that it would create employment and soon many could attain economic independence.

FUN FACT

Fasting was a protest technique that Gandhi believed in and he also was the one who started protest marches and his Dandi or salt march remains very popular incident in Indian History.

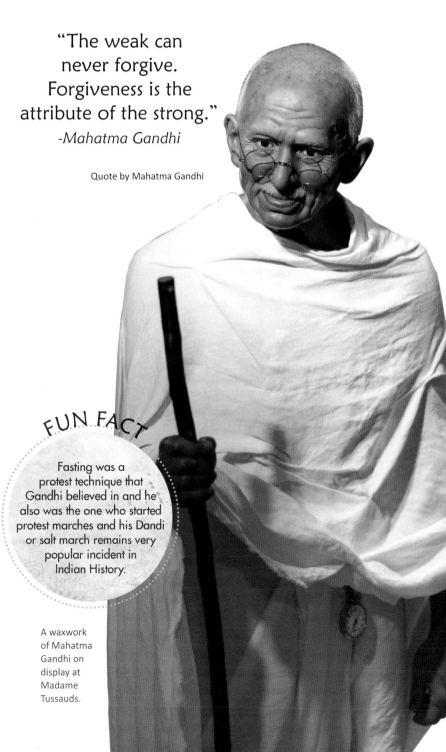

A waxwork of Mahatma Gandhi on display at Madame Tussauds.

Rise of the Muslim League

The Muslim League or the All India Muslim League was a political group that demanded for a separate Muslim state during the partition of British India in the year 1947. The Muslim League was a political organisation of India and Pakistan, and was founded in 1906 as the All-India Muslim League under Aga Khan III. The objective was simple to protect the political rights of Muslims in India. Founded in 1906 to preserve the rights of Indian Muslims, the Muslim League found favour with the British rulers. However, despite this show of encouragement from the British, the league called for a self-rule policy for India in 1913.

All India Muslim League.

Hindu–Muslim divide

Muhammad Ali Jinnah, the prominent leader from the Muslim league was a firm believer of Hindu–Muslim unity in a united and independent India. Only after 1940 that the league seemed to veer towards the formation of a separate Muslim state independent of British India. The fear within the league was that India in the present state would comprise many Hindus and India's Muslims would be a minority.

Decline of the Muslim league

Jinnah and the Muslim league spearheaded the struggle to partition British India into two different states, Hindu and Muslim. With the formation of Pakistan in 1947, the Muslim league became Pakistan's main political party and soon renamed the All Pakistan Muslim League. Gradually, the popularity of this league reduced in independent Pakistan and lost its power in East Pakistan or Bangladesh. A little later it again failed in West Pakistan and after numerous splits and factions in the 1960s the party disappeared by 1970.

Indian leaders at the Simla Conference (1946). From left to right: Rajendra Prasad, Muhammad Ali Jinnah, C. Rajagopalachari, Maulana Abul Kalam Azad.

Coin with the image of a portrait of Muhammad Ali Jinnah.

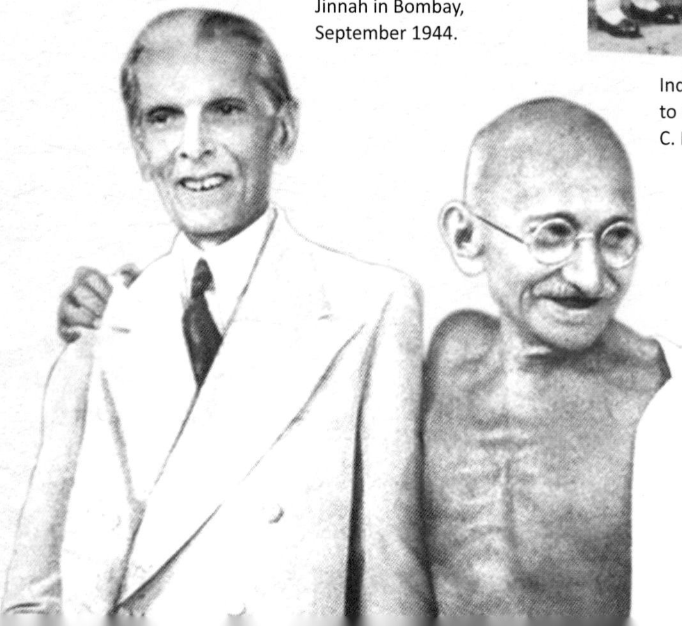

Gandhi and Jinnah in Bombay, September 1944.

FUN FACT

Jinnah forbade his doctor to disclose the fact that he was suffering from tuberculosis to the public. He was afraid that it would impact the freedom movement. However, Jinnah died of the same in 1948 and was buried in the heart of Karachi city.

Second Round Table Conference

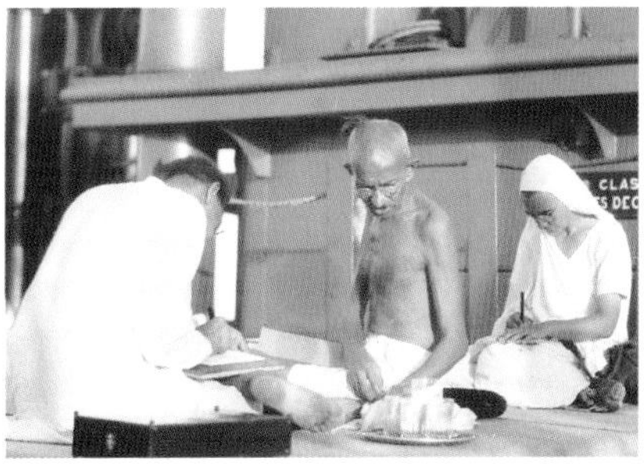

Gandhi and Mirabehn en route to London for the Round Table Conference, 1931.

The Simon Commission report did not provide adequate substance. The new Labour Government under Ramsay MacDonald in 1929 held a series of Round Table Conferences in London.

First Round Table Conference

The first Round Table Conference convened in 1931 did not have much impact. It spoke of the development of India as a federation under which transfer of defence and finance would happen. But it seemed to be recommendations only on paper and civil disobedience continued unabated. The British Government soon understood that the Indian National Congress would need to be part of any decision pertaining to the formation of an Indian Government.

Gandhi meets Lord Irwin

During the civil disobedience movement, Viceroy Lord Irwin met Gandhi to arrive at a compromise. They arranged for Congress' participation in the Second Round Table Conference with the condition that the civil disobedience movement would be discontinued and that the government would withdraw all ordinances issued against the Congress. It was also decided that the government would withdraw all prosecutions relating to all non-violent offences and that they would release persons who were jailed for their involvement in the movement.

Second Round Table Conference

The Second Round Table Conference was held in London from 7th September to 1st December, 1931. Gandhi participated on behalf of the Indian National Congress. Just weeks prior to the proposed conference, the conservatives had come to power and it was felt that Gandhi could not be the sole representative of all Indian people. The Second Round Table Conference did not seem to get any major results for India and soon struggles against the British rule continued, and Gandhi was arrested along with other Congress leaders.

1929: New Labour Government

1931: Second Round Table Conference

During the Federal Structure Sub-committee meeting presided over by Lord Sankey, London, November 1931 (Round Table Conference).

Impact of World War II on Indian Freedom Struggle

In 1939, when the German troops invaded Poland, Britain and France declared war against Germany on 3rd September, 1939 and the start of World War II accelerated the end of British rule in India. During the war, leaders from the Indian National Congress stated that if British wanted India's cooperation, it must have the right of self-determination.

1939: Britain and France declare war against Germany

1942: Sir Stafford Cripps comes to India

Limited Satyagraha

When the British refused to allow the right of self-determination for India, the provincial ministries under Congress resigned in 1939. By October 1940, they urged for a limited Satyagraha to ensure that it did not seriously hurt the war efforts. Many from Congress believed that a simple Satyagraha would not be enough to attain independence for India and aggression would be required.

Stafford Cripps Mission

In 1942, Britain faced pressure from USA and China to grant political power to India. With Burma's fall and rising pressure from Japan, Britain sent Sir Stafford Cripps to India in March 1942 to gain India's co-operation. The mission was also meant to convey to the local people that Britain would fulfil its past promise of a self-government by Indian people.

The mission also promised that post the war, immediate steps would be taken to put a body elected by the people in place to develop the constitution of India. However, the Stafford Cripps Mission assured dominion status with secession rights; immediate transfer of power was rejected. These assurances were rejected by the Indian leaders. Gandhi, as per the wishes of his Congress colleagues, called for a mass independent movement.

Sir Stafford Cripps

Silhouette of troops at Pandu Ghat, India, enroute Myitkyina, Burma.

FUN FACT

Indian revolutionary Udham Singh, as a child, had seen his brother's killing at the Jallianwala Baugh massacre. He wanted to seek vengeance for his brother's death and after 21 years he killed Michael O'Dwyer, the governor of Punjab who had supported the massacre. Udham Singh was arrested and hanged in 1940.

Quit India Movement

British Governor-General of India, Lord Linlithgow, had dragged the Indian army into World War II without consulting Indian leaders. While the Muslim League supported the war, the Congress had divided opinions on the subject.

After the failure of the Cripps Mission, the Indian National Congress passed the Quit India resolution at the 1942 Bombay session. The focus was on the slogan "do or die", which was derived from Gandhi's speech that called for freeing India or dying in the attempt of doing so.

Gandhi launched the Quit India Movement in his bid to get Britain to negotiate and agree to India's call for freedom. He issued this call from the grounds of Bombay, where Indians were asked to "do or die" towards attaining freedom for India. The British government declared the movement illegal, and soon, the most important leaders were arrested.

Netaji Subhash Chandra Bose and Members of the Azad Hind Fauj.

Role of Indian National Army

Captain Mohan Singh came up with the idea of the INA and urged for Japan's help. Indian prisoners of war were given by the Japanese to Mohan Singh, who gathered and trained them to form the INA.

By 1942, the first division of the INA was formed with 16,300 men. However, shortly after the formation, differences between Mohan Singh and the Japanese erupted and the Captain was captured. Along with Rashbehari Bose, Subhash Chandra Bose went to Tokyo, where he received assurances that Japan had no territorial aspirations in India.

Netaji Subhash Chandra Bose addressing a rally in Tokyo, 1945.

The INA was called the Azad Hind Fauj or "the Free India Army" and was re-organised with the creation of a second division. This time, it included a women's regiment, which was named the Rani Jhansi regiment.

INA losses and gains

The provisional government of free India declared war on Britain and captured large parts of Manipur. The Indian tricolour was raised on these captured lands. However, after the defeat of Japan and German forces, the INA had to retreat from Kohima. Many INA soldiers were arrested and died while fighting the British. Subhash Chandra Bose tried to escape to Japan, but he is said to have died in an air-crash on his way there.

Netaji Subhash Chandra Bose

Quit India Movement

Launched under the leadership of Gandhi in 1942, the Quit India Movement protested against Britain for sending Indian troops to fight in World War II and insisted on the immediate independence of India. This movement was also called the August Movement and was launched by Gandhi in his bid towards attaining complete freedom for India. It was a movement and a call for mass non-violent protest, where Britain was to withdraw completely from India.

Policemen trying to control protestors.

Protestors of the Quit India Movement.

Support for the movement

Gandhi felt that the presence of the British in India was provoking Japan to attack them. This reason, combined with all the other problems that India was facing at the hands of the British, led Gandhi to passionately call upon his countrymen. He asked Indians who wanted freedom to "strive" for it and he urged every Indian to "do or die" in the attempt to attain India's freedom.

The Quit India Movement began soon after the talks between the Congress and British were unsuccessful. Many Indian leaders, including Gandhi, were put in jail for supporting this movement. There were protest demonstrations. These demonstrations had several violent manifestations, some of which resulted in bomb attacks and violence.

However, the Quit India Movement wasn't a popular choice and many opposed it. Straying away from the Congress stand, the Muslim League supported the British and opposed the Quit India movement. Many Indian businessmen did not support the movement because they believed that it would affect their business returns. In fact, even within the country, the movement lacked student support because the students were supporting Subhash Chandra Bose's struggle. Therefore, this movement didn't have the kind of support it needed to succeed.

Period of violence and revolts

Britain's response to the protests was to implement fines and usage of bombs against protestors. The movement, which had its base in non-violence, soon developed to include several violent protests. In 1946, the Indian Royal Navy struck work and, soon, the sailors too joined the movement. They were followed by the air force and local police forces. Riots and revolts began, and the "do or die" slogan became the mantra of the people of India.

FUN FACT

The Quit India Movement had three phases. The first phase involved processions and strikes. The second phase involved raiding government buildings. The third phase saw mobs retaliating against the police.

Policemen trying to hit demonstrators during the Quit India Movement in Bombay.

Arrest of prominent leaders

The country was facing unrest much before the Quit India movement began. Around this time, the British government decided to curb the retaliations by arresting several prominent and senior leaders of the Indian National Congress.

As the protests continued, the British authorities began to impose stricter rules. They soon declared that the Indian National Congress was an illegal formation. This led to more protests as people flocked the streets with more demonstrations and retaliations. Slogans like "Do or Die" were chanted during these processions and the movement was locally known as the "Bharat Chhodho Andolan".

Revered leaders like Maulana Abul Kalam Azad, Netaji Subhash Chandra Bose, Mahatma Gandhi, Muhammad Ali Jinnah, Asoka Mehta, Jaya Prakas Narayan, Jawaharlal Nehru, Sardar Vallabhbhai Patel, Dr Rajendra Prasad and Chakravarti Rajgopalachari were involved in the Quit India Movement. Many of them were jailed for their participation.

The place where Kasturba Gandhi rests in peace.

Gandhi gets arrested

After the Quit India resolution was passed at the Bombay session of the Indian National Congress, the British responded by imprisoning Gandhi. He was detained at the Aga Khan Palace in Pune. Other members of the Congress Party's National Leadership were arrested and imprisoned at the Ahmednagar Fort and the Congress party was banned. However, this only served to agitate the masses, who burned down government buildings, resorted to violence against the police and gathered in large masses to protest against the British.

Period of protests

The British authorities arrested over 100,000 Indians across the country and levied heavy fines. In some cases, the protestors were publicly flogged. Many innocent demonstrators were wounded and some even lost their lives in police and army fire. Some leaders went underground and continued the freedom struggle. They broadcasted messages over secret radio stations and distributed leaflets. British authorities wanted to take some senior Congress leaders like Gandhi out of the country to another country like Yemen or South Africa, but finally chose not to do so. While under arrest, Gandhi's wife, Kasturba Gandhi, and his personal secretary, Mahadev Desai, died.

It was easy for the British to curb the Quit India Movement due to its lack of co-ordination and clarity, but it also gave them a clear indication that their time as the ruler of India was nearing its end.

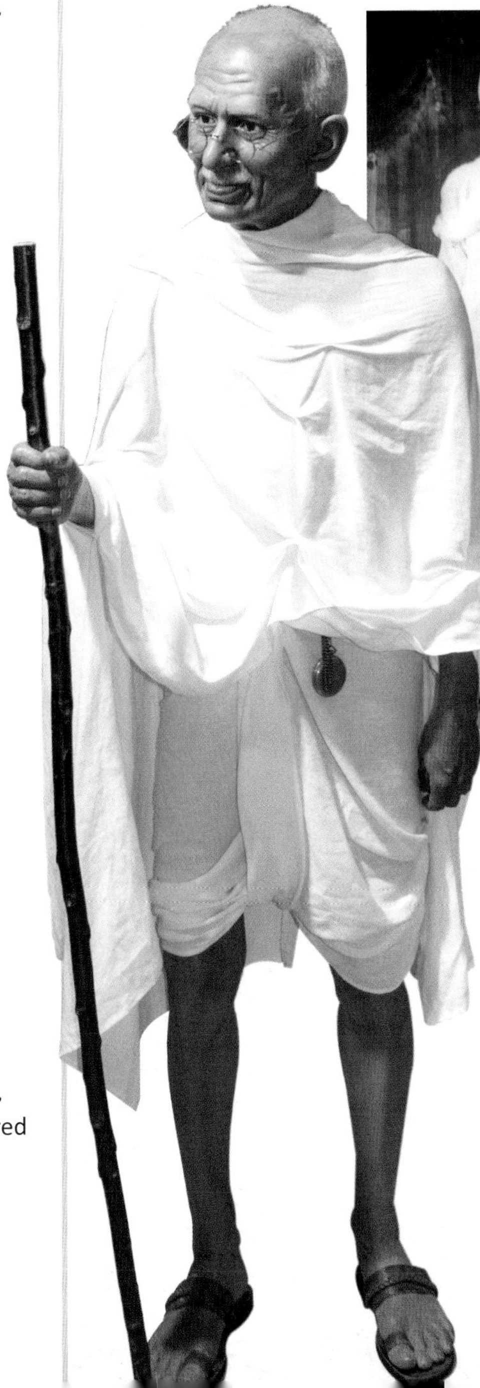

Gandhiji and Kasturba

FUN FACT

Mahatma Gandhi was nominated for the Nobel Peace Prize five times between 1937 and 1948. However, he never won the prize.

Partition of India

The struggle for independence against the British lasted for 90 long years. These years saw many rebellions, both small and large. The Indian National Congress spearheaded a major part of the freedom struggle, but the British authorities favoured the Muslim League. Eventually, the League demanded for a separate state and India was divided.

Reasons behind the partition

World War II fuelled a break in the relations between the British, Indian National Congress and Muslim League, because Britain expected India to be a part of the war and help by providing soldiers. However, the Congress opposed this as they saw no benefit for India to be part of the war. The Muslim League supported Britain because they wanted Britain's support in the creation of a Muslim nation for post-independent India.

Lord Mountbatten swears in Pandit Jawaharlal Nehru as the first Prime Minister of free India at the ceremony held at 8.30 am on 15th August, 1947.

Appeal for a unified India

Just before the end of the war, Winston Churchill lost the election and the Labour Party came into power. They supported India's call for an independent nation. Muslim League leader Muhammad Ali Jinnah campaigned for a separate Muslim state even as Jawaharlal Nehru asked for a unified India along with Gandhi. There was growing discontent between the Congress Party and the Muslim League—the latter had always strived to get more power for India. India's last British viceroy, Lord Mountbatten, had been given the duty to draw up the roadmap towards Britain's withdrawal from India. Nehru did not want to create two countries out of India and was against the partition, but finally accepted Mountbatten and the Muslim League's plan to divide India.

1857: First Indian mutiny against the British

1947: India gains freedom

Lord Mountbatten meets Nehru, Jinnah and other Leaders to plan the Partition of India.

Earl Mountbatten

India Granted Independence

Overcrowded train transferring refugees during the partition of India, 1947. This was considered to be the largest migration in human history.

In February 1947, Britain announced that India would be granted freedom by June 1948. Indian Viceroy Lord Louis Mountbatten asked for a unified India and requested the Hindus and Muslims to agree to the formation of such a country. Unfortunately, with violence erupting across the country, Mountbatten agreed to form two separate states and changed the date to 15th August, 1947.

Fixing of the border

The partition issue was largely debated and strongly opposed at first. However, once it was clear that the partition would be carried out, the task of fixing a border between the new states assumed grave importance.

Before the partition, the Muslims were living in two main regions in the north that were on the opposite sides of the country. Between these sections remained a huge Hindu population. Moreover, northern India also served as home to several other religions including Sikhs and Christians. To split the nation would also involve splitting the populations of these communities.

While the talks of partition were in progress, the Sikh community also asked for a nation of their own, but their demand was rejected. Finally, it was decided that the border for the two states would be made between Lahore and Amritsar.

The partition

This partition was highly controversial and not without blood; more than 500,000 on both sides lost their lives. Around 10 million people fled from either side to avoid the violence that came with the partition. Thousands of women were abducted during the partition. Cities were swarming with refugees as over 14 million people were crossing borders. Train compartments comprising thousands of refugees were destroyed and passengers were killed.

Pakistan was formed as a new country on 14th August, 1947. On the next day, India was granted its freedom and emerged as an independent country.

On 30th January, 1948, Gandhi was shot by Nathuram Ghodse because of his acceptance to create a multi-religious state.

Nathuram Ghodse

Statue of Gandhi in Bangalore.

Freedom at Midnight

The speech on "Tryst with Destiny" was delivered by Jawaharlal Nehru, independent India's first prime minister in the Indian Constituent Assembly on the eve of India's Independence during midnight on 14th August, 1947. It is considered as one of the greatest speeches as it captured the essence of India's freedom struggle, which, despite certain violent altercations, remained largely peaceful and non-violent against the British Empire in India.

FUN FACT

India awoke to freedom at midnight hour and the Constituent Assembly began its sitting at 11 pm with the singing of Vande Mataram by Sucheta Kripalani.

Excerpts from the speech

Many years ago, we made a tryst with destiny and now the time has come when we shall redeem our pledge, not wholly or in full measure, but very substantially. At the stroke of the midnight hour, when the world sleeps, India will awake to life and freedom. A moment comes, which comes, but rarely in history, when we step out from the old to the new, when an age ends, and when the soul of a nation, long suppressed, finds utterance.

It is fitting that at this solemn moment, we take the pledge of dedication to the service of India and her people, and to the still larger cause of humanity. At the dawn of history India started on her unending quest and trackless centuries, which are filled with her striving and the grandeur of her success and her failures. Through good and ill fortunes alike she has never lost sight of that quest or forgotten the ideals which gave her strength. We end today a period of ill fortunes and India discovers herself again.

The achievement we celebrate today is but a step, an opening of opportunity, to the greater triumphs and achievements that await us. Are we brave enough and wise enough to grasp this opportunity and accept the challenge of the future? Freedom and power bring responsibility. The responsibility rests upon this assembly, a sovereign body representing the sovereign people of India.

Independence Day

At 11:57 pm on the 14th of August, 1947, Pakistan was declared as a separate nation. Even today, this day is celebrated as Independence Day in Pakistan. About five minutes later, at 12:02, India was granted her freedom. It was a memorable moment that came after over an almost 100-year-long struggle for freedom against the British rule. It took many rebellions and the sacrifice of many brave lives, but India was finally a free country.

Jawaharlal Nehru gives his speech.

Before the birth of freedom, we have endured all the pains of labour and our hearts are heavy with the memory of this sorrow. Some of those pains continue even now. Nevertheless, the past is over and it is the future that beckons to us now. That future is not one of ease or resting, but of incessant striving so that we might fulfil the pledges we have so often taken and the one we shall take today. The service of India means the service of the millions who suffer. It means the ending of poverty and ignorance and disease and inequality of opportunity.

The future beckons to us. Whither do we go and what shall be our endeavour? To bring freedom and opportunity to the common man, to the peasants and workers of India; to fight and end poverty and ignorance and disease; to build up a prosperous, democratic and progressive nation, and to create social, economic and political institutions, which will ensure justice and fullness of life to every man and woman.

We have hard work ahead. There is no resting for any one of us till we redeem our pledge in full, till we make all the people of India what destiny intended them to be.

We are citizens of a great country, on the verge of bold advance, and we have to live up to that high standard. All of us, to whatever religion we may belong, are equally the children of India with equal rights, privileges and obligations. We cannot encourage communalism or narrow-mindedness, for no nation can be great whose people are narrow in thought or in action. To the nations and peoples of the world, we send greetings and pledge ourselves to co-operate with them in furthering peace, freedom and democracy. And to India, our much-loved motherland, the ancient, the eternal and the ever-new, we pay our reverent homage and we bind ourselves afresh to her service. Jai Hind.

Help the Refugees
AHUJA
Chandni Chowk, Delhi.
DELHI EDITION
The Hindustan Times
LARGEST CIRCULATION IN NORTHERN, NORTH-WESTERN AND CENTRAL INDIA
INDIA INDEPENDENT : BRITISH RULE ENDS
CONSTITUENT ASSEMBLY TAKES OVER
MOUNTBATTEN'S APPOINTMENT AS GOVERNOR-GENERAL ENDORSED
COLOURFUL CEREMONY MARKS BIRTH OF NATION
NEW STAR RISES IN THE EAST
LEADERS TELL NATION OF TASKS AHEAD
Attlee's Greetings To Nehru
Governors Sworn In As Free India Is Born
THE PLEDGE
THE NEW CABINET
HOMAGE TO THE FATHER OF THE NATION
Blessed Dawn of Independence!
Long Live Free India!

The Hindustan Times front page on 15th August, 1947 (Indian Independence day).

Jawaharlal Nehru became the first Prime Minister of independent India, while Sardar Vallabhai Patel became the Deputy Prime Minister. Together, they focussed on uniting the princely states as a part of India. Lord Mountbatten was invited to continue as the Governor General of India but he was replaced in the following year by Chakravarti Rajagopalachari.

While the country was in the throes of celebrating its independence, work had already begun on the drafting of its new constitution. This was done by the 26th of January, 1950, and the Republic of India was officially proclaimed. Dr Rajendra Prasad was elected as the first President of India.

Index

A

B

C

D

E

F

G

H

I

J

K

L

M

N

O

P

Q

R

S

T

U

V

W

Z